The passionate technique

The passionate technique

Strategic psychodrama with individuals, families, and groups

Antony Williams

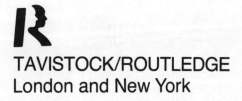

TAVISTOCK/ROUTLEDGE
London and New York

First published 1989
by Routledge
11 New Fetter Lane, London EC4P 4EE
29 West 35th Street, New York, NY 10001

© 1989 Antony Williams
Printed and bound in Great Britain by Mackays of Chatham PLC, Kent

British Library Cataloguing in Publication Data

Williams, Antony
The passionage technique: strategic
psychodrama with individuals, families
and groups.
1. Medicine.   Drama therapy
I. Title
616.89′1523

ISBN 0-415-00138-2
ISBN 0-415-00139-0 Pbk

Library of Congress Cataloging-in-Publication Data

Williams, Antony, 1941-
The passionate technique : strategic psychodrama with individuals,
families, and groups / Antony Williams.
p.   cm.
Includes index.
ISBN 0-415-00138-2.   ISBN 0-415-00139-0 (pbk.)
1. Psychodrama.   I. Title.
[DNLM: 1. Psychodrama—methods.   WM 430.5.P8 W721p]
RC489.P7W54 1989
616.89′1523—dc19
DNLM/DLC
for Library of Congress   88-18531
                                                            CIP

Contents

To Pam Hamilton

Acknowledgements

I want to thank the people who read and commented on various parts of this book: Liz Collins, Margaret Flynn, Mary Good, Claire Smith, Marina Strazdins, and Sally Trembath. Joady Brennan's strategic influence has been incalculable. I am grateful to my sparkling and generous sister, Diana, who was always asking if I were quoting her in my new book — well I am, Di. There are others, whom I will not mention by name, who heard out my ideas, cheered me up, corrected my ideology, lent their houses, opened the champagne, and suffered the onslaughts of the early versions. It's been fun, folks!

To my first teachers, Tom Wilson and Teena Lee Hucker, Lynette Clayton, and principal supervisor, Max Clayton, many of whose *bon mots* will be recognized through these pages, I am very grateful. I owe them much in terms of my present happiness with what I do, and my own students owe them much, too. Action methods are a godsend for teachers and illustrators of the human comedy, and if ever there is a book of students' rights, the right to have teachers who understand warm-up should be written into it.

My sincere thanks to Jenny Peek, who worked through forty fathoms of scrawl and produced each week forty pages of impressive neatness. I am also indebted to all the directors — the Duanes, Dukes, Dots, Dis, Dennises, and so on. In some cases they are obviously myself, and in others I trust I have done enough respectfully to disguise them. Even more kind have been the protagonists — the Prues, Pinos, Pauls, Priscillas, Patsys and even Pansys. I hope that their faith in this venture has been justified, and that you, the reader, are enriched from their allowing their story to be told.

Chapter one

Basic technique

Off the rails

Portia, a flamboyant, attractive, and overweight woman of 30, complains in the group that 'against all reason' she has given up the healthy life style that she had begun in the previous year. Now, she says, she uses cigarettes in the morning to 'kick-start the lungs'. She claims she drinks too much, eats too much junk food, and smokes too much dope. Somewhere or other, she went 'off the rails', as she put it.

Don, the director, asks Portia to construct some 'rails'. Portia chooses four people from the group, who lie on the floor in two parallel lines. Portia then stands between the lines and Don asks her when it was that she went off the rails. After some consideration, Portia replies that it was in August. Don asks her what was happening in August. At first Portia cannot remember. Then she recalls that a friend, Lucy, had applied for a job in her organization, and had been very angry when she missed out.

Don tells Portia to 'go off the rails'. She falls over to one side, and hides under a chair; objects representing food, drink, cigarettes, and drugs are supplied to her. She consumes them all, becoming distressed. The more distressed she is, the more rapidly and desperately she smokes, eats, and drinks. Don asks her whether she has been in this state before. Portia replies that it reminds her of a time when she was aged about 3, crouching behind the bathroom door eating bread while her parents were arguing in the kitchen.

The kitchen and bathroom scenes are established, and Portia chooses people from the group to play the roles of father and mother. Portia's parents are having a furious, hysterical argument. Her mother accuses her father of being 'no good' and repeatedly screams at him, 'I don't want to live any more.' Her father rages around impotently and says that he can't understand anything that is happening, that he is totally confused. Portia crouches behind the bathroom door stuffing bread into her mouth. She says she feels 'bad'. She begins to cry uncontrollably.

Her helplessness is apparent. In an aside to Don, she says that she is 'stuck'. Don asks her whether anyone could help her. She replies, 'There is no-one.' He asks her to choose someone from the group to act as herself viewing this scene. Portia steps outside the drama and witnesses Portia as a little girl in this stressful and overwhelming context. Soon this new role as witness is too passive for her. She becomes an indignant protector of the little girl, and calls out to the parents to stop. She insists that they pay attention to their daughter and stop hurting each other.

Don asks Portia to become in turn her mother and her father. In these roles, they are first outraged at this new, intrusive person's interference, and then they resume their fighting, ignoring any interruption. Back in role as herself at 3 years old, and with the help and loving encouragement of her protector, Portia grapples with them physically, and after a long struggle and much shouting, rolls them both out the door. She is triumphant, but also very sad. Don has the parents re-enter the scene, and Portia, weeping, tells her mother how she wished the latter had been more 'present' to her, and how her mother's depression and 'terrible marriage' got in the way of their ever being close.

Don then returns Portia to the first scene with the friend, Lucy, and re-establishes the four group members as 'rails'. Portia stands between the rails once more. Lucy fumes at her for causing her to miss out on the job. At first Portia begins to wheedle and explain, but after encouragement from her 'indignant protector', who is still watching over her, she exclaims: 'I'm not guilty, I'm not guilty. I might have managed things a little better, but I'm not guilty.' With authority and grace, she goes over to each of her parents, and says, 'I'm not guilty. I didn't cause you, or your hatred, or your messes. I'm not guilty.'

The drama ends with her standing between the rails once more as she embraces her 'witness' who turned into her protector. They promise not to be parted, and declare their mutual need and affection for each other. She pauses for a moment, still connected to the tissue of the past, but free of it. She then thanks the group members who have played various roles, and sits down with Don.

For the next 20 minutes or so, the group tell of the memories, emotions, and thoughts they had about their own lives while Portia was enacting her drama. The entire session, including the 'sharing' at the end, lasts about 90 minutes.

Since action is the essence of psychodrama, it is tempting simply to present the dramas here, one after the other, and allow you to judge them for yourself. After all, they are stories in their own right, chaste and compact, in some ways beyond explanation and analysis. They are human documents with their own imaginative resonance, their own speech forms, and their own value as aesthetic products. They have created a moral and emotional atmosphere of a place and a time, and endowed events with their true meaning. They are an expression of human passion.

Honestly enacted psychodramas speak to our capacity for wonder and delight, to the sense of mystery and awe in our lives, arousing our sense of pity, beauty, pain, and fellowship with all creation. They can awaken a sense of solidarity, as Conrad (1914, 1974) says in another context, 'that knits together the loneliness of innumerable hearts, to the solidarity in dreams, in joy, in sorrow, in aspirations, in illusions, in hope, in fear, which binds men to each other, which binds together all humanity — the dead to the living and the living to the unborn'. I will call this usage of psychodrama 'psychodrama as revelation'.

Let us now begin with some terms and descriptions: psychodrama is a process where someone acts out personally relevant situations in a group setting. These situations might be distressful, in which case the person will try to alter them, or they might be satisfactory, in which case the drama simply celebrates them. Psychodramas are not solely concerned with anger, pain, or the 'darker' emotions, but can be for the simple purposes of illustration or enhancement. Most psychodramas, like Portia's, contain an affirmation beyond their tragic narrative simply from setting out the narrative itself before others who share one's basic humanity. Psychodramas that are true-to-being present on stage our efforts to live with our own human strangeness.

These first two chapters are intended as 'primers' for the seriously curious about psychodrama's basic processes. Subsequent chapters are more speculative and concern the mutual influence that systems therapies and psychodramatic practice might be made to have on each other. For fuller accounts of the basic process, excellent introductions have been provided by Blatner (1973), Fine (1978), Goldman and Morrison (1984), Kahn (1964), Leveton (1977), Starr (1977), and of course Moreno himself in his three volumes simply called *Psychodrama* (vol. I, 1946, 1964, 1972; vol. II, 1959, and vol. III, 1969). Bischof (1970) has provided an 'approved' account of Moreno's personality theory, and Hare (1986) has elaborated his contribution to social psychology.

The language of psychodrama

Psychodramas are like partisan plays: with apparent naturalism, they chronicle people's lives, deaths, loves, their hatred and suppression, their transcendence, their couplings and uncouplings. The other group members, the audience, discern in the psychodramatic narrative an echo of themselves. The plays are not finished products, like plays in a theatre, but poetic,

3

dramatic works evolving on stage before the audience's eyes. They watch its process of development, step by step, from its beginnings to the moment of catharsis and integration. In Aristotelian drama, the 'catharsis' (the exercise of fear and pity that liberated one from those very emotions) took place in the audience. In psychodrama, the place of catharsis moves from spectator to the stage, to the actors themselves. Rare is the psychodrama, however, where the audience is not moved as well; the catharsis becomes total, involving actors and audience.

People who act out the situations, *protagonists*, express their phenomenal world outwardly in scenes, just as in a play. 'Protagonist' was the title of the chief actor in Greek tragedy: 'Protagonist means man in a frenzy, a madman. A theater for psychodrama is thus a theater of the madman, an audience of madmen looks at one of them, living out his life on stage' (Moreno, 1964, p. 12). A *scene* is a term used to indicate a time and place that is being presented in a session. A scene may be elaborately constructed, or can be a mere fragment suggesting a real or imaginary time and space. The scene helps the person *warm-up* to that time and place.

A passage from the diary of Cocteau, the French playwright, illustrates the link between a scene and a warm-up: finding himself in his childhood neighbourhood, Cocteau tries to recapture lost memories of walking along a wall and tracing his finger along it, as he did as a child. The memories are few and lifeless. He is disappointed. Then suddenly, he remembers that as a child he had trailed his finger along the wall at a different level, over different stones. Cocteau bends down, closes his eyes, and trails his finger over the wall. He writes:

> Just as the needle picks up the melody from the record, I obtained a melody of the past with my hand. I found everything; my cape, the leather satchel, the names of my friends and of my teachers, certain expressions I had used, the sound of my grandfather's voice, the smell of his beard, the smell of my sister's dresses and of my mother's gown.

> (Cited in Van den Berg, 1975, p. 212)

A child has a different perspective from that of the adult, as Cocteau found. By re-expressing the event that gave rise to that perspective, the experience can be re-evaluated in terms of the adult world. At the wall Cocteau is simultaneously child and adult. Like Cocteau, protagonists fit into the groove of the past as in a record, they 'pick up the melody of the past'. Ultimately they re-evaluate it in terms of the present, usually by having altered that melody in the enacted scene from the past, as Portia did in her kitchen and, as we shall see, so many protagonists do. After these first two introductory chapters, some nonstandard ways of altering that melody will be suggested.

The first scene of a drama usually takes place in the present, and around the presenting problem. Portia's first scene was in fact an imaginary one derived from acting out her metaphor of 'going off the rails'. A first scene usually contains insufficient information for an understanding of the difficulty, and subsequent scenes, sometimes as many as four, take the action first to other parts of the person's life, and then, perhaps, into the recent or distant past. In Portia's drama, the second scene occurred with Lucy, and was only briefly enacted, while the third scene took place in the family kitchen when Portia was aged about 3.

The scenes are enacted on a 'stage', which may be a formal raised platform, but is more usually a section of the room cleared for that purpose. The protagonist's physical world is expressed outwardly by means of chairs to represent objects — doorways, benches, walls, beds, TV sets, stoves (a surprising number of psychodramas are enacted in people's kitchens), sofas or dining tables. The props in psychodrama are thus very simple — usually half a dozen chairs or so. Group members, called *auxiliaries*, represent relevant persons, whether these be relatives, spouses, friends, teachers, bosses, or even parts of the self. An 'auxiliary' is the term for anyone besides the director and the protagonist who takes part in a drama. In keeping with the dramaturgical nature of the process, the therapist or group leader is called a *director*. Auxiliaries assist the director in producing a full experience and satisfactory resolution of whatever is dramatized by the protagonist.

One of the scenes may be from early childhood, where the origins of the primary feelings and indeed of the presenting problem itself is thought to lie. The aim of the presentation is not so much analysis as a deeply felt reliving of the relevant experiences. In the core scene, the director may encourage protagonists to give full expression to their experience, which could be one of rage, intolerable grief, or a wonderful unity with another person. The emotional events of the drama are experienced, rather than merely talked about. At the level of passion, a psychodrama needs only to reach the secret springs of human emotions; these secret springs are often difficult to tap, but when protagonists do find them, their qualities of freshness and purity are quite evident. Although the experience of 'the abyss' might have been very painful, protagonists after a drama usually exhibit a lovely calm, shown even by physical changes in their face and body. They seem to have snatched back a fragment of life, and it shows. It is difficult to doubt the veracity of the change, at least at the time, and audience members are usually intensely involved with and moved by the protagonist. The experience seems to carry its own authentication, sealed by the evocative nature of the images and language.

The powerful synthesis of sensory and perceptual information helps form new meanings and organizes experience in new ways. According to psychodramatic theory, the change has come because protagonists have at last enacted roles that are inwardly truthful and appropriate to the original situation. The spontaneity involved in the new interaction illustrates and changes the core dynamic of the original dysfunctional interaction and creates new perceptions, responses, and interactional patterns. Directors hope to create a powerful framework that will give new meaning to experience, and go on influencing protagonists' lives long after the drama is over.

We shall be making the point throughout this book that passion is not a 'thing in itself' but is fundamentally relational; it is used strategically to help people define themselves in interactions and can be very significant in understanding and changing relationship dynamics. The passion that emerges in strategic psychodrama is understood cybernetically — it has not resided somewhere 'in' the person, full-blown but out of awareness. Rather, it is newly synthesized in interaction with the director and the group. Strategic psychodrama uses the drama as a staging area for change in the person's everyday life, rather than the place where change is to occur. Emotionally charged situations are reframed or relabelled in ways that lead to new structures in relationships. The emphasis is more 'outside' than 'inside'. But now let us return to our description of a conventional psychodrama.

When the core scene is complete, protagonists are led out of that scene back to the present. Usually some attempt is made to link the presenting problem with the core scene — perhaps by replaying the first scene. So Portia ended up 'on the rails' again, but not before she had confronted Lucy in a manner where she was fully 'present', rather than being a guilty, hiding child. In revisiting the first scene, protagonists have the advantage of the new roles that they developed in the course of the drama, as we shall see in the drama of 'Wiping the sink' in the next chapter, and in numerous others reported more fully in this book. The final moment of the drama, therefore, tends to be present-oriented.

Protagonists' perceptions of themselves and others are acted out so that they may experience outwardly the truth that they experience inwardly. They not merely tell, but enact their memories, their dreams, their fantasies in the theatre of therapy, so that they may live more effectively in the theatre of life. Apart from the interview-in-role, directors seldom interpret during the drama, but gather information from the action itself; they attend to significant cues, watching for patterns and repeated actions. Protagonists are encouraged to maximize all expression and action, rather than reduce them: so-called delusions, hallucinations, soliloquies, and fantasies are not only allowed but actually encouraged as part of the production.

The aim of psychodrama as revelation is to find the forms, the colours, and the light of what is fundamental and enduring in people's lives — the very truth of their existence as it appears to them. A drama presents 'what is there' and also creates 'what is there'. Dramas can fail as revelation by being derivative, ornamental, and lifeless; they can also fail therapeutically if these qualities are dominant. Psychodrama as revelation helps people to develop new capacities, to become more expressive and creative in their daily lives, especially in their relationships. Dramas can fail therapeutically and as revelation by not arousing protagonists to the truth in their lives, and by not presenting adequate pathways to spontaneity. The revelatory and therapeutic meanings of spontaneity will be elaborated in Chapters 4 and 5.

As revelation and as therapy, dramas work on people's 'act hunger' — their drive towards fulfilment of the desires and impulses at the core of the self and at the core of their interactions with others. The director helps protagonists towards a symbolic fulfilment of their act hunger, which is usually to express a fundamental part of their psychological truth. Kellerman (1987, p. 79) suggests that while drama may be a healing experience, and while psychotherapy may be dramatically satisfying, 'psychodrama cannot be categorized simply as theatre. No matter how much we attempt to dilute what is done in psychodrama, it is definitely a form of treatment.' It is with precisely this question that this book is most concerned — whether a therapy can be a passionate technique. But for the moment, let us continue with our basic definitions and processes.

In the act itself, protagonists usually have no clear idea of what they are doing. They are alternatively delighted and terrified by glimpses of potentiality, of promise, and the sweet joys of uncomplicated action. They move in and out of time, and in and out of the conventional structures of reality. Being a protagonist gives them a passionate sense of what they are, somehow more deeply and explicitly than they usually experience in their everyday reality. In the moment of spontaneous action, life is at last simple. So when Portia confronted her parents, she experienced more fully her own guilt at their distress, but also her rage that they were as they were to each other, and heedless of her needs as a 3-year-old. As she acts out the anger to her parents, her need for them and the frustration that they are not adequately present to her also becomes evident.

Blatner (1973) draws attention to the psychotherapeutic maxim: 'Don't ventilate the hostility without protagonists also experiencing their dependency.' That is, the protagonist's need for something (let us say, love or acknowledgement) is frustrated in some way by the significant other; people's frustration and apparent hatred is usually more accessible than their need, and hence the layer of anger must be experienced before the layer of love can be even seen. In Portia's enactment, therefore, we do not have anger or hatred as the real basis of the drama, even though those emotions occupied much of the narration. Thwarted love is the underlying theme. She is blocked from the love and stability that a 3-year-old might reasonably expect from parents and tries to comfort herself with food. The catharsis of rage usually triggers a catharsis of longing: so Portia weeps, then rages before she can weep in a different fashion. And then, it seems, she can cope with conflict and demands.

7

Only some of Portia's drama concerned what 'actually happened'. The narrative of Lucy's anger and disappointment with Portia was probably realistic enough, but the narrative of the fight in the kitchen is doubtless made up of a mixture of memory of that fight overlaid by memories of other and similar fights and experiences, and her own reflections on the experiences. We shall discuss the constructed nature of therapeutic reality more fully in Chapter 3 in a drama called 'Dale's dilemma'. For the moment, though, it is clear that the rest of Portia's drama was overtly fantasy, where actions and dialogue clearly occurred for the first time on the psychodramatic stage. This is called in psychodrama *surplus reality* — the reality that did not actually happen, but which possibly 'should have'. It is constructed according to the psychological reality of the time, and according to how reality 'should' have been. Portia is only 3 years old; it is not only not advisable for her to confront her parents in the way she did in the drama, it is not possible either. But the primitive reality is there: she is angry and she is suffering unbearable loss. So the protagonist's hopes, fears, impulses, hurts, judgements, and world view are brought to the stage. On stage, protagonists live through and enact all of these as fully as they can; for a while, Portia can experiment with a rather alarming kind of utopia where the only morality is the truth as she sees it.

After a drama, the session closes with *sharing*. The props are no longer tables, double beds, stoves, refrigerators, etc., but have returned to their rightful status of humble and ordinary chairs. The auxiliaries have been de-roled, acknowledged for who they actually are as group members, and have sat down in the circle. The protagonist and director rejoin the group, and sharing begins. Sharing is not an informal chat, or a means of processing the drama, but is a semi-formal linking of the group's feelings and responses to the narrative and emotions of the drama.

Group members are given to understand that this is not the time for analysing, interpreting, or advice-giving, but a means of integrating themselves with the protagonist and the protagonist with them. The protagonist may have been 'on stage' for one or two hours, for the most part heavily involved in another place and time, and relatively oblivious to the group's presence and to current space and time. Their deepest experiences, most terrible fears, most traumatic moments may well have been enacted. They themselves may have been totally consumed with rage, fear, or melting tenderness, showing these to the group while at the same time being largely unaware of the group. In the sharing, protagonists 'come back to earth'. They realize, through companionship, that they are not alone with these feelings and experiences, and incorporate the acceptance by the group of their glories and weaknesses, their eccentricities and singularities. At the end of a drama, in fact, no matter how ugly the scenes depicted, or how frail and human protagonists think themselves, group members are usually in awe of the power of the human spirit and the grandeur and beauty of the person who has shown his or her life. Protagonists of honestly enacted dramas become somehow grand figures — generous, laughing, raging, fearful and weeping — bearers of all the parables and paradoxes of humanity itself.

Many of Moreno's key concepts were not those of an individual on his or her own, but concepts that relate to social organization or interpersonal space: roles, for example, were essentially defined as interactive, as we shall see in Chapter 4. *Tele* was another important term. It was the process of interaction between individuals. Tele is 'the simplest unit of feeling transmitted from one individual to another' (Moreno, 1953, p. 159). It is the emotional feeling tone that exists in almost all human relationships. But the word itself is Greek meaning 'far' or 'far off', or in Moreno's slightly altered sense, 'distance'. Unlike empathy, it is a two-way process, the flow of feeling between two or more persons. Tele, as opposed to transference, is not a repetition from the past, but a spontaneous process which is appropriate in the present here and now (Kellerman, 1979).

Social atom was another organizational/interactive concept, but one that, unlike tele, does not have positive or negative poles. It is the 'smallest living unit' — one that cannot be divided. Tele describes the feeling tone, social atom describes the structure. Modern usage, or at least certainly the usage in this book, is to consider the social atom as all the significant relationships that a person has at a given time. Thus a current social atom may consist of spouse, sister-in-law, father, first best friend, second best friend, work, the dog, the Catholic Church, and a former lover. A person's social atom when they were a child will be obviously different: included may be all immediate family members, a favourite aunt, some friends, school, a particular teacher, and the family pet. We each, therefore, see ourselves as the nucleus of a little world; 'social atom' is a convenient way to describe or map out that world.

Essential philosophy

The originator and driving force behind psychodrama was Jacob Moreno, a Rumanian psychiatrist born in 1892 who received his medical degree from the University of Vienna in 1917. During his student days he developed a deep interest in the work now known as psychodrama. He began to devise a form of role playing between 1909 and 1911, and he became involved in group psychotherapy while still a young man. In fact, he is said to have originated group therapy, and to have coined the term. In 1922 he had a stage especially adapted to spontaneity work — Das Stegreiftheater — spontaneity theatre. The first actors in his 'company' were children, but gradually they were replaced by adults. In Moreno's spontaneity theatre, striving after perfection was rejected in favour of being-in-the-moment-of-creation. Adventure and radicalism were the keys:

The difference between my own stage construction and those of the Russians was that their stages, however revolutionary in the external form, were still dedicated to the rehearsed production, being therefore revolutionary in external expression and in content of the drama, whereas the revolution I advocated was completed, including the audience, the actors, the playwright and producers, in other words, the people themselves, and not only forms of presentation.

(Moreno, 1964, p. 100)

Members of the theatrical community in the theatre of spontaneity were urged to return to some kind of original, dynamic, unifying innocence (Ginn, 1974). The spoken word, which for the legitimate actor was the point of departure, is for the spontaneity player the end-stage. The spontaneity player actually begins with the spontaneity state:

The legitimate role player has to be untrained and deconserved before he can become a spontaneity player. Here we have another reason why so many 'non'-actors pass the test for spontaneity work successfully. Their fountainhead is life itself and not the written plays of conventional theatre.

(Moreno, 1964, p. 74)

Moreno's Stegreiftheater closed down, possibly because of the complexity of the task (of having actors whose 'fountainhead is life itself'), and the difficulty of training not only actors but audiences out of their embedded preconceptions about theatre. Before his sort of theatre could succeed, he argued, the attitude of the public would need to be changed. 'This would require a total revolution of our culture, a creative revolution' (Moreno, 1947, p. 7). But simultaneously with the work of the Stegreiftheater came Moreno's recognition of the 'therapeutic' benefits of his procedures on participants and audience: what if spontaneity, so vital, so interesting, and such fun, was actually the key to 'mental health'? Moreno watched his actors carefully, and occasionally observed a beneficial overflow from the stage to their personal lives: spontaneity was paying off at home.

The spontaneity movement was essentially religious and transformational. Moreno maintains that he chose 'the course of the theatre instead of founding a religious sect, joining a monastry or developing a system of theology' (Moreno, 1947, p. 3). Between 1908 and 1914 he underwent a Hassidic period: he changed his name from Levi to Moreno, which was also a family name and meant 'chief rabbi'. He and four other young men formed a 'religion of the encounter'. They were committed to anonymity (Moreno did not last long at that!), to loving and giving, and to a direct and concrete life in the community. They would take no money for their services, but any gifts received went into a fund for the 'House of Encounter', which was a shelter for displaced people in Vienna in the tumultuous period before World War 1.

Moreno began to apply his transcendental ideas and the insights he gained from expressed spontaneity in the theatre to therapy. In therapy, in theatre, and in religion, people gather to heal themselves and one another, to connect with their own existence. They seek meaning, commonality, and redemption. In spontaneity the 'two selves' — the conscious analytic teller and the unconscious doer — come together so that they function as one harmonious whole. Action flows smoothly and freely; action and evaluation of action is automatic and hence unproblematic. Moreno consistently maintains that the highest value of spontaneity and creativity is a totally spontaneous being, the 'godhead'.

> In the psychodramatic world, the fact of embodiment is central, axiomatic and universal. Everyone can portray his own version of God through his own actions and so communicate his own version to others. That was the simple meaning of my first book, in which I proclaimed the 'I-God' ... But it is the I which matters; it is the I which was provocative and new. And it is the I-God with whom we are all connected ... It is amusing to think retroactively that my proclamation of the I was considered as the most outstanding manifestation of megalomania from my side. Actually, when the I-God is universalized, as it is in my book, the whole God concept becomes one of humbleness, weakness and inferiority, a micromania rather than a megalomania. God has never been so lowly described and so universal in his dependence as he is in my book.
>
> (Moreno, 1969, p. 21)

In 1925 Moreno emigrated to the United States, where he began private practice as a psychiatrist in 1928. He married a woman called Zerka Toeman, who co-authored volumes II and III of *Psychodrama* with him. As Zerka Moreno, she had a profound influence on the psychodrama movement. Moreno favoured a 'horizontal' social-systems approach to psychodrama, while Zerka Moreno favoured a 'vertical' approach that concentrated on a primal past experience. This latter cathartic approach provided the training basis for the modern generation of students, and is today considered 'classical' (Fox, 1987).

Moreno set up a private teaching and treatment centre at Beacon, in New York State, whence he taught and wrote prodigiously until his death in 1974. He believed that his techniques were more advanced than Freud's: through the spontaneity of psychodrama both client and therapist could actively participate in lifelike situations and change behaviours *in situ*, as it were. Moreno's concept of the highly functioning person was based on the idea of the multirole personality — a person who was flexible and adaptive, who could act appropriately in whatever situation life served up.

> The problem is not that of abandoning the fantasy world or vice versa
> — but of establishing means by which the individual can gain full
> mastery over the situation, living in both tracks, but being able to shift
> from one to the other — this is spontaneity.
>
> (Moreno, 1964, p. 72)

Spontaneity is the 'here and now'; it is 'Man in action, man thrown into action, the moment not a part of history but history as a part of the moment' (Moreno, 1956, p. 60). A certain degree of unpredictability always exists in life. If one could know the future, there would be no need for spontaneity — a fixed pattern of behaviour might be worked out to meet all oncoming problems. But since the future cannot be known, one must be ready for anything. Even an infant just after birth already operates spontaneously by initiating demands for food, changes of clothes, and human contact. In adults, lack of spontaneity generates anxiety; as spontaneity increases, anxiety diminishes: the person is able to 'handle' the next moment — indeed, to create it. The person not only adapts to new situations, but responds constructively to them. He or she not only meets new situations, but creates them.

Moreno valued the becoming, the actualizing, the creating, the actual experience of creativity. In its highest form, spontaneity leads to creation, which may be simply a new way of behaving for an individual or group, or it may be a product, such as a painting, a poem, an invention, or a building. If spontaneous output is genuine and consistent, there usually occurs a creative act, the results of which may be new to the individual, but not necessarily to the rest of the world: they may be something so simple as a new relationship between two people. Thus true creativity can be found in daily living.

> Spontaneity and creativity are thus categories of a different order;
> creativity belongs to the categories of substance — it is the arch
> substance — spontaneity to the categories of catalyzer — it is the arch
> catalyzer.
>
> (Moreno, 1953, p. 40)

For this reason, perhaps, action was essential in his approach to therapy: his focus on the group, on intense encounter, and on action was much more revolutionary in the psychiatric world of the 1920s and 1930s than it appears to us now. Action was synonomous with interaction; since role flexibility was the goal, and since roles are nearly always interpersonal, psychodrama was established as essentially an interpersonal therapy. As far back as 1916 Moreno used diagrams to indicate the space and movements between psychodrama actors, much in the same way that Lewin was to adopt them in 1936.

Even his notion of the unconscious was dynamic and interpersonal, and he was thus critical of Freud's emphasis on 'the' unconscious as an entity. Psychodrama directors have followed this dynamic but rather simple view; they tend to regard material not so much as 'buried' in the unconscious but rather that some meanings are not available to people for a number of reasons. In this light, the so-called 'repressed' material is merely an extension of a current structure, rather than existing in a different state altogether. Psychodrama emphasizes the extension and creation of meaning rather than the excavation of something buried in the unconscious that contains the meaning. Directors enter with the protagonist into an experience that may not at the time make sense, and leave the integration for another time (the 'processing' of a drama). Moreno postulated a common unconscious, or a 'co-unconscious'. To encourage experimentation in their clients, directors themselves need to be able to experiment: spontaneity must be two-way. He was thus a wonderful champion of recursiveness between therapist and client (Campernolle, 1981). The recursive nature of therapeutic interaction will be one of the themes of this book.

Moreno considered his psychological system superior to that of the 'big three' — Freud, Jung, and Adler. These authors were criticized, rather hastily, perhaps, for not having a theoretic foundation based on 'logic', and more substantively for their clinical methods not going conceptually beyond the individual being analysed. He regarded his own treatment of interpersonal groups to be far wider, and to include 'a total understanding of human behaviour'. In fact, he thought the formulations of creativity/spontaneity were the root forms of all behaviour, including the entire behaviour of the universe itself.

Although quite widely celebrated in his own lifetime, Moreno never received the recognition for which he yearned (e.g. Moreno, 1953). He called his methods 'therapy for fallen Gods', and thought of himself, perhaps, as a not-so-fallen god. He was not a person to aim low in his therapy, as some of his titles suggest: *Words of the father*, or 'Psychopathology and psychotherapy of the cosmos', or 'Psychodrama of Adolf Hitler', or 'Ave Creator'. Moreno's vision was essentially a theological one (Kraus, 1984) which got translated into therapy and is now practised as such — a point that will become a focus of this book. Many find the naïve grandeur of his ambitions for the movement he founded warming and *sympatico*; it was not likely to win him many accolades in the scientific community, however, although his 'science' of sociometry made a very strong impact in the 1940s and 1950s:

He is now remembered, if at all, as part of an early classic period of social psychology. This is in sharp contrast to his development of the group therapeutic method of psychodrama, which is still practised in the manner he initiated.

(Hare, 1986, p. 90–1)

He edited *Sociometry* between 1936 and 1956, and also used the journal *Group Psychotherapy* as a major outlet for his writings. He was largely self-published and some of his works have a somewhat self-congratulatory flavour (see, for instance, Moreno, Moreno, and Moreno, 1963; Moreno, Moreno, and Moreno, 1964; Moreno, Z., 1967; 1968). He reprinted his own work frequently, often under another title or amalgamated with new work (Fox, 1987).

Moreno had the courage to create his own world, and urged others to do likewise. But he also endured a prolonged cultural trauma: he had some-how to reconcile his optimism and messianism with the fresh evidence each day that the world was not improving as predicted. He ambitioned psycho-drama and sociodrama, not only as a 'third revolution' in psychological practice (Moreno, 1964), but with a place in the political and social process as well (Masserman and Moreno, 1957; Moreno, 1968). The opening words of *Who shall survive?* are: 'A true therapeutic procedure cannot have less an objective than the whole of mankind' (Moreno, 1953). The uncon-scious was the lowest common denominator of humankind, and spon-taneity was the highest function. He saw the destiny of the twentieth century as dependent on the successful unfolding of people's relationship to their spontaneity. When the evidence seemed to be against this happen-ing, his character led him to look even more determinedly for unambiguous answers.

His ambitions for psychodrama and sociometry have not so far been fulfilled, and maybe they never will be. Although most psychological professionals and even many lay people have heard of psychodrama, on a world scale the full process of psychodrama (as distinct from action methods) is little used as a clinical modality. It made some impact in Europe (Leutz, 1973) and is widely popular in the Latin American coun-tries. Nevertheless, it has hardly been the 'third psychiatric revolution' that Moreno predicted. Even its founding house at Beacon has been sold. While the movement has many newsletters of local associations, there is only one refereed journal in English. Psychodrama is rarely taught in university-level psychology, psychiatry, or social-work courses, and does not seem to be the subject of much outcome or conceptual research, either in the English-language *Psychodrama Journal* or in other scientific publications. It receives no significant citations as a personality theory (Bischof, 1970). At most, bits and pieces have been stripped off Moreno's genius, and applied in clinical settings as 'action methods', adjunctive techniques to other ways of doing therapy. It has always been thus, from the days of group therapy on, and a considerable part of Moreno's writings have been devoted to crying 'Thief!'

Chapter two

A passion for action

When you set out for Ithaka
ask that your way be long,
full of adventure, full of instruction.

C.P. Cavafy

The essence of action methods is action. 'Action methods' are ways of understanding and acting, derived from psychodrama, that do not involve a full psychodrama as such. Role reversal is an action method, for example, and so is the 'empty chair technique' and various forms of sociometry. Action methods send a verbal narrative into space and time. They produce dialogue. They seize on 'messages from the unconscious' by making use of small bodily movements and 'maximizing' them. Thus a twitch of the mouth, a sigh, a clenched fist, or a tapping of the toe is repeated, repeated, and enlarged. The tapping of a foot may become a stamping, and the stamping a jumping or kicking.

Naturally enough, this sort of behaviour changes what might have started out as a rather staid and stuck dialogue (let us say between a man and his boss) into something quite different. While jumping up and down, protagonists are likely to have quite new thoughts and say quite new things to the other person than they had before, or even than they would 'in reality'. Verisimilitude is not the point: the psychological reality of the interaction is enlarged, even if the content cannot quite be repeated outside the therapy room.

The methods have the ability to get quickly to the emotional and interactional 'heart of the matter'. Let us say that a man says he is having 'trouble' with his son. He is asked by the director for two words that might describe him. 'Weak and bland' is the instant reply. He is then asked for a word or symbol to describe his relationship with his son. 'It's like trying to catch a fly with chopsticks', he says. The director then asks the person to choose someone to be the fly, and a chase around the room ensues, with the man snapping at the fly as if he were a pair of chopsticks. He role-reverses as the fly and feels what it is like to be such an adroit escapist. The action may stop at this first scene, and be self-contained (a vignette), or it may provide a take-off pad from which the protagonist is already compelled to view events in a new way. The enactment, while imaginative and enjoyable, also presses a point: it is difficult to keep quite the same opinions or world view after one has become a pair of chopsticks, or has buzzed around the room like a fly. A new orientation is called for, a new start on the problem and its habitual solution.

Concretization

Concretization is the term used most frequently for the acting-out of a metaphor unwittingly produced by the protagonist or deliberately introduced by the director. A metaphor, says Gordon (1978), is a novel representation of something old. Metaphors tend to compact information, expand perception, evoke emotion, and permit expression of experiences that could not otherwise be expressed (Billow, 1977). Concretization is a major part of the method, giving it not only warmth and vitality, but also much of its clinical and diagnostic strength.

While full psychodramas usually imply interactions with the 'other', action methods also lend themselves to encounter with the self. By means of concretization and dramatization, the self may be represented dramatically either by another person, or by a chair or other object. The implication of using the dramatic method with the self is that the self is a system. The object is thrown 'outside' the speaking self in order that the relationship aspect of self with self may be manifested and then developed.

As soon as the self, or part of the self, becomes 'outside' in an object or other person, that is, when it is concretized, the quality of relationship with the self must change as the person is required to enter a dramatic dialogue. A new perspective is necessitated by the format of the drama itself. The format for such an encounter is: 'Choose an object that represents you ... Interact with that object in some way ... Extend this interaction so that it may be witnessed by others.' The following example is derived from the above general formula wherein people externalize a 'part of the self' and then address it:

Everyone, take off one of your shoes — the shoe from the foot that you'll lead with next year. Pick it up and hold it in your hand. It's January the first, next year. Sight along the shoe to where you want to go — see that place and that state. Now, do to the shoe whatever needs to be done to help it get there — it may need little gentle pushes, it may need shaking, it may simply need pointing, or it may need some mess cleaned off so it's not so heavy. I don't know. Only you can know that.

The shoe takes on the reality of the self about to embark on a new course of action. Participants are asked to do to the shoe 'whatever needs to be done'; — by implication, the way they treat the shoe (gentle pushes, shaking, etc.) is the way they need to treat themselves in order to get what they want in the coming year. If instructions on how to treat oneself were given directly to the person, however, it is likely that they would be ignored or have little impact. They would not have the same imaginative resonance or trancelike quality that is lent by the process of dialogue and enactment. In later chapters, when the concept of 'double description' has been introduced, the therapeutic effectiveness of the dialogue with the self in the form of a shoe may become more intelligible. Double description is not a term commonly found in the psychodrama canon, however, and at this stage we are preferring to remain within the traditional psychodramatic framework.

Let us take another example, this time not at the start of a drama, as in the case of Portia's 'rails' or the man who chased the fly with 'chopsticks', but from during a drama itself. The protagonist is walking around her family (represented by five auxiliaries), who are grouped in a circle. It is the second scene of this particular drama, and the protagonist is 'stuck'; she does not know what to do or say. The director asks:

D: *What are relationships in this family like?*
P: *They stink.*
D: *What would the spirit of the relationship be?*
P: *Like a sewer.*
D: *Set up a sewer, and let's see who is in it.*

Although we will not report the remainder of this drama, suffice it to say that the sudden shift brought about by concretizing the metaphor sets the protagonist in a new direction as she deals with her family as a sewer and its members as turds, tampons, spent tea leaves, used bits of paper, and so on. In concretizing a metaphor, the director is not immediately striving for 'insight', but rather for a new vision, a form of thinking and being radically different from the habitual, which presumably has landed the protagonist in trouble in the first place. Insight, if it comes at all, follows the action. The issue is first presented in dramatic terms, and later, if at all, analysed in terms of role states in a particular time and place. Seeing her family as a 'sewer' is not journey's end, but the protagonist has certainly left the sealed main road and is now jolting along an unfamiliar bush track, not knowing what will come next, even though she co-creates what comes next. The sewer metaphor has been a 'way of speaking in which one thing is expressed in terms of another, whereby this bringing together throws new light on the character of what is being described' (Kopp, 1971, p. 17).

The immediacy and urgency of action methods spring in large part from their being both physical and visual. Interactions find not only a verbal but also a bodily expression, which may be gross, such as shouting, dancing, vomiting, or hugging, or may be relatively imperceptible, such as the twitching of a muscle, or the clenching of a fist, or a trembling in the voice. Using involuntary movements of the body helps protagonists to get in touch with their primary feelings and to intensify them when appropriate. The physical expression of emotion, especially when manifested interpersonally and in a scene, gives clues to the structure of relationships and the restricted or adequate roles that are being portrayed.

Directors can heighten the emotional tone of an interaction by asking the protagonist to 'put your body in the shape of the feeling' or to 'sculpt with your body you in the interaction right now'. When people are talking about an event it is usually possible for them to control both the interaction and the emotional impact that the event has made. But when they become warmed-up actors in a scene, the as-ifness of the experience becomes more pronounced, and they begin to behave, think, and feel as they would in actual life situations. The physical and verbal cues are maximized — taken to the limit — and then fed into interaction with another person.

Wiping the sink

Now that Portia's 'Off the rails' drama may have receded from memory somewhat, it may be helpful to present another outline of a 'typical' psychodrama. This one involves two scenes — one in the present, and one in the past that is linked to the first scene. Many further psychodramas will be described in detail throughout the book, with their systemic implications drawn out, or a particular teaching point being made. 'Wiping the sink' is still a 'taster' to impart the general idea of a drama, and to become familiar with its sometimes strange language. The narrative of the drama of 'Wiping the sink' will be interspersed with explanation of terminology and some of the basic procedures and 'rules' will be indicated.

A group, let us say a personal-growth psychodrama group, has met about six times. Its members are by now familiar with the psychodrama format. After half an hour or so of discussion, a theme or central concern emerges: it is that of overreacting in a guilty fashion to apparently small criticisms. Phyllis is chosen by the group as protagonist. (All protagonists' names in this book will begin with 'P' and all directors' names will begin with 'D' so that the reader knows who is who in the sometimes complex narrative of a drama.) Phyllis had joined the conversation with an anecdote about herself in the workplace. Although a tireless worker, she has been accused by a colleague of being 'half-hearted' in her consultancy to a self-help grief group. Let us use Phyllis's drama to reiterate and follow through some of the terms and typical procedures of a psychodrama.

Dot encourages Phyllis to make a contract with her about the purpose of the drama. Phyllis says that she wants to know why she feels so 'hopeless'. She begins to set the scene in the staff room of the hospital where she works. She uses chairs to establish the benches, the sink, the refrigerator, and the central table and chairs. When she and the group are fully 'there', or warmed up to the scene, she is asked to choose someone from the group (an auxiliary) to represent Larry, the man who was angry with her.

19

'Larry' knows what to say and do by means of *role reversal*. In their argument, Phyllis continually changes between being herself and Larry, and after she has spoken Larry's part, the auxiliary steps in and says more or less the same words, until the role is established and ad-libbing can take over. Then auxiliaries can experience the protagonist in the 'now' and authentically respond to that experience from the role. If the auxiliary gets too far off the track in the ad-libbing, or if an important change in direction occurs, role reversal is again used until the new ad-libbing is reliable. The process will be illustrated many times in this book, and will become completely familiar to the reader, if it is not already.

The auxiliary takes up not only the words but also the physical posture of the other. If there is a fight, or an embrace, or a beating, they find the amount of force that is required by role reversal, and then give this back to the protagonist with the same amount of strength to create a full experience for them. If protagonists push softly, so do the auxiliaries in role reversal; if they punch hard, so do the auxiliaries, leaving it up to the director to see that no-one is hurt.

Auxiliaries physically change places with the protagonist and repeat the words that the protagonist has spoken so that protagonists can hear their own words while in the role of the other. The protagonist is not the only person to benefit from a drama; by taking up roles of the other, auxiliaries broaden their life experience, gain a deep connection with others, and have the freedom to express themselves in ways they may normally avoid. They might enact the roles, over several sessions, of clinging grandmother, drunken husband, *ingénue*, lonely dead brother, or *femme fatale*. When it is not fun, it is at least broadening.

Goldman and Morrison (1984, p. 18) suggest five specific purposes for role reversal: (1) At the simplest level, role reversal is necessary to obtain information known only to the protagonist. (2) Role reversal is also used when it is necessary for the protagonist to understand and feel the sensibility of the other. (3) It is used to help the protagonist see self through the eyes of the other, thus leading to awareness of the effects of one's own behaviour and being. (4) It can be used to accelerate protagonists' spontaneity and free-up their thinking: a wife may see her husband as putting too many limits on the relationship. In role reversal as him, she feels what it is like to put on those limits, and may actually wish to put more on, or less as the case may be. (5) Finally, it can be used when the protagonist is the only one in a position to be able to answer a question about the self. For example, in scenes of reconciliation or interactions with reversed 'wisdom figures' such as a deceased relative, Jesus Christ, a part of the self, or others (see 'The relative influence of Peggy's monster', p. 129; 'Dale's dilemma', p. 40 'The women who couldn't get in' p. 104, etc) protagonists ask advice of 'the other' or seek to be reconciled with the other. It is imperative that the director role-reverse the protagonist into the other for the answer, rather than allowing the auxiliary to ad-lib the reply. Thus the person becomes, of course, their own wisdom figure, even while speaking or acting as Jesus Christ or a loving and grown-up self.

Dot is puzzled as Phyllis then re-enacts the scene with Larry. While the scene is 'authentic' enough, there is a question as to why Phyllis should be so upset by such a small event. There are few clues in the scene that suggest a contact with Phyllis's own core issues or themes. The argument with Larry might lend itself later to role training or 'assertiveness' training, but at the moment there appears to be something very incomplete about it.

Phyllis tells Dot that the feeling is just like the one she had as a young girl in her family. A new scene is created, in which Phyllis is 7 years old. She has just been doing the washing-up, and is standing by the sink, wiping it over and over. Dot conducts the interview-in-role, *addressing Phyllis as a 7-year-old, and warming her up to the role of a child in that particular household. She asks questions about her family, and finds that Phyllis's elder sister has just been diagnosed as an incurable epileptic. She is having fits of increasing frequency and severity after a head injury two years previously.*

Auxiliaries are chosen to represent the parents and the sister, who are all in the sitting room next to the kitchen. Again by the use of role reversal an interaction is developed between Phyllis and her parents, first centering on her father and then on her mother. As this dialogue never actually happened, it is an example of what psychodrama calls 'surplus reality'. Phyllis is bewildered, and continually feels at fault for her sister's illness. The parents react in a most emotionally constricted way. They are unable to explain anything to her, and do not notice the guilt and rage that she is experiencing.

Phyllis becomes more and more frustrated in her attempts to gain recognition and love. She flies at her mother, bringing her to the floor. When (in role reversal) her mother protests at this unusual behaviour, she muzzles her, and tells her off for ignoring her and for showing so little understanding of what was happening to her. Her mother weeps, and says that she too feels guilty and bewildered — she just does not seem to have the resources to cope with such a sick child, she explains. Phyllis wavers; she is very persuaded by her own empathy with her mother's plight. But this is partly the quality that led her into difficulties in the first place. She cannot afford to take on the whole world at this stage, no matter how realistic are her mother's difficulties. With the encouragement of the group, she operates once more from 'total, subjective one-sidedness', and acts from a primitive subjectivity. It is most liberating. She muzzles her mother once more, casts a withering look at her father, and tells her mother that she is only little and that she herself needs to be helped, rather than having to help all the time.

Another auxiliary is chosen to portray Phyllis at the sink, endlessly wiping it. The auxiliary is acting as a mirror, portraying the actions and unconscious of Phyllis at a distance so that she can see herself. Phyllis 'stands out' of the drama beside the director, observing herself. She moves back into the scene and once again kneels on the floor beside her mother. She addresses the auxiliary who is portraying herself in the role of 'guilty servant'. With her hand still over her mother's mouth, she says: 'Stop! You've done enough.' In role reversal, as the guilty servant, she hears these words coming to her. She looks stunned, then relieved. The two Phyllises embrace. Finally, Dot introduces Larry to the scene. Phyllis shouts at him: 'It is enough. I've done enough.' She is elated by her discovery. The drama ends, and the group share from their experience the parts of their lives that have been prominent for them in Phyllis's drama.

A fortnight later, in the processing of the drama, the major auxiliaries — sister, mother, father, and guilty servant — speak of their experiences of being in those roles. Phyllis reports on her activities and feelings in the intervening time — she notes that she has been perfectly calm in her meetings with Larry, and that her attitudes towards her patients have been gentler. She has also been able to study — a quite unexpected outcome. It would appear that the new role — calm self-appreciator, perhaps, which was conveyed by the words 'I've done enough', has persisted and filtered through into many areas of her life.

The goal of psychodrama is spontaneity — a new and adequate way of action where feelings, belief, and behaviour are not conflicted. In the spontaneity state, everything seems to come together in the sweet joys of uncomplicated action. The formerly bowed and stuck protagonist may laugh, shout, cry, rage, or fall on another person in utter ecstasy — or do all of those one after another. Alternatively, spontaneity might arrive in the form of a quiet 'uh-huh' — a 'got it' experience, as when Phyllis said, 'I've done enough.' She was not at that stage spinning around the room in an elevated state, but the statement nevertheless went deep with her. As Zerka Moreno remarks, psychodrama 'is just as much a method of restraint as it is a method of expression' (Z. Moreno, 1969).

The enactment of a scene, and then the move into 'surplus reality' is designed to throw protagonists into a different state where alternatives are available to them other than their preferred modes of transaction. A spontaneous person is more sensorily aware of the data of experience from the 'external' world. These data give clues to the flow of experience and what should be done about it — what reactions are creative and appropriate. In a state of spontaneity, people experience their own needs and environmental possibilities fully and clearly from moment to moment, whilst working on a creative integration of the two.

Spontaneity involves a different world view — one that no longer needs the cognitive, affective, and behavioural state that has been the basis of experience for that person previously. The protagonist's symbolic universe becomes more flexible or adaptive as a result of taking on new roles, and becoming those roles. Phyllis's old roles, for example, seemed to be dominated by those of guilty servant and bewildered child. By entering for a while the role of, say, demanding 7-year-old, she was able to progress to those of calm self-appreciator and freed spirit.

Most psychodramas, and certainly most systemic psychodramas, assume that a person's inner self is inextricably entwined with the selves of others. Directors search as soon as possible for the transactional component of a role. In the early stages of a drama, protagonists tend to act out roles from their so-called 'neurotic system'; they may indeed have had little choice about these roles when they were very young — remember Portia aged 3 in the bathroom, or Phyllis aged 7 by the sink — because of the physical and emotional power of the adult world, or because they were then too little to have any other way of thinking and reacting to events. Their continuance of these roles into adult life, however, presents even more of a problem, but one that may be amenable to new sorts of experience. The goal of a drama is to develop a more adaptive role system in the protagonist and to bring that system into contact with their old role system. A strategic psycho-drama aims to promote new definitions in the system that will lead to rapid and durable changes in functioning, as we shall see.

At the end of a drama, the person is usually warmed up to confident, humorous, compassionate, or determined roles in themselves. Thus the two 'Phyllises' hug each other, or Portia stands between the rails once more. There is an internal reconciliation and an end to conflict — a developing self-love. Furthermore, a new form of relationship with other people is evident — with Phyllis's mother, for example and with Larry and the patients.

Sometimes dramas begin with a metaphor that is concretized and then acted out (as in 'Off the rails', p. 1), and sometimes they begin with a problem, as with 'Wiping the sink'. The metaphor might lead into a problem, or the problem into a metaphor. These dramas may develop a surreal quality as they progress. Their imagery can be startling and hyperbolic, or as friendly and cosy as a picnic in a forest. In the two dramas outlined so far, the problem is to help protagonists with their warm-up, to help them visualize, and to free-up the emotional and psychological 'truth' as it is experienced. But with other protagonists the problem is different; the visualization involved and the degree of warm-up is overwhelming, making the task to keep the protagonists 'grounded' so that they can complete and integrate their work. 'The snakes behind the wall' is one of the latter types of drama.

The snakes behind the wall

Pansy, the protagonist of this drama, is a thin, alert woman in her thirties, the mother of two children. The drama takes place in the context of a 'personal-growth' group that is being run on a sessional basis in a large country town. The membership consists of several first-timers, country housewives, welfare workers, social workers, and teachers.

Pansy had attended the group once before, so the session to be described is her second-ever psychodrama experience. Even though new to the medium, she had shown herself an excellent auxiliary and double, but she had never been a protagonist, nor had she revealed much of herself to the group. When Di, the director, had asked what was 'on top' for her on this particular morning, she replied that she did not really know why she came to the group, but she thought it might have something to do with 'the fear'. 'What fear?' the director asked. Pansy's eyes took a faraway look: 'The snakes', she said, 'I used to have nightmares about them when I was a little girl.'

The change in her appearance was remarkable, and caused some fear even in Di and certainly in the rest of the group; the members looked at each other and shifted uncomfortably. 'What snakes?' asked Di. 'The snakes behind the wall over there', replied Pansy, her eyes wide and staring. 'Let's have a look at those old snakes,' said Di getting to her feet. 'Do you feel solid with me?' She holds Pansy's gaze, and looks at her very seriously. Pansy pauses, focuses on Di's face, and says that she does.

Di is already setting limits around the drama and the protagonist. Although she reported later that she was 'quite frightened' by Pansy's apparently altered state and strong powers of hallucination, she believed that she would be able to help Pansy move productively between a present-time focus, at the same time allowing her to experience whatever it was that was so troubling. She uses language such as 'those old snakes' to demonstrate that the snakes had no power over Di herself, and she takes unusual steps such as asking Pansy whether she feels 'solid' with her to help Pansy relate to her directly before the drama begins, and to 'ground' her.

She says to Pansy, 'Why don't we set up a wall in front of that wall?' In front of the real wall of the room is erected a psychodramatic wall made of chairs. Although rather slight in build, Pansy chooses the heaviest armchairs, and throws them into place with considerable ease. She is, to say the least, warmed up. Di then encourages Pansy to choose five or six people from the group to be snakes. Pansy does this with some difficulty, as even the word 'snakes', or the thought of them, causes her intense anxiety. She stands in front of 'the wall' staring at the snakes, who are moving around in energetic arabesques, which seem to imply patterns of smoothly evil force.

The auxiliaries are relishing their splendidly evil role; it is fun to be so bad, once in a while. That is, every so often it can be liberating to give full vent to one's own evil or 'shadow selves' given a suitably safe environment. Pansy is not having fun, however. When asked to role-reverse as one of the snakes, she refuses, saying that it is 'impossible'.

Pansy is clearly very afraid as she experiences the nightmarish quality of that time in the past. Di realizes that she will need to continue to be a 'container' for her, setting firm limits to the drama, and taking more control of the action than she would normally be inclined to do. She does this by making the directives for role reversal very crisp, and by having her voice almost bark directions, so that Pansy, at least to some degree, is reminded of the present time and place; that there is, after all, an 'adult' present who is in charge.

Pansy singles out one of the snakes as having 'angry eyes'. She at last has allayed her fears sufficiently to allow herself to role-reverse with it; the action in itself has already brought some relief and some sense of mastery. In role as the snake, she presents a vicious countenance to the world beyond the wall; she sways and glares beyond her boundaries.

Sn: *Pooey humans! Pooey and full of mess!*
Di: *Is she (pointing to the auxiliary playing Pansy) included?*
Sn: *She certainly is. She's just like the rest of them.*
Di: *Say that to her.*
Sn: *You're just like the rest of them. Making a mess and hurting each other. I hate you all. The only clean things are birds.*

Back as herself, by role reversal, Pansy is shaken by the snake's hatred, and cries in a jagged and tormented fashion. She says that she too would like to be like a bird, 'flying high above everything'. Di considers that at this stage there would be a real risk that Pansy might like, all too well, 'flying high' above everything, and that it might be difficult to get her to make contact with the ground again. Rather than taking up the action cue (of having Pansy be a bird and 'flying high') she decides that there has been adequate acting of metaphor already.

Di conjectures that if the snake is angry at 'people' for hurting each other and making messes, these people must be from Pansy's original social atom, and that the hurting probably took place when she was quite young. Ignoring the 'anal' references in the snake's diatribe, Di asks Pansy to set up a scene where people in her family were hurting each other. In doing this she challenges the notion of a purely 'internal' context to the problem that might be implied by making a pooey mess when one is little, although to concretize this metaphor would also have been legitimate.

There are many paths a director can take when presented with the hundreds of words and images that people produce in discourse. The context is never quite 'outside' or completely 'inside'. To be sure, the snakes are a 'part' of Pansy but they are likely to make most sense in a context between her and someone else. Strategic psychodrama, as we shall see, regards the self as a subsystem, and the individual as part of a larger organism. Each person within the larger organism arranges the others' reality; no-one is entirely a cause, or entirely an effect.

Pansy's family is comprised of father, mother, Pansy, a sister nearly two years younger, and an infant. Father and mother are 'always fighting', and when they do fight, Pansy becomes afraid, and hides. In this particular dispute, father and mother are having one of their sulking fights, where they do not speak to each other. Pansy is hiding behind a door, with her toy koala, played by an auxiliary. The director asks what she is doing.

Pa: I'm going to cut his ears off.
Di: Why's that?
Pa: He's pretty.
Di: How come you want to cut his ears off, then?
Pa: I want to make him like me.
Di: Like you. What are you like?
Pa: I'm ugly!
Di: What?
Pa: (Shouting and crying at the same time) I'm ugly. Ugly. Oooh!
Di: What do you cut his ears off with?
Pa: Scissors.
Di: Better get yourself a nice big pair.
Pa: (Searches around the room until she finds two broomsticks which she joins together to make a grotesquely large pair of scissors. She begins to cut the ears off the koala.)
Di: Here comes your mother!
Pa: (Crying) Go away! I'm ugly, I'm skinny, and I'm stupid.
Mo: If you were a good girl, you wouldn't get into trouble.
Pa: Go away.
Mo: Don't be bad.
Di: Reverse roles as the snake.

The snake hisses around, and comes out from behind the barrier. Pansy is so distressed that she goes into a state of role confusion between herself and the snake. The director allows this, thinking that probably the roles are not so different anyway. Pansy says that it is no good being a snake, they just hurt things 'just like I hurt my baby cocky'.

Di's hunch that the snake is linked with Pansy's anger at someone in her family is neither confirmed nor disconfirmed, at this stage, though it is evident that her early directorial intervention regarding the expression of anger has been premature. Pansy is not yet warmed up to anger to the extent that she can express it directly as herself, or indirectly as the snake. She is more preoccupied at the moment with guilt and fear, leading to a symbolic self-mutilation.

Di suggests that they now go to the scene where she hurts her baby cockatoo. This scene is constructed: it takes place on the rear verandah of a typical farmhouse, with tankstand, clothesline, working boots, etc. Apparently the cocky had 'not been eating', and Pansy, aged 3, is attempting to persuade it to have some food. She places a grub in its mouth, but the bird cannot swallow, and just keeps it there in its beak. She shoves the grub down the bird's throat, using a stick. In role reversal as the bird, she falls over and dies. Back as herself, she is wild with grief. Her tears go on for some time. Di prompts her to apologize to the bird for killing it, thus bringing in the notion of reparation, which is different from guilt and grief, but which, like grief, has a healing quality. In her younger days, Di found herself quite influenced by Kleinian psychotherapy.

Pansy apologizes to the cocky, at some length and with great feeling. When asked if she wishes to bury the bird, she says no, that she wants its spirit to fly free. Di asks where that spirit is now. Pansy replies that it is flying high above everything, riding on a cloud, partly supported by it. When a role reversal is suggested, she says that she is quite content just watching, and that she can experience all she needs from her present position. This is so obviously the truth that Di does not persist. The 'flying high above everything' that Pansy has mentioned at the beginning of the drama is now linked with this scene, which is itself linked with death and transcendence.

Pansy now returns to the koala and apologizes to it for mistreating it. She begins to laugh at how crazy it is to live in her family. Her mother reprimands her, and she deflates once again. Di suggests that it is now time for 'the revenge of the snakes'. By this time Pansy is fully ready to take on the role of angry snake. With the other snakes she launches an all-out attack on the mother, hissing and striking. 'I can't help it if I'm skinny. I can't help it if I'm ugly. It's not my fault! It's not my fault!'

She drops her role as the snake, and without suggestion from Di grows up to adult status. She shouts at her mother for daring to tell her how to raise her own daughters, and lists examples of the incompetent mothering that she herself has received. She carries on, stabbing her mother in the breast with her finger, and stating her own beliefs in parenting and the nature of childhood. Suddenly, it is done. 'It's all over now', she says. 'I don't think

I'm going to be afraid of those snakes again.' Di sees little need to point out what the snakes meant. Their meaning is now obvious.

The 'diagnosis' that Pansy had hitherto applied herself had assumed a problem that was 'internal' to her. The psychodrama separates Pansy from the problem by externalizing it within a scene. That is, the very setting up of a scene and populating it carries the implicit assumption that this problem began at a particular time and in an interpersonal context. The problem is not intrinsic to the protagonist, but is interactional or relational. Bateson (1979) remarks that it makes no sense to talk about 'dependency' or 'aggressiveness' or 'pride', and so on. All such words have their roots in what happens between persons not in something-or-other inside the person: 'If you want to talk about, say, "pride", you must talk about two persons or two groups and what happens between them' (p. 133).

Pansy's problem has been externalized and placed between another person, her mother, and herself. Although the problem is still 'her' anger, it is found to have its origins at a particular time and in a particular context. Furthermore, she has inherited from her family a particular perspective — a transmitted universe. This universe has the advantage of being a known territory, but it also imposes limitations that do not have to be there. It has prevented her from exploring different worlds, and of changing perspectives on the one she does inhabit. The drama offers her an extension, an alternative, a modification of her known boundaries.

The lady of Spain

Peta, the protagonist of this transgenerational epic, is an attractive, serious-looking woman in her early thirties who works as a psychologist in a position of high responsibility in the community. She won the group's interest by saying, in the group warm-up phase, that she had realized that she was somewhat secretive, and she recognized that her mother was a bit secretive too. I'd just like to explore this,' she said.

The group elected Peta as protagonist in a formal manner by 'sociometric choice'. That is, after she and one or two others tell of the issues that concern them, they sit in front of the group and declare their readiness to be protagonists. The remaining group members then come out and stand behind the person whose theme seems to trigger something in themselves. The group is asked to choose 'selfishly' in these instances, not on the basis of any popularity poll, or because they feel sorry for the speaker, but according to a hunch that if this person were protagonist in a psychodrama, some of their own questions would be answered too. Such a basis for choice helps to ensure that the protagonist is truly representing the group's themes at that time (see the section on central concern p. 52).

Also standing for the protagonist role was Pino ('The clockmaker's son', see Chapter 9), who said that he was feeling 'very frustrated and without potency'. Pino's own drama is recounted later in the chapter on transference. In fact, Pino at this stage gave a more elaborate and more emotional discourse on his difficulty than did Peta. The formal sociometric choice nevertheless went to Peta, presumably by reason of some kind of group 'unconscious process'. Pino's prospective drama about 'not being powerful' was, in a sense, validated by the group's failing to choose him, and was to be suggested again in the course of Peta's drama itself, where Pino becomes the 'disappearing auxiliary' who never gets to say his lines. As so often occurs in a psychodrama group, the themes acted out in the psychodrama are also present in the group roles that members take.

In the preliminary interview for the drama, Peta was asked if any pictures came into her mind that might have to do with her theme. She replied that she had a vague image of a scene with her brother when she was about 10 years old, but that it didn't seem to have anything to do with secrets or secretiveness. The director encouraged her none the less to go ahead with that scene, assuring her that if nothing came of it, another would occur readily enough that might be more relevant. Peta rather perfunctorily sets up the kitchen of a villa outside Madrid, where the family had a holiday house. The director asks her to look out the window. She begins to warm up to herself as a young girl as she gazes out over the kitchen bench, noting various features outside. She points to a neighbouring villa, which she describes:

P: *They're both the same, really — the only difference between theirs and ours is that they've looked after the garden, whereas ours has never been developed and is all dry and withered.*
D: *Just like this family?*
P: *Yes, that's very true.*

Peta chooses Pino as an auxiliary to be her brother Nick 'who got all the attention'. The scene consists of her raising a tin-opener above her head, just about to stab Nick. Her mother, Mary, is nearby in the kitchen, hovering ineffectually, a little appalled at this latest manifestation of family nastiness. Peta portrays Mary as a rather lost woman beneath whose maternalism seems to lie a desperate wistfulness, a pervasive disappointment with life.

Dennis now extends the interview with mother, having in mind Peta's original statement about the link between her secretiveness and her mother's. At this stage the director has no explicit hypothesis. So far he is presented with an air of disappointment and an opening scene of potential violence where a sister is trying to stab her brother. Someone else is getting the attention that rightfully belongs to oneself; perhaps this will become a family theme, perhaps not. There are also some family secrets, the point of which will probably not be the content of the secrets, but the alliances that support them. The evocative garden next door, the original tableau of a stabbing, and the strange sadness of the mother suggests that this will be a drama saturated with forms and meanings that may only imperfectly be understood.

The director role-reverses Peta to Mother, and begins the interview-in-role of Mary. Mary is full of complaints about her family, and comments despondently on this latest manifestation of trouble between brother and sister as being typical of the family's troubles and the wearying nature of life in general. The director suggests to the mother that this probably was not really what she had hoped for when she got married. The mother readily agrees, looking somewhat relieved that someone appears to be appreciative of her as a hoping person. Dennis asks her to set up her dream of the marriage. From this time on, throughout the drama, Peta stays in role as Mary, the mother, and the scene with the brother is not returned to until the very end of the drama (to Pino's chagrin — see Chapter 9).

The mother arranges her dream sculpture of herself and her husband. In the tableau, he gazes at her adoringly, and has his arm around her shoulders. She also has children, 'Six, or maybe even ten'. They are all little, and either play with each other engagingly, or look up at her in a cute fashion. It is almost a scene from a nineteenth-century genre painting. Her dream of family kitsch is totally lacking in vibrancy. Nevertheless, its elements are likely powerfully to affect her emotional satisfaction, or lack of it, and her vision of what reality ought to be. Her vision of reality, and her actual reality seem very much at odds.

Dennis next asks her to establish her version of the family relationships as they actually are, again by means of a sculpture. The family is arranged thus: Frank (her husband) is sent to a corner of the room and faces the wall. He is busy and remote. The three children, including Peta, stand like statues, separated from each other and from their mother, who runs around the outside of the group distractedly. Occasionally she makes little darts in towards each of them, asking for their love and begging them not to leave her. In this sculpture, her own character seems to shrivel into pathos and self-recrimination.

The sculpture appears in some way unbalanced and incomplete, although there is plenty of action and dramatic interplay. Dennis asks if there could possibly be anyone else in the sculpture. Mary replies that she prays to God a lot. Dennis asks her to select someone from the group to be God. She does, and places him in another corner, facing her. From the formal qual-

ities of the sculpture, it already seems that there might be a symbolic parallel between the position of her husband and that of God, or at least that God is part of this family.

The mother begins to pray to 'God' in the corner. She goes very close to him, and rocks back and forth on her knees: 'Make me tolerant, make me good, give me comfort, don't let me be unhappy,' she cries, over and over, still rocking.

From the structure of the sculpture, and from a kind of ambiguous sexuality between Mary and God, the director forms the hypothesis that Mary, disappointed by the failure of her dream, has substituted the fantasy husband, God, for the real one, Frank. As later events reveal, this hypothesis is partially incorrect; it turns out to be a fruitful rather than a strictly accurate surmise. But by being able to be ruled out it leads to the formation of new hypotheses and new pathways for distinction and action. An invalid hypothesis is only dangerous if the director sticks to it rigidly, despite its disconfirmation.

The director suggests that maybe Mary (mother) might like to get a little closer to God. She does. They embrace. They embrace some more. They fall to the floor, rolling over and over. Mary wraps her legs around God's. She has thrown away the little toy chisels that she used on the sentimental family sculpture, and is now carving her scene with fists and elbows and belly. The director suggests that Mary might wish to make love to God on his celestial couch. At this stage, the auxiliary playing God objects, saying, 'No, I won't be in that.' The director responds immediately to Mary:

D: That's not quite what you want either, is it?
M: No.
D: You want someone else.
M: I want my daddy.
D: Get your daddy and your mommy here.

An interview-in-role then takes place with Mary's father. The drama has now moved to the second generation, to Peta's mother's relationship with Peta's grandfather. It is as if Mary is the protagonist, rather than Peta. The drama seems to have arrived 'naturally' at its present point, yet clearly it has reached this stage through a mixture of spontaneous sequences and steering from Peta and Dennis. The protagonist and director appear to share a 'co-unconscious'. This term was coined by Moreno principally to refer to couples who had been together for a long time; when they came to therapy, Moreno surmized that the therapist had to deal with the consciousness of A, the consciousness of B, the unconscious of A, the unconscious of B, and their co-unconscious — a somewhat independent 'third' unconscious of the relationship itself.

The notion of co-unconscious, however, need not necessarily be restricted to people who have been together for a long time. When directors co-imagine a scene, the process is more than an empathic one; it is a joining, perhaps, of the symbolizing actions of two minds. When protagonists speak about an aspect of their life, the director may form an image, and convey it to them. They may have no trouble acting within that image, and are not puzzled by it, and do not reject it. In turn, they themselves create more images that the director further acts upon. Director and protagonist operate in a kind of chain reaction, with the director monitoring whether he or she has gone too far beyond the protagonist's 'network of presuppositions' that restrain them from seeing the world in any other way than the way they already see it. We shall have much to say on restraints and networks of presuppositions in subsequent chapters.

We had left the 'Lady of Spain' at the point where the director asked Mary (Peta's mother) to bring forth her own father and mother — that is, Peta's grandparents. At this stage, therefore, the drama moves into the family-of-origin one generation up. Peta (as Mary) makes the selection of grandfather and grandmother. When interviewed in role as the grandfather (Mary's father), one of the first things that Grandpa says is that he never saw his wife naked until she was 72 years old. She had slipped in the bath, necessitating his entry to the bathroom to help her.

The theme of repression, including sexual repression, that had been first hinted at when Peta described the sterility of the garden, and that was evidenced in the family sculpture that Mary set up, and also in her behaviour with God, is repeated through generations. Of all things to mention first, Grandpa mentions the bath scene. The drama at this stage could have taken several directions: marital therapy for Grandpa and Grandma, sealing off that spouse 'holon' from the children and effecting repair work within that marriage, or 'structural' therapy towards the role of Grandpa as parent, thus keeping continuity with Mary's struggle with God. This latter course was the one adopted. The application of 'structural therapy' to psychodrama will be explained more fully in Chapter 6.

Mary begins an angry confrontation with her father, telling him that he never gave her anything she wanted and that he gave all his tenderness to her sister. The director asks for an auxiliary to be chosen to act as the sister, Sally. Mary then confronts her father and sister together. In the role reversal, Grandpa (played by Peta) acts with extreme reserve towards Mary and great affection towards Sally.

The two major themes of the drama are re-established: the longing for union and the secret rival, who is presumed to be receiving more affection.

The director concludes that further fighting between Mary and her father will not be productive for the time being. The physical dispute between them has taken Mary's (Peta's) spontaneity as far as possible at that stage, and to maximize that battle further does not seem to be a realistic option, although it may well be that this avenue could be better travelled in further work with Peta.

The director suggests to Grandpa that he 'parent' Mary to the best of his ability. Peta (as Grandpa) at first does this very awkwardly and roughly — it seems that she has no clear idea of how such loving and expressive parenting could be done. But after frequent role reversal and coaching from the group, she beings to be more expressive as Grandpa. In role reversal as daughter Mary, she sits on her father's knee, lapping up all this affection. A charming and peaceful vignette is established, with father talking to daughter, soothing her, cuddling her.

The director then nods to Sally, Mary's sister. The auxiliary playing Sally proves to be an excellent spontaneous actor, butting in on the scene, feigning illness, wheedling, seducing, manipulating, and in short, trying to do anything that will distract her father from his new-found relationship. Grandpa is nonplussed, but after a while Peta, in role reversal as him, is able to deal with Sally's anxiety, promise her equal time later, send her off to her mother, and return his attentions to Mary.

Mary, as daughter, begins to repeat the behaviour with her father that she had manifested with God. She entwines her legs with her father's, and seems to want to climb inside him. She cannot seem to get close enough. She wants no separation at all from him. The director remarks empathically on these actions, saying, 'It's hard to get close enough' and 'It's almost as if you want to be him.' Mary agrees, and does more entwining and burrowing. The movement does not appear to be so much sexual as a desire for unity, a desire to be not separate. No doubt its manifestations in the family, had they been expressed by Mary and allowed by the father, could easily have become sexual, and perhaps here is the clue to mother's secret.

In role reversal as Grandpa, Peta does not allow Mary to be one with him. Grandpa now allows the feelings and the longings, but draws limits. He empathizes with Mary, tells her he is not going to leave her just yet, and that even when he does, because he has to work and to attend to his own life and that of the rest of his family, he will always be her father. He says that it is impossible for her to be him, or him her, but that that it is possible to be close but individual. There is more talk between them. Mary is much quieter now, sitting calmly and rather alertly on her father's lap. This section of the drama seems finished. The sister, Sally, at the director's nod, re-enters, wheedling. Both father and Mary deal with her firmly but kindly. Father sends her off, promising time with her soon.

The director gets an auxiliary to be Mary in that scene, and asks that it be maintained as a tableau in the spot where it occurred. The whole scene becomes a 'mirror' to be observed from without. He then asks for the mother's social atom to be re-established in the part of the stage where it was originally set up, and chooses three extra auxiliaries to be Mary, Peta, and her brother. He asks Peta, her brother, and her mother to re-create the original scene in Spain, with Peta about to stab Pino, while Mary ineffectually stands near.

Peta raises her hand once more. But she seems now not to be very interested in the gesture, and the director decides to make this, too, a tableau. He removes Peta for a mirroring exercise, choosing an auxiliary for the original scene. Peta then has the opportunity to observe from the mirroring position four scenes: herself in the stabbing scene, her mother's social atom, her mother writhing with God in the corner, and her mother receiving adequate parenting from her grandfather. During the whole drama, Peta had not once done an action as herself, not even following through with the stabbing. She says, from the mirror position, 'If mum had had that (adequate parenting), I wouldn't have needed to do that' (the stabbing). Peta appears calm and relieved, even though she had had no catharsis 'as herself', and had acted almost the entire drama in the roles of other members of her family.

It is difficult to say with certainty why this result should be so. A possible explanation may be that all the roles enacted on the psychodrama stage are somehow roles of the protagonist, even though the narrative is apparently historical, and the drama is 'populated' with other characters. Integration of any two or more people in the drama, therefore, implies integration within the self of those roles. Live theatre, a film, a novel, or a horror story work in a similar manner, perhaps: human beings are so empathic, so tribal, so connected, that a 'part' of them goes into the narrative of any involving story concerning other human beings. When the story, film, or play is resolved, the integration between the split-off bits occurs also in the reader or watcher. Psychodrama generally offers a much stronger experience than this, however: the story is one's own, and one becomes an actor in it. Thought and feeling are joined by the terrifying power of action. To explain the phenomena of Peta's drama we are led into the concept of roles and internal representations, which shall be discussed more fully in Chapter 4.

Chapter three

Focusing passion: the contract

The truth may snare us at times
but we can never snare truth

Bradford Keeney

Once a protagonist has been selected, directors merge their unconscious with that of the protagonist at the beginning of a drama, and begin to utilize their own fantasies in relation to the emergent psychodramatic family. These fantasies are introduced to the drama first in the form of words and images, then later in terms of actions or scenes. Further associations are created, and an intensification of the therapeutic process occurs. Of all skills of the therapeutic repertoire, psychodramatists are most adept producing interactions that open the heart. Psychodramas unfurl all the great passions — pride, pity, greed, rage, compassion, and love — and let them flap and strain like sails, bearing the protagonist forward into unknown territory.

In the long run, psychodrama deals with the problems and glories of love — rapturous, unrequited, paternal/maternal, filial, patriotic, or spiritual. Most of the rationale for hypotheses in systems theory, too, seems to concern love or loyalty: people act out of their connectedness, even though their actions may be severely dysfunctional. By setting these emotions in space and time, that is, by producing them as drama, directors themselves need to cope with the feelings that are attendant on a role, and are involved in the state of spontaneity. What will actually happen in the drama, once this state has been reached, is usually uncharted territory.

Directors ask themselves four questions at the start of a drama: (1) What is the central concern of the group and how does it show itself? (2) What is the contract with the protagonist? (3) What is the central theme of the drama as it emerges, and the essential roles of the protagonist in the drama? (4) What have been the roles emerging in the group in the sharing phase after the last drama?

At the beginning of a session, the prime director roles are those of inter-actor, social investigator, and hypothesizer. Directors need to interact with the group, attending to sociometric isolates and building communication bridges between people. They look for alliances and coalitions within the group (alliances and coalitions in groups is a major theme of the author's companion volume to this book, *Forbidden agendas*. Directors note what people say and do, searching for patterns, and mentally testing these patterns for relevance to the concerns of the group. They assume that all events in the group are a response to demands from the members' original and contemporary social atoms, as well as the demands of the current group system. This interplay of the archaic and the now, the 'out there' and the here forms the operating dynamic of the system.

A formal, central-concern model was developed by Enneis of St Elizabeth's Hospital, Washington, DC, and has been used there successfully for 25 years (Buchanan, 1980). Essentially it is a mixture of what we will later term 'group-as-a-whole' theory and psychodramatic understandings of the warming-up process. Both these strands are incorporated in Moreno's belief that a protagonist must serve as a vehicle for the group concern. Hence the theme of a drama must be a truly experienced problem of most of the group members. To ensure that this happens, directors listen carefully to what is going on in the group, taking note of the sociometric interplay as well as the manifest content. They structure the resulting group interactions so that a 'true' protagonist will emerge whose theme relates to that of the central concern. The drama's content links with spontaneous productions that have occurred since the very beginning of the session. The three essential elements in the formal model are contract, theme, and topical concern. Each of these will now be expanded to some degree.

Contracting before a drama

Although the goal for the group is something worked out between director and group members, final responsibility for accepting it rests with the director. Group members may ask for something that the director knows is impossible; if he or she even half agrees to the impossible goal, the therapy is implicitly defined as a failure from the outset. Directors need to negotiate with a protagonist who attempts to set up a 'global' contract that has little chance of success, and to help them settle for one that is more within reach. The global ideal need not be ignored, of course. It is kept in mind as a goal, albeit one whose very out-of-reachness may be the actual source of the problem. To accept it, however, may serve to hook the protagonist further into failed attempted solutions.

Before an individual psychodrama, a member may announce that he or she wants to 'resolve the issues of my marriage', for example, or he or she may attempt a contract to 'become self-confident and at ease socially'. It is unwise for a director to take on such a contract for a single session, although these goals may be attainable over a term. Having been set such a global task, the director might say: 'We can't do that in one session, but what you're hoping for seems very valuable. Where could we make a start? What would be a sign that you were more self-confident? If you were more self-confident, in whose company would that take place?' Or even: 'How underconfident are you now? A hundred per cent? Sixty? What would you settle on as being a reasonable goal — something that would suit your sort of person?' Usually such negotiation by the therapist is completely acceptable to the client, who, with some relief, sets about renegotiating.

As well as directors building 'success', however minor, into the contract, they also are modelling appropriate limits. When the drama begins, directors encourage protagonists to enter an experience that does not at the moment make sense. The road is created at every point. The experience may not make sense, but the contract needs to. Thus the 'rationality' of the psychodramatic process is reserved for contracting, interview-in-role, and processing. It is used to prevent the director and protagonist entering a relationship that is structurally unsound. The boundaries set by the contract then allow the therapeutic phase to put rationality aside for the while, and permit the dynamic forces of the drama to have a full play.

At the contract stage, directors' tasks usually include the following. They need:

(a) understanding as to which difficulties have been cleared out of the way in making the contract operable with the protagonist and the group;

(b) an initial hypothesis from what is already known about the protagonist: the major roles in his or her personality, particularly which roles are overdeveloped, underdeveloped, conflicted, absent, or adequate;

(c) some idea of the areas of the protagonist's functioning that are going to be observed in the action. For example, what roles do they mobilize when people try to get close? What do they do when others do not behave in the way they want or expect?

(d) to develop a rationale for the dramatic production and reasons for the rationale in terms of the person's social atom in which the roles are operative, and the effects of these roles in his or her social system.

Second-order cybernetics

For directors acting strategically, the problem to be worked on needs to be put in solvable and probably interactive form. Strategic therapists (e.g. Fisch, Weakland, and Segal, 1982) suggest that when asked what they want to do, people will usually launch into a description of presumed underlying matters, presenting them as the 'real problem'. Actually, the therapeutic debate over what constitutes a real problem, and therefore 'real therapy' is probably a futile one. Naïve realism is no less a danger to strategic therapists than it is to psychodramatists, since all therapists co-create their clients' maps of reality. Competent therapists from all persuasions can and do play an active part in the client's reconstruction of experience. Psycho-drama itself is a very strong constructor of experience. The question becomes: what experience is it most helpful to construct?

A strategic director might become quite problem-focused at the inter-view stage, and ask questions like 'What are you doing now that because of your problem, you'd like to stop doing, or do differently?' Or 'What would you like to do that your problem stops you doing at this stage of your life?' The answers to these questions can themselves take the form of psycho-dramatic enactments. The idealized solution, for instance, can be enacted; or the actual nature of the problem, and other people's participation in it, can be shown clearly, and in action. In a series of psychodramas, at least, the 'problem' should be something that can be 'objectively' agreed upon, so that an assessment can be made if the difficulty has actually been influ-enced. People are helped to change, *inter alia*, by seeing how they have already changed. For any single psychodrama, such as a first-time psycho-drama at a weekend workshop, the appropriate contract may be somewhat less outcome-oriented and more exploratory. A series of sessions, however, should lead to more than exploration — otherwise the psychodrama will no longer be 'strategic' and the sessions with the director run the risk of becoming haphazard 'awareness'-orientated procedures, with little build-up or follow through.

In terms of the central-concern model, the director on any given day needs to be mindful of the general contract of the group (such as the contracts in an obesity group, a training group, or a substance-abuse group) as well as individual contracts that people have made. In a group that has been meeting for some time, directors need to remember the overt and covert 'agendas' of each member, whilst not locking them further into their restrictive solutions by reifying them. Each person is new each minute; but sometimes it takes more than a minute to change.

Moreno was more conscious than most therapists of his time of the co-creation of reality by the therapist and client. He insisted on the inter-personal nature of therapy, and was critical of Harry Stack Sullivan calling his own therapy 'interpersonal'. Moreno maintained that when there was only one patient facing a professional therapeutic agent it was a 'moot question' as to whether this could be considered 'treatment' of inter-personal relations.

In order to talk cogently about treatment of interpersonal relations there must be *two* patients present, and a third, the therapist, who may be able then more genuinely to remain uninvolved, a participant observer and an interpreter to both parties, or ... the therapist must himself become a participant actor, although not formally, 'psychologically' a patient. When there are two patients, not one, they can give therapy to each other, each in accord with his ability and his needs. Admittedly, to function in the role of the professional therapist and at the same time mobilize his own private personality in order to help another individual requires careful strategy.

(Moreno, 1959, pp. 55–6)

Psychodramatic enactments give the impression of being presentations of the protagonists' own systems. This impression is an incomplete one, however. In joining with the protagonist in a psychodrama, directors create a new system, which might be called the protagonist—director system. The director's inclusion and participation in the system makes up the 'reality' of what is presented. Director and protagonist operate in a recursive process to co-create reality in the form of a psychodrama. The insistence on the observer's role in the complete description of the system is the contribution of second-order cybernetics, although Moreno hinted at such a view at least as early as 1959.

First-order cybernetics emphasized the homeostatic and adaptive properties of systems, while in second-order cybernetics (Howe and von Foerster, 1974) it is the observer (director) who draws distinctions that create 'reality' (MacKinnon and James, 1987). Second-order cybernetics emphasizes the observer's inclusion and participation in the system, and includes such concepts as self-reference, recursive process, and construction of reality. All psychodramas are the product of distinctions that are made, in part, by the director: interactions among family-of-origin members, for example, are transactions that occur in the context of the session, in the present, and in relation to the therapist and the group, as well as being the pinpointed dialogue between the family participants in the there-and-then.

Even the choice of a scene is a construction of one or other party drawing distinctions — it is the selection of the system considered relevant. The director and protagonist together construct and bind together an ecology of ideas through language and through action (Hoffman, 1985). The psychodrama is not an 'object' that can be controlled or programmed from the outside. Rather, like the system itself that it purports to describe, it is an ecology of ideas, the boundaries of which have been shaped by many decisions, including the decision to enact this rather than that psychodrama.

Therefore, belief in the 'truth' portrayed by a psychodrama can safely be laid to rest: neither the director nor the protagonist can know the 'truth' about the problem or the events portrayed. Both of them take the protagonist's version of events (itself a construction) and together rework it to new meanings and a new truth. The 'reworking' does not simply refer to the 'surplus-reality' section of the drama or the interpretation given it afterwards. The reworking includes the warm-up of the group, the selection of the protagonist, and every decision that the director and protagonist make thereafter.

Dale's dilemma

Pilar, the protagonist in this drama, is a large, colourful, and witty woman. She has attended several psychodrama workshops, and likes to use the method in her job as a welfare officer. Under Dale's leadership, the group had developed a central concern of 'being suppressed'. Such a concern is common in psychodrama groups, and itself needs questioning, as we shall see later. Dale had himself chosen Pilar as protagonist, and sat with her for the initial interview holding her hand. He begins to negotiate a contract with her to 'examine' certain of her roles that operate dysfunctionally when success/failure situations present themselves.

D: *What is it that we'll be attempting in this drama? What do you want out of this session?*
P: *I want to get rid of that part that squashes me and sets me up to fail.*

As we shall later observe, Dale is diverted in his contracting attempts with Pilar into a difficult and unhelpful contract (to 'get rid of' a part of her, the part that she claimed was squashing her and holding her down). Dale is caught between the idea of psychodrama as a form of enchantment, and as a clinical modality. He is therefore reluctant to break the intimate atmosphere between himself and the protagonist that has been established in the group and by the very selection of the protagonist. His understandable desire to join Pilar in creating from the outset a magical world where everything can come true had repercussions throughout the drama. At the outset Dale was in a dilemma, however, caught between not wanting to dampen his own and the protagonist's emerging spontaneity and sense of magical freedom, and yet needing to establish a role system between himself and Pilar that would be the most helpful — caught between passion and technique.

Dale is faced with the vital question of whether he should accept the presenting problem of the protagonist, even though he knows that the protagonist's ambition is difficult or perhaps even impossible to achieve, or should he use his commonsense and clinical experience to moderate the protagonist in her aims? This issue goes back, perhaps, to a division in Moreno's own development — that between his sociometric thinking, and his desire to support the protagonist's 'total subjective one-sidedness'. If Dale opts for the latter, does that support relate to Pilar at the contracting stage, or only after she has actually entered the psychodrama? It is difficult for Dale to answer this on the spot, as Pilar presents him with her ambition.

The problem Dale 'sees' is very dependent on what Dale does. Psychoanalysts, for example, would most likely regard Pilar as having a quite different set of problems because they would 'do' things differently from the outset. Pilar would be on a couch, for example, rather than on a stage. She would be alone, rather than in a group. What becomes Pilar's problem, and its solution, is a co-product of Dale and Pilar. Pilar may have come to believe she had a very different set of problems were she in Primal Therapy, or if she lived in the fourteenth century. In psychodrama, directors always moderate the phenomenal world of the protagonist simply by their form of enquiring about it, and thereafter by supporting it and giving it physical shape and movement in time. Even the narrative of the psychodrama, just telling the story, becomes a joint production between protagonist and director, as we have already suggested. The question for directors is what the nature of their influence should be. Is it simply to make the lived world of the protagonist more concrete and conscious, and thereby more manageable? Sometimes the mere production of a scene and development of it in surplus reality is in fact enough to help protagonists redefine their system so that it becomes more functional. But even in the case of mere production, the construction of reality is a joint process.

Directors 'follow/lead' (Seeman and Weiner, 1985): they pick up cues given by the protagonists' display of their phenomenal reality, and attempt to clear a path or lay down supportive emotional tracks ahead so that the protagonists' perceptions may improve and achieve their full concreteness. Psychodramas have the quality of a trance or an awake dream — the unconscious made into conscious experience. In tracking the unconscious, the director cannot go where the protagonist is not ready to go or does not want to go. Moves made by the director that have not first been indicated by the protagonist will either be ignored by the protagonist, or be greeted by puzzlement and corresponding loss of warm-up. The alliance between director and protagonist may also suffer and need repair.

What are the cues being put out by this protagonist? What particular path should be cleared? Is it possible that Pilar's top-dog/underdog dialogue ('get rid of') might be the essential dysfunctional process? Or perhaps it is legitimate to go with the content of the protagonist's imagination and develop their 'megalomania normalis'. Actually, even this description is not adequately circular. Dale does not create Pilar's reality, nor Pilar Dale's. Dale's dilemma is where to draw the distinctions that will create the therapeutic reality:

P: I want to get rid of that part of me that squashes me and sets me up to fail.
D: You want to have a relationship with it?
P: I want to get rid of it.

Dale accepts Pilar's statement, and after some negotiating, a scene is established. It is at a country hotel, late at night. The next day, Pilar has to *launch a project at work. She needs to be fit and alert. Dale role-reverses Pilar as the bartender and interviews him. He says that Pilar is 'some drinker' and that he is mixing her a drink that would 'kill a brown dog'. It is a mixture of whisky and two liqueurs, double size. Pilar is seated at a corner of the bar, hunched over, and swinging one foot. In the bar are some regulars, and the local football team. Pilar eagerly awaits her drink, though it is not the first bar she has been to that night, and it is far from her first drink.*

Having evoked the bar scene, Dale then takes the drama to an 'intra-psychic' dimension. He ignores the footballers and the other restraints on Pilar behaving in any other way than the way she did. But at several inter-personal levels, Pilar's behaviour makes sense. Dale, however, joins Pilar in wanting to punish and get rid of a part of herself. In so doing, he risks putting the full force of a psychodrama behind a dysfunctional and possibly unnecessary polarity. The part that Pilar wants to be rid of is as much her 'map' of the world as the virtuous part that wants to do the ridding.

D: *While you're here there's a person telling you you can get blind drunk.*
    (An auxiliary is chosen for this role, who lies under the bar stool)
P: *And there's a person saying I can have anything I want.*

Dale lies on the ground like a wrestling umpire to interview Pilar-below-the-stool. He has loosened up now, becoming more easy and flamboyant. Pilar tells him that her serious side is 'much more important'.

D: *Do you know about her up there?*
P2: *'Course I do — she totals me.*
D: *Express yourself to her.*
P2: *I don't know how to be strong.*
D: *Reverse roles.*
P1: *(Sitting on bar stool) I don't give a f.... You're bound to lose. I'm going to have a joint and a nightcap.*

Dale further interviews Pilar-below-the-stool:

P2: *If I get into that I might feel a lot of sadness. I'm scared to enquire where that punishing stuff came from. She knows what my real pleasure is. It's not good enough for me. I had to wreck myself. Nothing's ever enough.*
D: *She's been wrecking you.*
P2: *I want to develop personally and not be stifled.*

In this interchange, it is almost as if Pilar is acting as a 'little psychiatrist' to herself, and some of her statements at this stage have the air of therapeutic cliché. Although superficially anguished, they are probably not the stuff of life. In fact, they may even be part of the problem, part of the good girl/ bad girl polarity that is widening. Dale is fully within his brief as a director for producing the split in concrete form on stage — after all, it has already been part of Pilar's dialogue in the initial interview, but the conflict has been accepted as totally 'internal', and there seem to be few options other than to escalate it.

Not so. After a little more dialogue between the virtuous and evil Pilar, Dale asks Pilar to come out of the scene and to watch it from the outside ('the mirror'). He thus creates a role outside of these two interagents. In this new role, Pilar can see her two 'selves' at the bar. She says:

I just want to change my lifestyle. I've got so many hooks into this old one. Considering where I came from, I've been really successful. I'm outgoing, I've worked successfully in the hotel industry. I'm used to operating like this. *But it's time to change. I have an overwhelming inner sadness. (To Pilar on the stool) Why can't you accept the inner part of me?*

D: *Yes, why can't she?*
P: *She came from internalized rejection. She needed to survive. I've got a bit of an identity now. (Cries)*

At this point, Dale leads into the second scene. But there are elements from the first that are not well explored; he may have rushed too quickly into the role of therapist, when that of social investigator might have been far more useful. If one follows two notions: that psychodrama is an inter-personal therapy, and that people will usually go to a scene that is relevant, and put them together, this scene is bound to be interpersonally relevant in some way, and not just intrapsychically relevant. Pilar is in a scene where she wants to change. But the restraints on change — why she remains as she is, and for whose sake — are unexplored. Instead Dale goes with the original contract — to get rid of something, and so sides with the polarity that is already there in nearly every smoker, drinker, binge eater, and so on. He does not appear to value 'Pilar on the stool' as also being 'the real her', but joins the dissociation. 'I don't know why I do it, but I do it. I hate this part of me and want to crush it.'

Dale takes little account of Pilar saying that considering where she came from, she has been 'really successful'. Nor of her statement that she has 'so many hooks' into being the way she is. What are these hooks? Are they all bad? In fact, she vividly and dramatically demonstrates some of the rewards for her role on the bar stool: she is surrounded by people; she is very witty, making the director, the footballers, and the audience laugh; she kicks her heels with pleasure against the bar stool at the thought of being served her exotic nightcap. Her behaviour is in many respects highly functional

— it is a way of being related to people, it is her current and partially successful pattern of joining others. The interpersonal restraints on change are ignored, however, and no dialogue is developed except for a sentence or two to the barman. The director acts as if the intrapsychic battle (good vs bad self) is the sole or real issue.

D: *Let's go back a little to a moment when this feeling was really strong. Does any picture come to your mind?*
P: *(Crying) My childhood. In the kitchen on the farm.*

The scene of the farmhouse kitchen is set up, with attention paid to the position of the windows, the island bench, the stove, etc. Dale works briskly, using professional short cuts, as in his first question:

D: *What's a word to describe the feeling in the room right now?*
P: *Tense.*
D: *(Using voice to create atmosphere and heighten drama) Tense.*
P: *I've just boiled the spuds dry. I forgot about them. (Cries)*
D: *You're going to be punished. Where's your mum?*
P: *In the dairy.*
D: *Choose someone to be mother. (Pilar does so) Point to the direction of the dairy. (Pilar points)*
P: *All the other kids are here too. They're all saying, 'You'll be in trouble'. There's six kids in six and a half years, so they're all eleven months apart. Diana and Carol are 5 and 6. I'm about 4. Those two are down in the onion paddock.*
D: *Where's dad?*
P: *Walking around. Pacing in and out of the house and up and down in the garden.*
D: *What's your daddy's name?*
P: *(Incredulous) Daddy! Huh!*
D: *Well, what do you call him?*
P: *C..tface.*

When a protagonist is very 'warmed up' the details of a scene become less important. Dale uses refined devices such as asking Pilar to 'Point to the direction of the dairy' both to warm the protagonist up to that state and that place, and yet not to establish too many alternative 'scenes' that could be messy and confusing. We are there in an instant, because if someone points *to* something, they must already *be* somewhere to do the pointing. 'What's a word to describe this ...?' is also a nice form of shorthand, and saves unnecessary interviewing while at the same time deepening the sense of the essential emotional atmosphere. The scene had doubtless been triggered in the director's mind by questioning the 'I can have anything

I want' Pilar on the bar stool: 'Where did she come from?' Obviously from rejection, and the struggle to survive.

Pilar at 3 or 4 years old has boiled the potatoes dry, and fears a beating or scolding from mother, who is harrassed from the responsibilities of her large family, and the necessity to run a dairy farm without the aid of her husband, who is 'in and out of mental hospitals'. Father is introduced, also economically, and for the rest of the scene paces up and down, in communion with himself only. Pilar is in the doorway stuffing biscuits into her mouth. The other younger sisters are frightened at the impending row between mother and Pilar, and a little relieved that it is Pilar and not they who will be punished. As Michelle says complacently of Pilar: 'She mucks up. She's in a world of her own.' The mother is walking towards the house. Dale stops her. In the interview that Dale conducts with the mother outside the kitchen door just before she enters the room, Mother says that she is 'sick of living'.

Mo: *(Entering kitchen) The potatoes are boiled dry! Pilar! Pilar! (Rushes on Pilar) I'm going to belt the shit out of you, you stupid little girl. (Does so)*
D: *Reverse roles with Michelle, your sister.*

The scene is then re-enacted, this time with a richer idea of the social consequences of the action, as the sister's possible participation is explored. It is a blind alley, however, and the action reverts to Mother and Pilar again. A lead has been followed, and Dale has initiated a social-atom exploration that does not have the effect of deepening the warm-up, so he cuts his losses and returns to the main actors:

Mo: *(Slapping Pilar with her hand) Go to your bed and read.*
P: *(In bedroom) I just sit here and think how f....d it all is. I'm tired. We're all tired. We don't have any fun.*

Dale then interviews Pilar about the resources available to her. There appear to be very few: father is not available because he is mad, mother is worn down and harassed, and the other children have their own problems just keeping up and trying to compete for the limited affection that *is* available. Dale encourages Pilar to talk to her father, who is still pacing up and down in frenetic self-absorption.

P: *I don't want to be here. (Crying)*
D: *Louder!*
P: *I don't want to be here.*
D: *Again.*
P: *(Shouting) I don't want to be here! I hate it here. There's nothing here — Dad's crazy. There's no cuddles. There's nothing for me.*

Here Dale is using the standard technique of 'maximization', in the hope that Pilar will 'break through' from her former role of passive eater and overburdened young child to some new state that will be adequate to the situation. The warm-up is fuller and the protagonist is more integrated than in the bar scene. One can almost count on this in a family-of-origin psycho-drama, though one must be careful not to make it a stock in trade simply because it 'works' nearly every time. Because people do warm up so readily and so fully to their original social atom, they need sometimes to be 'pro-tected', as it were, against this being a point of therapeutic exploitation. In Pilar's case, however, the original family scene is relevant.

At the age of 3 or 4, Pilar has actually very few options but to do what she did, given the family circumstances and the fact that she was only 4 years old. The biscuit-eating itself may have been a fruitful avenue for exploration, given the suggestion contained in the scene and its possible link to overweight Pilar on the bar stool ordering yet another drink. Four-year-old Pilar tries to comfort herself and perhaps ward off evil by food as she huddles in the kitchen doorway.

Not every lead has to be followed in a psychodrama, however. A drama is so symbolically rich that it will constantly throw up elements and images that are relevant to the protagonist's functioning, but need not be taken up at the time. So Dale decides that he wants to hear mother's reaction to the outspoken rage that Pilar is expressing to father and to the unfair world in general. Role reversal needs to follow the maximization of a particular affective state, and leads into a further enactment, now at the level of 'sur-plus reality'.

All the actors are now working fully in psychodramatic reality, and have left the so-called 'historical' narrative behind. Pilar has never actually said to anyone, 'I don't want to be here' etc., when she was a child. But even the apparently historical narrative, of course, is a construction of reality built up from the protagonist's memory in interaction with the director and the group, as we have already noted. Had any of us been there in 1954, we may have seen events quite differently. Had Pilar been a protagonist with a different director, the psychodrama would have been almost completely different, even the apparently 'historical' sections. All psychodrama is surplus reality, but some sections are more surplus than others.

In order to organize information, and thereby condense differences, which are the basis of meaning, individuals develop *maps*, which are codes for meaning, and *grids*, by which distinctions will be made. These maps, while they may have some fit with the territory, are nevertheless not the territory. They are constructions by the observer. While the content of the constructions frequently changes, remark MacKinnon and James (1987), the rules of transformation, that is, of how the maps are constructed, remain relatively stable. A psychodrama can change the particular meaning of one event or behaviour, can introduce entirely new behaviours, or can change the rules of transformation themselves. For Dale to have changed the rules of transformation, he would have had to have started at the initial interview, and challenged Pilar's version of reality at that stage. As it is, she is getting a new version of reality, but not necessarily new rules by which she transforms data itself. He asks Pilar to reverse roles with her mother, and interviews her:

Mo: *She's a bit crazy. I mean, the other children toe the line.*
D: *(Heated) Express yourself to her.*
Mo: *(To Pilar) You're an annoyance to me.*
P: *I hate it here!*
D: *(Sharply) Reverse roles!*
Mo: *Well I hate it too.*
P: *(To director) I'd never have this conversation.*
D: *(Authoritatively, so that she maintains the new reality of the psychodrama) I know. Well, you're having it now. Get on with it.*
Mo: *Where would we go?*
P: *I want to go with Uncle John.*

Pilar has now introduced a 'wisdom figure' into the drama. In dramas that take place in early childhood, the child either has to act effectively with emotions that had to be suppressed at the time in order that she could survive, or she has to find help from some source. This help can come from someone who was there at the time, such as a sibling, an aunt, or an animal, or it can come in the form of the protagonist's adult self helping out her little self, or from a figure in history, literature, or religion. There is no reason why, if all else fails, Jesus, or the Angel Gabriel, or Mahatma Gandhi cannot be invoked, if such figures accord with the protagonist's belief system as heroes or helpers or wisdom figures. The director has recognized that Pilar has chosen a wisdom figure, and decides to steer the drama in this direction. Other directors may have continued the dialogue with mother, until new roles were developed with her. Such a course undoubtedly would have meant further and bigger fighting with her, probably physically. In a typical psychodrama, this fight would eventuate in a new form of dialogue with the parent and the development of more loving roles in both parties.

D: *Talk to him. (Uncle John)*
P: *This family's all a big front. Not just when we have visitors, but all the time. It's really lonely, even though there's a lot of people. I sleep in me clothes all the time so I can go and get the cops and the doctor in the night if Dad goes really crazy. Sometimes he gets us all up and makes us march around the farm. We're too scared not to. You can't certify without a doctor and Dad has to be actively crazy for the*

47

*doctor to certify him, because the bins are all full and he's afraid
he'll be sued. We always try to look after Mum, even though I don't
like her very much. She can't help it.*

Pilar then struggles at the 'reality' level with whether Uncle John can really
help her. She explains to Dale that he already has eight children of his own,
and could not possibly take her in. For Pilar to be taken in to her uncle's
house is not so necessary as for her to receive some tenderness and age-
appropriate care from someone. After a short interchange, the director
says:

D: *Uncle John, you've got eight kids of your own, so you know what
     kids need. Talk to me about what kids need.*
J: *They need lots of nurturing and care, and TLC and all that.*
D: *You get your kids and you hug them and hold them, do you?*
J: *Sure I do.*
D: *Show us how you do that.*

Here the director has decided that Uncle John (that is, Pilar) needs warming up to the nurturing role, given that these roles appear to have been so
lacking in the family of origin. Had he asked Uncle John (Pilar) immediately to nurture Pilar, he (she) may not have been able to do so. So Uncle
John is 'warmed up' to the nurturing role by nurturing his own family. One
more will not make much of a difference, perhaps. In fact, the warmed-up
Uncle John does accept Pilar.

D: *John, you're an expert in cuddles. Do it the right way. (To Pilar) You
     like this, eh?*
P: *I just want to stay like this forever.*
D: *Take it into your heart, and you can.*
P: *I don't care if I die. I just want to stay like this. I don't get recognized.
     Mum only hollers how the biscuit tin is empty — doesn't recognize
     how I'm really frightened and not allowed to cry. And I want to cry! (Sar-
     castic) Might upset your father, might upset your father. (Angry) Might
     upset yourself, more like it. You might get to know how upset you are.*

*Pilar stays in Uncle John's arms for a while more, and the drama winds
down. The 'sharing' is conducted with Pilar still held in Uncle John's arms,
and the group draws round closely. Although this scene gives the
impression of great sweetness and closeness, there is a danger for the
protagonist of blurring the psychodrama and 'reality'. There is also a risk
that group members themselves may not appreciate being Pilar's 'psychodramatic space' whilst at the same time being expected to share from their
reality-selves. Long-term difficulties from this practice may be those of*

making people angry without their knowing why, or else of creating excessive group dependency, encouraging people to prefer the sheltered world of the group to the harsh, outside realities. It may aid the impression of a 'magical solution' being available — that is, that the group will be exactly as Pilar wants it to be, and can reinforce the 'I can have anything I want' idea that Pilar had about drinking in the bar. If Pilar turns from nightcaps to psychodrama for her kicks, she probably will not have made much progress with the role that she is trying to 'get rid of'.

Theme

The theme of a group refers to the affective dimensions that the group faces at a particular time — its primary emotion. This notion is common across the group literature, whether a 'focal conflict' (Whitaker and Lieberman, 1964) or a 'common denominator' or a 'common unconscious fantasy' is the term used. To discern the theme on a given occasion, directors need to 'tune out' from content and hear or feel the dominant emotion. They need to understand the common unconscious fantasy (let us say, that all our needs will be met by one ideal person) as well as the specific reactions of each participant to it.

Group leaders have little choice but to be part of the group situation and theme, as we shall discuss in the companion volume to this book on group work. Therapists need to embody a cybernetic epistemology of patterns that characterize living and mental processes. 'Otherwise, we treat ourselves and our contexts of living as though they were heaps of bricks subject to locomotion' (Keeney, 1983, p. 96). At the same time, leaders are relying on their professional skill as psychodramatists to be able to act differently from the rest of the group; that they are not always saved or protected by this will be the theme of the chapters on 'transference'. Moreno's notion that the most spontaneous member of a group is the leader of the group still has currency in modern group work, and is a more 'cybernetic' one than even many modern psychiatric concepts.

Dominant emotions have a fairly limited basic range: fear, hate, joy, and love, perhaps. But in practice, the group is seldom given over to the one outstanding affective dimension, and an overlay of feelings will be manifest. For example, the group overtly may be expressing anger towards the leader, but this anger could be complicated by feelings of isolation and abandonment which might have nothing to do with the leader. Or the group may be fighting with each other a good deal, but it would be rash to interpret the dominant emotion as rage or 'oedipal rivalry' (see 'The clockmaker's son', Chapter 9 and 'The woman who wasn't born', Chapter 10). A more accurate interpretation of events may be that the arguments come from a new atmosphere of confidence and trust in the group, and that the members are reacting to a more comfortable, familial atmosphere where squabbles are possible. The interpretation conveyed to the group, there-fore, might be that the members are feeling confident and trusting. This interpretation itself is a construction of reality, of course.

Directors, then, think around the following issues:

1. Where will they draw distinctions that will create 'reality'?
2. What function does the expressed theme of the group play in stabi-lizing their existent roles?
3. What is the meaning-system in which the problem is embedded, and how does such a system include the director?
4. How are director and group bound together in this theme, and therefore what is the therapeutic dilemma?
5. What will be the consequences of change, if any?

Let us turn to an example from a group in order to discern some of the themes that may be operating (or are typically constructed between direc-tor and group). Only the selection of protagonist section is narrated here — the full drama of 'Paul's pain' will be continued in Chapter 8 on the problem-solution cycle.

Paul's pain

The setting is a first-year psychodrama training group. The members of the group are fairly high-functioning people, usually very eager for skills acqui-sition. A conversational group warm-up occurs; in this particular session the group seems to be more than usually concerned with personal issues of a painful nature. One woman, for example, talks of swinging between complacency and craven fear about her work; when she is not highly occupied, she feels 'empty inside'. Another talks of recent attacks of panic: of waking in the middle of the night and wishing her husband or anyone in the household were awake, too. Another talks of her 'reality whirring round and round' since she returned from overseas: job, primary relationship, money, direction of professional and creative development, so that she is constantly in a state of 'nothingness', unable to move. Another member agrees that this is very relevant for her, though she declines to give details.

Paul, a vigorous man in his thirties then speaks again. He says that he had, in the last couple of days, gotten into a 'no-win' interaction with his partner, where he felt, and she agreed, that he 'had a lot to work on'. Another man chimes in enthusiastically: he had been the subject of what he now saw was a kind of 'attack' by two women friends of his, who were questioning how he lived his relationship with his lover, how he brought up his children, and other aspects of his personal life. When asked why he had felt the need to get into such conversations, the man replies that he had wanted to remain 'open and non-defensive'. Others chime in with similar views: The group themes seem to centre around emptiness, confused apathy, and feeling pain as a result of interactions where one is made out to be 'bad', or one makes oneself out to be 'bad' in some way.

Any of these three themes would have provided a basis for a well-supported individual drama, given that the two main ones: emptiness/panic and no-win interactions seem to be something like 'valuing the self' or even 'defending the self'. The theme of apathy/confusion is probably also linked to this main theme (what issue in psychology isn't?), but the link is more tenuous and people's comments were not so strongly directed to that theme.

The themes of a group are often tied to developmental stages in the group, (e.g. Bion, 1961; Braaten, 1974; Tuckman, 1965) such as dependency/independence, fight/flight, abandonment. Care needs to be taken lest these concepts are reified, and that a non-recursive meaning system is not developed that is punishing and inflexible. 'Fight' and 'flight' are events that take place between persons, rather than within persons. Problems need to be expanded to derive their definitions from patterns of interaction.

Bateson (1979) uses the notion of 'context' — that is, pattern through time. The patterns and sequences of experiences are built into each group member's map of the world, which then becomes the context for further experience. Rather than thinking too tightly in terms of group developmental stages, one can view the development of a theme through time as this relates to each member's current map. Using a co-evolutionary framework, directors can track the evolution of a theme as it evolves (including its evolution with the director) with the pattern of relationships and beliefs over time. The current context also includes the group's own beliefs about its history. The aim of a group-as-a-whole interpretation, as we shall later observe, is to draw attention to the theme as it relates to a particular event in the group, such as fight. Where an intervention has been successful, or psychodrama well selected, the theme of the group tends to change. Over the life of the group, the director's task is to help the members restructure their thematic responses in the direction of greater spontaneity and potency.

Cybernetic explanations help directors avoid their own subjective experience of lineal causality. They are urged to more complex descriptions of events in the group, as well as focusing on dyadic or triadic behavioural patterns in the present or the recent past. After the drama of 'Paul's pain' the sharing concerned changes that the group had made in valuing itself as a group, and changes that members had made in self-valuing. They were able to redefine 'being open' to appropriately setting limits on what other people could do with them. As one woman put it: 'I've always been a bit of an attacker. And I sure could feel pain and go down a hole. But it had never occurred to me before that it was OK to nip some things in the bud. I was wedded to attack or collapse.'

Topical concern

The topical concern of the group is derived from two streams called the 'manifest content' and the 'matrix of identity', in psychodrama language. The topical concern is the broad area of focus produced by the group members' interactions with one another. The manifest content comprises the actual words spoken by the group members as they interact, such as complaints about the accommodation, acknowledgements of a birthday, enquiries about someone who has been absent the last two sessions. It also includes members' more metaphoric language, such as 'This place is the pits', or 'I can't get across to anyone today', or 'I always feel so tremendously happy when I see you'. As well as being clues to the manifest content, such expressions are also action cues that might be profitable to enact. Directors can make immediate use of these metaphors to deepen the action warm-up; for example, they can ask the whole group to enact 'not being able to get across'.

The matrix of identity concerns the protagonist's beliefs about the origin of the problem — where it was born, as it were. Again, one is dealing with the protagonist's map of reality, rather than with reality itself. There is no possibility of doing otherwise, of course. In working with the matrix of identity, directors develop appropriate statements by the members that may have initially been broadly expressed. The idea is to track the context of the statement and the other persons who may be involved, so that a cybernetic explanation might evolve. If someone says that 'society is phoney', for example, the director may attempt to relate the statement to specific individuals in society, either now in the group, or in the speaker's past where the person has felt 'phoney'. That is, directors make general/particular, and now/then links. Penn (1982, p. 272) describes this process as one in which therapists draw an arc beginning in the present and moving to the past (or vice versa), so that they can fix a point 'in the history of the system when important coalitions underwent a shift and the consequent adaptation to that change became problematic'. They identify a merger between the individual's own matrix of identity and the here-and-now of the group situation, and suggest this merger to the group members in a way that makes sense to them.

Through the integration of the contract — the manifest content and the matrix of identity — the director is able to formulate a central-concern statement. This statement is best couched in dialectical terms, for reasons that have already been given. It should be broad enough to encompass all group members, but specific enough to relate to each individual and his or her matrix of identity. When the concern is stated to the group in dialectical terms, rigid thinking of the members is diminished; their restrictive solutions ('resistance') can go to either pole of the dialectic instead, or else travel between each pole like a ping-pong ball: 'Will I/won't I? This is true/no, this is false. I am like this/no, I'm not.'

The central-concern statement can often be formulated in the first quarter of an hour or so of the group's interaction, although Buchanan (1980) points out that in new groups or chronic regressed groups, there may be insufficient development of sociometric links and group cohesiveness to uncover the central concern so quickly. That is, a number of themes might be thrown up, and it is hard to see which one most represents the group. This itself can be stated in a way that will help people define themselves. That is, the very fact of members not communicating freely, or the sense of an underlying confusion and crisis in the group can in itself lead to the formulation of a central-concern statement around those issues.

There's a feeling of crisis in the group today — a stillness, just like the still-ness before a storm. People want to reach out to each other, but it's almost as if they would need permission to do that, almost as if they fear someone would stop them. This may or may not be a very productive time, just now; a moment that may be very like similar crisis times in your outside lives when the atmosphere seems dangerous, when something in your relation-ships isn't quite right.

From time to time, directors may prefer to delay the statement, to make no unifying comment at all. On such occasions, they continue to raise the interactions between the group members, rather than immediately leading from the central-concern statement into a psychodrama. The central-concern statement can be made, the dilemma posed, and reactions to that dilemma sought from members. When one person reacts, another can be asked to react to that person, and so on round the circle until, perhaps, a new central concern is reached. This procedure is preferable to directors 'bailing the group out' of its anxiety by 'putting on a psychodrama'. While it is perfectly appropriate and part of the directors' role to lead the group out of the wilderness from time to time, they need also to resist the temptation to be Moses reincarnated. It is not unknown in this author's experience for whole sessions profitably to be spent in developing and then defining the basic assumption of the group, and to track the alliances and coalitions around those assumptions. This procedure, called strategic socio-metry is described in full in the companion volume on group work.

Thus, to delay the psychodrama is by no means a failure — rather, it allows for a deepening of the group process to go on, without which any psychodrama that is offered may be 'cloudy', resulting in sociometric isolation for the protagonist, or a reinforcement of the protagonist's restrictive solutions. Such protagonists, having done such a 'good' drama, may wonder why they feel so poor and unsupported at the end. In effect, the group may have engineered the presentation of a drama to avoid the real and painful group issues that are taking place, and that are best settled in the here-and-now. In its demand for a psychodrama when the going is tough, a group can act like a family in trouble, which switches on the TV or focuses on the dog rather than come to grips with a family issue that has led them into stuck thinking.

The central-concern statement is sometimes, but not always, a warm-up to a psychodrama, then. Essentially, it allows the group members to focus on specific issues, and to clarify their stances around them. The director, having formulated the concern statement, then highlights the interactive nature of the concern:

It seems to me that people in the group today are concerned about creativity. Most of you feel that your lives have become stuck in some way, and that you need to make a breakthrough. Perhaps someone, now or in the past, has seemed to stop you from breaking out. You want to express yourself more fully, but you're afraid to. You end up stuck. Bill, here, says that he's never had a creative moment in his whole life. How do you relate to that, Sue? What do you make of Sue's comment, Jack?

In this example, the director focuses the concerns of the group on one issue, here, the broad one of creativity. He or she can continue to focus on the central concern of the group whilst drawing more and more people into the system around it. At the same time, a search is going on in the group for a suitable protagonist.

A combination of the central-concern model and circular questioning (see the chapter 'Strategic sociometry' in *Forbidden Agendas*) generally ensures that a protagonist is clearly identified; someone undeniably demonstrates their connection with the theme, and a good balance of expression of disturbing and reactive motive. The method generates a warming-up process around a particular issue, and a protagonist who is truly working on behalf of the group issue. The method also tends to by-pass the necessity for formal sociometric choice of protagonists, outlined in Chapter 2. Although this formal method is tried and true in the psycho-dramatic world, and is often very useful, such formality in choosing is rarely necessary if the director has correctly located the pressing issue and has determined the informal sociometry within the system.

Summary

1. There is discussion and interaction between group members.

2. The director mentally identifies the concerns being expressed.

3. The director:

    (a) observes who is most warmed-up to those concerns;
    (b) verbalizes these observations;
    (c) validates his or her perceptions by checking with the group;
    (d) generates broad concepts connecting apparently unrelated issues that have been spoken of;
    (e) ties them in to a dialectical framework;
    (f) asks people in the group to connect with this framework;
    (g) uses a series of circular questions further to connect people.

4. A protagonist emerges from the group interaction. Directors can then present to the group their reasons for selecting the particular protagonist and ask the group if they support such a choice. This procedure helps support the protagonist, particularly one who is feeling a little anxious or isolated. Effectively, it acts as a confirmation of the group sociometry.

Chapter four

Interviewing for a role

All the world's a stage
And all the men and women merely players

As You Like It

Morenian definitions of a role

Carl Whitaker maintains that Moreno was 'probably more clearly responsible for the move from individual therapy to the understanding of interpersonal components of psychological living than any other single psychiatrist in the field' (cited in Fox, 1987, p. vlll). Moreno suggested that we were all actors on the stage of life, and at the same time he exposed our considerable stage phobia — or one may say, life phobia. The idea of 'role' was central in Moreno's theory of personality. Roles were not masks or a kind of 'top-up' to the core self, but actually constituted the self: 'Role playing is prior to the emergence of the self. Roles do not emerge from the self but the self emerges from roles' (Moreno, 1964, p. 157). The word 'role' is therefore not opposed to the word 'real', or associated with masks or forms of insincerity. A role is 'the functioning form the individual assumes in the specific moment he reacts to a specific situation in which other persons or objects are involved' (Moreno, 1964, p. iv).

The choice is not between playing a role and not playing a role — one has no choice in play-acting. The choice is only between one role and another. Bentley (1972) notes that the famous expression 'all the world's a stage, and all the men and women merely players' may have been derived from a motto in Latin on the wall of Shakespeare's own theatre, the Globe: *Totus mundum facit histrionem.* While Shakespeare popularized the expression, the concept of our playing roles in life is a good deal older, it seems. In Greek and Roman theatre, the parts for the actors were written on 'rolls' and read by the prompters to the actors. Like 'catharsis', 'tele', and 'protagonist', the notion of role is one of those difficult parts of Morenian terminology that he borrowed from Greek theatre to create a new language for psychiatry. Sometimes the technical psychodramatic use of terms, however, and their connotation to other contexts, tend to clash. 'Role' and 'protagonist' are terms from the theatre, but the theatre in this case is everyday life. 'Role' reinforces the idea that we are improvising actors, who can change the middle or end of any script that is handed to us.

We are actors, not from falsehood, but from truth; our truth becomes more manifest the more we are in touch with our spontaneity. If we persist with our old script when there is a chance for improvisation, we become rigid. The number of roles available to us becomes limited; our flexibility to adapt to a changed situation is restricted. Our personal system becomes closed, and probably the social systems within which we operate, such as our family, job, or circle of friends may also become closed.

Let us examine the elements in the Morenian definition of roles given earlier. Firstly, it is a functioning form, that is, an action or a position taken up — a way of being. Secondly, roles are developed in a specific moment: one's role relations, even to the same other person, therefore, are not permanent. Thirdly, they arise in reaction to a specific situation: that is, roles are determined by context. A person may take up the role of aggrieved husband at home, but he is unlikely to adopt that role on a soccer field. A woman may be a tough union rep at work, but may be a nurturing mother to her infant when she comes home. If people attempt fixedly to maintain a role from one context to another, they and those around them can experience considerable distress. Nurturing mother may not be an appropriate role state for someone negotiating a log of claims, and tough union rep may not always fit the mother–child interaction. Evidently the context and the time are highly significant in determining what an appropriate role should be. Finally, in Moreno's definition, 'other persons or objects are involved': that is, roles imply an interaction between person and object, or person and person. Basil Fawlty beats his broken-down car with a branch; a father takes his daughter to the beach; a priest says Mass before a large congregation — in each case, the role is a feature of an interaction.

From 1936, the start of his treatment centre at Beacon Hill, north of New York City, Moreno attempted to treat not only the individual sent for therapy, but members of the patient's social atom as well — the spouse, the parents, the organization, the lover, the children. He himself believed that a role is completely enacted when the person comes into living contact with another role played by another actor. He thought that the universe was not simply a bundle of wild forces, but that infinite creativity tied us all together, and bound us in responsibility for all things. 'Everything belongs to me and I belong to everybody', he said.

We are at our 'fullest' when living contact is made, when the 'I' playing the role feels that the other role is 'thou' and not 'it' — one can see the influence of Martin Buber here, and in fact Buber was an early contributor to a little magazine that Moreno founded. When we are walled off from each other we still enact certain roles, of course, but they may be inappropriate, cutting us off from an adequate warm-up to ourselves and others. Perceiving the other as 'it' usually obscures important systemic information — feedback — which allows systems continually to adjust. We do need 'its' in our lives as well as 'thous' (otherwise we would become rapidly exhausted with the intensity of things simply by buying a bus ticket or walking through a city street) but too often the 'thous' that we do really need, and therefore the 'I-s' that we need, have become 'its', and our response to life is unnecessarily flattened and constrained.

Five components of a role

Psychodrama as therapy or as revelation aims to push back old boundaries and help people enter new territory. It operates by a kind of peripheral vision, enriching, distorting, and ultimately transforming what commonsense would otherwise present. The protagonist's unconscious processes are usually believed to be trustworthy, taking them to scenes that are relevant and allowing the production itself to leap ahead of analysis. But not always. Dramas can also be unhelpfully chaotic, or repetitively caught, or trivial and sentimentalizing. The protagonist's spontaneity needs to be assisted by the director's skill and knowledge that is based on an analysis of protagonists' roles as they interact with relevant others.

Analysis of behaviour generally answers three questions: What does the person believe? What is the feeling state? And what is actually said or done? Such an analysis, however helpful, can still neglect the notion of role as being interactional. The systemic view demands five rather than the traditional three components of a role in order to conduct an adequate role analysis. The components, actually implicit in Moreno's definition given at the start of this chapter are: context, behaviour, belief, feeling, and consequences. The three-part analysis tends to produce excessively intrapsychic and non-interactional understandings, whereas a five-part analysis leads directly into systemic thinking. Contextual, behavioural, belief, affective, and consequential aspects of a role are deduced by means of the enactment itself, and by means of the interview-in-role. Although the present section concentrates on the verbal interview, it must be kept in mind that the five components of a role often fall out 'naturally' in the course of the production. The presentation of the five components via enactment rather than by interview will be frequently demonstrated in the reports of later dramas.

Context

It is said that Konrad Lorenz unwittingly attracted a curious crowd when he used to waddle through high grass and quack. His behaviour no doubt seemed weird to those who did not know that he was an ethologist imprinting himself on the ducklings who were following him. From this example it is plain that understanding the contexts of action implies making higher-order distinctions than simple descriptions of action. For example, 'driving a car' is a higher order distinction than 'turning the steering wheel'; or 'a game of football' is a higher order distinction than 'kicking a piece of inflated leather'; or 'an exercise to learn about circular causality' is a higher order distinction than 'pushing a chair around a room and then pushing a person around a room'. An examination of the contexts of action provides the link between a simple and otherwise unintelligible action and the social organization that gives it meaning. As Bateson (1979) noted, the context reveals how the reactions of individuals to the reactions of other individuals are organized in time. Just as turning a wheel is given meaning by the higher order distinction of driving a car, so guilty person is given meaning by describing a mother's interactions with her daughter, when a double description is produced.

Tracking the sequence of behaviour around a role provides a detailed environment for understanding all actions and interactions that go to co-create the role. Investigating the context of a role implies an initial enquiry about what the other members of the social atom do and say when the protagonist is in a given scene. Such enquiry often reveals the coalition positions of the other members. For example: What does father do when mother runs to her room in tears? Have there been any events in the household recently which have been a bit unusual? are questions that help to establish the context of a role. Other leads that may be helpful in establishing context could be questions that refer to the family's developmental stage: mother might run to her room in tears because all her children have left home and she is now faced only with her husband for company for the next twenty-five years. If such is the case, then the context of mother's tears is crucial for understanding the role of the crying mother.

Directors who think consistently in systems terms can not only be more penetrating and efficient at getting to the heart of the family-construct system, but the work itself tends to be tighter, more efficient, and more dramatically satisfying. To save tedious role reversals, and to maintain a systems orientation, an overview of the main characters is requested. After the significant people have been identified, a 'gossiping in the presence of others' method can be used for the interview before the enactment. 'Gossiping' asks one member in the family to comment on the relationship of another two. Let us suppose that the scene takes place in the family dining room when the protagonist is 15 years old. The director can ask:

D: What is happening in this scene?
P: There is a big family row because I came home late.
D: Who are you interacting with?
P: My father.
D: Who else is significant in this scene?
P: Grandmother, my father, my mother, and my brother Andrew.

D: What does your grandmother think of the relationship between your father and your mother?

The last question about the grandmother's estimate of relationship between father and mother is the gossiping question. This form of questioning also tends to keep the action neat, and if well timed does not cut across the protagonist's warm-up. In fact, preliminary contextual questions can help protagonists get on with the action, rather than having continually to go back to establish relevant detail. The action component can be spoilt both by too much initial verbal material, which leads to intellectualization and douses the warm-up, and too little, which results in the continual need to return to contextual explanation.

Directors do need to cover certain common elements in an interview for a role or a warm-up to a scene. The list presented below is not intended to be exhaustive or for that matter to be gone through every time. Sometimes only one or two details are sufficient to establish what is essential.

1. *Location in time: the year, how old the person is, the season, day, and time. What has just been happening to this person or in this family? Is this the first time there has been such an interaction?*

2. *Location in space: whether the scene is in the country or city, in a house or out of doors. What is the immediate environment? The director can induce a sort of 'action trance' by asking the protagonist such questions, so that the important objects need not always be established by direct questions but can emerge from the action and the production itself:*

   Come up to this scene now. Go to the door. Close your eyes. What is the most important object in this scene? How does this object feel? How does it smell? You are only little: crouch down now and think of the scene from that level.

3. *Awareness of self and other persons, in terms of size, stature, condition, ways of moving, and nicknames.*

4. *Identification of significant others and a review of role relations. What are the coalition alignments around the problem in the present? Who is most/least upset by the problem? Who feels most helpless, for example? To whom do they appeal when they feel helpless?*

Let us suppose that Dot is interviewing Penny with the intention of helping her notice some of the differences and changes in her life, especially when these took place, and who was around when they did take place. That is, she is looking for the *matrix of identity* of Penny's present roles (see previous chapter, p. 52).

D: So, you're six years old? What sort of little girl are you? Are you an active girl? Do you like to climb trees?

P: No, but I like to sit in the tree in our back garden where no-one can find me.

D: Mmmm. Who do you hide from most often?

P: My mommy and my brother. I like hearing them call out.

D: If someone did find you, who would you like it to be?

P: Jesus, 'cos he's my friend. He understands.

D: Does anyone in the family understand you nearly as well as Jesus?

P: My dad, but he's dead.

D: (Switching tack) How tall are you? Show me. Are you going to school? What are you wearing?

P: My check uniform because it's summer, and my brown shoes, and I've got a tartan schoolbag.

D: Have you! What's inside? Open it up and show me what's inside.

In this preliminary interview, Dot is attempting to create a sense of lived reality, and an appropriate 'regression', so that Penny's 6-year-old self is established. If this interview were being conducted in the context of a psychodrama, she would have established what Moreno calls the *locus nascendi*, the place where it all began, the environment, the space. She has also found that Penny hides 'most often' from her mother and her brother. She knows that Penny can talk to Jesus, her 'friend', and that Jesus may be a wisdom figure who could be useful later in the drama to give Penny advice, perhaps, or to support her. The most understanding family member is her father, who is dead. She stores that information away, too. It is likely to become a major theme that provides the true context for Penny's hiding.

The therapeutic questions can follow these practical and earthy details. For example, Dot might follow up on Penny's spontaneous mention of hiding from mother and brother (Why hiding? Why not hiding from step-father and sister too?), or might actually follow a pre-arranged path, such as tracking Penny's beliefs about fathers through her 42 years, or her sense of herself as worthy, or whatever. Again in Morenian terms, this process would be called an enquiry into the *status nascendi* — how something grows and develops. The essence of the standard interview for a role, then, is the establishment of place, time, and relevant others.

Let us consider another interview segment that establishes the operation of two roles in one person. Most of us have several roles operating in rapid sequence as our 'self talk' switches back and forth from daydream to denigration to coping strategies. Di is interviewing Patsy, who is grappling to maintain her feelings of self-confidence against feelings of being rejected.

D: Do you have a time in mind when these things occur most strongly to you? What is one time when you have stepped out?

P: *It's a routine I make myself before I step out.*

D: *Is there anyone at home when you step out?*

P: *No.*

D: *Does it take place in the bedroom or the living room?*

P: *In the car.*

D: *What kind of car?*

P: *It's a Camry, gold, with press-button windows.*

D: *Reverse roles and be a Camry. Feel it in your body. Mmm. You look nice.*

P: *Yes, I've got red strips down each side, and press-button windows. I'm square, professional-looking, but smart.*

D: *Square, professional-looking, but smart! Reverse roles. How about you sit in your car, Patsy.*

P: *I'm sitting in my car, peak traffic going the other way. Feeling inadequate relationshipwise, so I imagine I'll phone a bloke and ask him to dinner.... He is way away ... doesn't know I exist. (Sighs) No good waiting for things to happen — have to make them happen. (Mimes phone) Oh hi, Steve, how about coming to my place for dinner?*

P: *(As Steve, loses steam) (Aside) I'm not used to this directness. How will I get out of this one?*

D: *What would a square, professional-looking, but smart person do, Patsy?*

P: *They'd pick up his tone, and tell him to get lost, the ambivalent shit!*

D: *What is the difference between a square, professional-looking, but smart person, and yourself? Choose someone to be the person. Address her about your differences.*

Di has established a context within which Patsy moves into the drama. She knows that Patsy is alone. She does not yet know the coalition alignments in her social atom that may have ensured that she be so. She has the first understandings of the type of role relations that Patsy has with herself and with a likely candidate for a date. She has established a double description between Patsy and a person who is professional-looking but smart, and is on her way to getting a description of the problem from the other. From this new description, which contrasts with Patsy's original view, she will create 'news of difference' wherein new responses can unfold.

Behaviour

Even the most obvious component of a role, the behavioural component, is not always established by the enactment itself. Prior to a drama, director and protagonist develop a common understanding of what might happen in the drama. The director focuses the enquiry onto what people say and do in relation to the problem, rather than settling for generalities. Detailed information about behaviour can reveal important distortions or contradictions that are the key to understanding the systemic functioning of the behaviour. Especially when using action methods one-to-one, the therapist can profit by taking a slow-motion picture of events leading up to, during, and after the problem that is the focus.

Let us say that Perry, a member of a therapy group, complains that he has been feeling 'helpless' lately. Upon closer questioning, it appears that the helplessness occurs particularly when his girl friend, Jan, spends a lot of time at netball and at her studies. Perry tends to talk in generalities about this issue, and is straining to get on with a scene where he can psychodramatically 'explode' at Jan for letting him down. This may indeed be the way to go. But there is time yet, and it will do no harm to hold Perry back a while longer, to check whether old and dysfunctional roles are not merely being reinforced. Indeed, further questioning reveals that Perry always goes home to see his mother when he feels helpless, and that Jan 'has to collect him there because she does not have enough money for a taxi to get home'. Jan 'has to' chase him, and, in addition, earn the opprobrium of her future mother-in-law for neglect.

In action methods, no less than in any other method of therapy, the therapist needs to be persistent in tracking a particular behavioural sequence. What is the context? What behaviour follows what? What are the feelings involved? Whom do they affect? Who does what next? What happens then? In this way, the director asks Perry the sorts of questions that focus mostly on what Perry does. The director is concentrating on the behavioural level of the role, and thereby inevitably on its context.

D: What do you do when you feel helpless?
P: Nothing much. I feel so ... so powerless.
D: When was the last time you felt like that?
P: Oh, it happens all the time.
D: Think of a time recently when it was really bad. Where was it?
P: In my flat.
D: In your flat. Who else was there?
P: No-one. Jan was out as usual.
D: How long had she been gone?
P: It seemed like ages. I'm always being left.
D: Be Jan for a moment, and walk out. (Etc.)

Prior to the enactment, then, the director has gained relevant information concerning the person towards whom the role is enacted, and when the role is enacted. The drama can then relate to major dilemmas in Perry's life, and is likely to be more systemically sound than if Perry were simply to rage against Jan, say. The director tries to understand, respect, connect, and produce relevant social-atom transactions. Protagonists themselves cannot always make these connections, as the continuation of dysfunctional family behaviour actually may require that they be unaware of them.

When the fuller story eventually emerges, the director might hypothesize that the systemic function of Perry's behaviour was that his mother would not feel lonely, and the function of Jan's repeated calling on him at his mother's place was to show that there would never be another woman standing between a son and his mother. These hypotheses would be tested by further enactments, and further role analyses of the context, feelings, beliefs, and effects of the actions. Directors run the occupational hazard of becoming 'intimacy freaks' — indeed, the prospect of participating in many people's intimate worlds may often draw them to the profession in the first place. The danger for the client is that the therapist will join their own role system, especially at the emotional level, to the detriment of even the simplest enquiry of who did what to whom, and what happened next. Clients themselves often are not able to make these distinctions, in their focus on emotional meanings.

Let us take another illustration of the importance of finding out 'what happened'. Philippa presents for therapy with the complaint that her husband, Paddy, is 'always getting drunk'. Enquiry about Paddy's drinking habits reveals that he comes home at night, begins a conversation with his wife, and then goes out to the pub. Further enquiry about what the couple say and do suggests that Philippa first complains to him bitterly about his behaviour, and then withdraws. The more bitterly she complains/ withdraws, the more he seems inclined to go out. When asked what her hypothesis is about Paddy's behaviour, Philippa says that she is probably being 'too soft' on him, and that she needs to make her feelings 'clearer' to him.

From the director's viewpoint it is easy to see that the complaining/ withdrawal and the drinking may be bound up with each other. It would be yet another linear solution, however, to suggest that the complaints or with-drawal cause the drinking, just as it would be to suggest that the drinking causes the complaints. If the roles of drinker and complainer are held to be 'inside' each party, either Paddy or Philippa could be treated for drinking or complaining. If, however, a double description is created, then Duke (the director) would be more inclined to treat the 'drinking-withdrawing relationship system'. Double description is a higher order of description than single description, or even two single descriptions placed side by side. The practice of double description will be described more fully in Chapter 7.

A third factor becomes evident from the contextual and behavioural interview. When Duke asks when Paddy's serious drinking problem seemed to begin, Philippa says that it began after the birth of their youngest son. Over the history of the marriage, all the children were quite frightened by Paddy's drinking, and drew closer to Philippa, to the extent that any possible separation could not be countenanced. At the time of Philippa's presenting for therapy, all the children have left home save the youngest son, who stays to 'protect' the mother from the drunken, and by now verbally violent father. Is this the reason for Paddy's drinking? Perhaps not, although the factor involving the youngest child certainly widens out the definition of the family system, and any 'solution' in the psychodrama that did not involve this factor might not be very successful.

The view from every side of the relationship, the numerous double descriptions, must be juxtaposed to generate a sense of the relationship as a whole. It would seem that there was at least one point in the history of the system when important coalitions (husband–wife) underwent a shift (the birth of the first child; all the siblings save one leaving home) and the consequent adaptation to that shift became problematic for the family. The double descriptions required are quite complicated. The therapist may seek circular information on the differences in relationships the family has experienced before and after the problem began. Father's solution of drinking is connected to mother's solution of withdrawing, which is connected to the son's solution of drawing close to mother. The problem and solution interactions are recursively related. Nearly all of this information has been gleaned from questions about context and behaviour — tracking the sequence around the problem, and enquiry about the beginning of the problem and the attempted solutions to it. The information is relatively easy to obtain, and in most instances is well worth the trouble.

Beliefs

The ability to select out and respond to information about difference depends to a large degree on the recipients' restraints, their 'network of presuppositions' that exist largely out of consciousness. Yet the 'beliefs', or personal constructs pertaining to a role are the elements least likely to emerge directly by enactment. Sometimes they cannot even be deduced from the enactment: after all, people rarely state their beliefs directly, or even think of them as such. Those people who do go around saying 'I believe ...' are usually, and maybe rightly, considered to be bores. Since the interaction itself, then, may not yield sufficient information on the construct systems of the participants, a direct verbal interview often becomes necessary. Interviews around beliefs usually take place when an interaction has begun, and the context of the interaction is beginning to emerge. It is of little use to ask people about their beliefs until they are warmed up to a role, whereas the context and the behaviour may be established from the outset.

The director wants to find out what are the personal constructs of the protagonist and who are the major actors who have steered the protagonist's life in this particular direction. Changing old code books and the establishment of new ideas is a prime goal of therapy. The enactment, the interview-in-role, and therapy itself all contribute to the selection and endurance of new ideas in the therapeutic system. Directors might ask themselves:

> What are the restraints on change in the system? If the protagonist did change, would he or she be 'disloyal' to someone else in the social atom, betraying them or perhaps betraying a personal code? If they acted differently, would they be going against a family injunction to behave in a certain way? For example, in this family is to be depressed a sign of noble character because depression demonstrates 'sensitivity'?

It is only for the sake of analysis that roles are broken up into belief, affect, behaviour, context, and effect. In reality, of course, these all merge into each other. Roles are not 'things', and nor are the components of roles 'things'. Roles are a construction on experience, a way of making sense of complicated data, a form of distinction that turns behaviour into information for the therapist. To analyse the 'affective' component of a role, then, is something of an artifice, given that emotions always have a content, a context, a set of beliefs around them that gives them shape, and have an effect on the roles that other people take up. Similarly, beliefs or cognitions are rarely emotionally neutral: they stem from or lead to behaviour, and always take place in a cultural as well as a personal context. All of them — beliefs, feelings, behaviours, contexts, and effects are simply distinctions made upon an otherwise unintelligible mass of experience. They are ways of ordering and responding to reality.

The belief aspect of a role is one of the most complex factors involved in a role assessment. Behavioural cycles in individuals, families, and groups are governed by a belief system that filters into most aspects of daily life, and guides the members in much of what they do. It is composed of attitudes, assumptions, prejudices, convictions, and expectations. Beliefs *are* the network of presuppositions that 'restrain' a person from taking action other than the action they do take. Because they are largely out of awareness, they are difficult to discern, far less change. That is why only sometimes directors hit the jackpot about people's beliefs by asking directly, 'What do you believe?'

In a stable system such as a family, people's individual beliefs interlock to form a whole set of governing premises, the 'family construct system' (Procter, 1985). When dealing with a whole system, it is not only the individual beliefs or the assumptions of any particular members that are crucial, but how these are linked to form the operating rules of the system. Change, which is what a therapist is usually driving at, exacts a price, and raises questions of what the repercussions will be in the rest of the system. Whole systems are not necessarily amenable to changing their operating rules.

People's beliefs in a system can be the chief reason why the system cannot change; members are restrained by their personal constructs or beliefs from acting in any other way than the way in which they do act. They may believe they are doing the right thing already, but not 'hard' enough, as we saw in the section on 'behaviour' with Philippa's belief about her husband Paddy who drank too much. Family members presenting for therapy tend to think that one designated member is guilty or crazy, and that that person needs to change, rather than themselves or other members. Again the example of Philippa and Paddy springs to mind: each of them has a single description of the complaining/drinking system. The premiss is that the symptom or person is a 'foreign element' outside the system and can be changed separately. Even the crazy or guilty member believes that. So if Paddy's drinking can be 'fixed', the system will have no further problem. The principal challenge to the therapist becomes not how to eliminate the symptom, but to find what would happen if it is eliminated. What price has to be paid, who will pay it, and is it worth it? These are questions relevant to the network of presuppositions, or personal constructs, or beliefs surrounding a role for which change is demanded.

The steel band

A group member, Prue, complains that she has a severe headache, like a 'steel band' around her head. According to standard procedure, this steel band is first concretized by the director who asks Prue to choose an auxiliary, A_1, from the group to be that pressure. Again in standard procedure, a role reversal is required, and Prue herself acts as the pressure on A_1, who now represents her. When Prue is applying the pressure to her satisfaction, the interview-in-role as 'Pressure' begins.

D:	*Who are you?*
Pressure:	*I'm the pressure on Prue's head.*
D:	*How long have you been around?*
Pressure:	*Oh, years now.*
D:	*Looks like she really needs you.*
Pressure:	*She certainly does — I stop her getting too cocky.*
D:	*Is that what you're here for?*
Pressure:	*Yes, she gets too big for her boots sometimes and I have to come along.*
D:	*What does she have to do to make you go away?*
Pressure:	*She has to sit tight, shut up, and stop flirting.*
D:	*Is this how girls (sic) should be?*
Pressure:	*Certainly — girls don't count — they should wait to be noticed.*
D:	*Tell that to Prue.*
Pressure:	*You've got to sit tight, shut up, and stop flirting.*
D:	*Keep telling her. (She does so)*

D: *Reverse roles*

The role of the 'Pressure' has now been partially established with respect to a central belief, which seems to concern the upbringing of women. Two direct questions are asked about Pressure's beliefs: 'Is that what you're here for?' and 'Is this how girls should be?' Note that the role reversal did not take place straight after the interview, but after a brief enactment. Protagonists moving into a new role then have something to which they can respond, which will thus more easily bring out their own roles. In the case of Prue, the auxiliary now takes up the role of 'pressure' so that Prue can experience that role as being 'outside' her, and a double description is thereby created.

Pressure: *You've got to sit tight, shut up, and stop flirting.*
D: *Reverse roles. Respond to that.*
Prue: *Aaah, it's awful.*
D: *Keep going; respond to that pressure.*

At this stage, it is preferable to encourage Prue to continue the enactment rather than to commence an interview with the director, which will tend to divert her attention away from relevant matters in her social atom and on to her relationship with the director. Prue would develop a quite different set of roles towards the director than towards the 'pressure'; her roles as interviewee are not relevant at this point, though these will be the one's activated if the director overinterviews. Generally speaking, the interviewing should be merely enough to gain direction for a satisfactory enactment.

Prue: *It's awful, I just can't stand it.*
D: *Express yourself directly to the Pressure.*
Prue: *Go away please, just go away and leave me alone. (Begins to sob)*
D: *More.*
Prue: *Go away, go away, go away.*

Now that Prue's set of roles have begun to emerge (a role title for which may be tormented, impotent victim) it is time to see what the response is by the 'pressure'. Another role reversal is called for. Prue, in role reversal as pressure, keeps up her sadistic restrictions upon the weeping auxiliary. There is no let-up — rather an increase in torment. A theme is beginning to emerge.

Papp (1983, p. 4) defines a theme as a 'specific emotionally laden issue around which there is a recurring conflict'. There are many such themes in any family or group: dependence versus independence; responsibility versus irresponsibility; repression versus spontaneity; closeness versus distance. In a complementary dyad, usually one person assumes the role of responsible person, and the other assumes the role of irresponsible one; one will try to gain emotional closeness, and the other will evade this. In the case of Prue and her pressure, let us say that a theme is emerging of 'control versus release'. Possibly this dialectic had been a family theme when Prue was a little girl, and now the two sides of the conflict are embodied in the one person — Prue.

Let us revisit Prue in her mini drama, which has moved on somewhat. The 'pressure' has identified itself as Prue's elder brother. This phenomenon is completely common in psychodrama: a particular feeling ('iron-band pressure') is given concrete form and is acted out by an auxiliary. After the interaction has developed, and after careful interviewing by the director, a family-of-origin figure may be identified, and a group member chosen to play the role of that person. Identification of a family member produces another choice point for the director — whether to set the enactment with the member in a particular scene around a particular incident at an historic time, say when she was aged 7, or 12, or 15, or to attempt to resolve the drama in vignette form, without a scene or particular time. In the latter case, Prue simple 'meets' her family in a neutral space and at an indeterminate time — more like the present than anything else. History is actually created, rather than recreated, as it purports to be in a time-and-place psychodrama.

Comprehension of the beliefs in the system (in this case so far between Prue and her brother) and the ensuing themes is not only arrived at through direct questioning, although this method has its place, as we have seen. The deduction of a theme and a core belief is based on observation of the enactment: listening for metaphorical language, tracking behavioural sequences, and picking up key attitudinal statements, such as 'You've got to ...' and 'just go away leave me alone'. The 'girls don't count' statement may or may not be crucial: it was said in interview with the director, rather than to Prue, and has a conventional ring to it. Even an auxiliary role (such as a 'pressure') enacts a different set of roles towards the director than it may towards Prue. 'Girls don't count' may be a very deep family theme — and the eventual core of the drama, or it may be a statement made with half an eye to the audience and half an eye to avoiding the deep pain in the family by diverting it to conventional sexual politics. The director simply does not know until the interaction is more fully developed.

Understanding the belief component of a role is critical in attaining a comprehensive definition that can allow the role system to change. Beliefs are the key to the unconscious networks of presuppositions that provide the restraints on spontaneity and new action. It is fallacious to conceive of spontaneity as a bizarre form of acting out or simple impulse release. Moreno suggests that warming-up to a spontaneous state leads to and is aimed at more or less highly organized patterns of conduct. He remarks that spontaneity is often 'erroneously' thought of as being more closely allied to emotion and actions than to thought and rest: 'Spontaneity can be present in a person when he is thinking just as well as when he is feeling, when he is at rest just as well as when he is in action' (Moreno, 1964).

Feelings

In Chapter 7 it will be suggested that change cannot occur until the person-in-the-system feels adequately and accurately 'defined'. Only then can their perception of the problem and the consequent perception of solutions begin to be helpful. In psychodramatic work, altering the perception of the problem enables spontaneity to take place: the new map itself invites fresh solutions. In fact, if the drama is well laid out, one often does not need to search for solutions — a new way of construing the problem itself brings its own solution.

People's emotional experiences need to be part of this new definition, since emotions are primary sources of information about one's experience of the world. Indeed, affective experience is extremely salient, to the extent that it often overrides other information. Emotion is the direct experience of the self; it is a crucial regulator of action and furnishes the basis of awareness of what is important to the person. Because it is so dominant, therefore, emotional experience can be a powerful tool for changing perceptions and meanings. 'New' emotional experience can provide an organizing and integrative framework for the creation of meaning, especially meaning that refers to significant others in one's social atom.

Clearly, then, the affective or emotional level of a role is highly important. To evoke and clarify (define) the feeling component of a role is vital, so that once acknowledged and recognized it may then change (if change is required). This definition does not imply, as we shall show later, asking the person 'How do you feel?' Rather, the feeling is usually hinted at or subtly expressed by the protagonist, and then enlarged and enacted with the help of the director. The enactment of the feeling ultimately defines it and thereby clears the way for change. An interview for the 'feeling' component of a role, therefore, attempts as much to aid direct expression as to provide information to the protagonist. In fact, these two can be one and the same.

Pia, a woman of about 40, is complaining to the group that her world is collapsing around her. Her husband's business is about to go bust, and she is faced with the fifth move in seven years if the bankruptcy court puts an order on her house. Her husband will not talk to her, her children are showing signs of distress, and, to top it all off, her father-in-law, Freddie, has had a stroke and she is left with his care. In the segment to be presented below, Pia has already, in psychodramatic form, represented the house, financial security, and the children. Auxiliaries are on stage in these roles.

D: *Where to now?*
P: *Freddie, I guess. He's had a severe stroke, and needs twenty-four hour care. (To Freddie): I wish you'd just die. (Cries)*
D: *Say it again.*
P: *I wish you'd just die. I wish you'd just die in your sleep, and then we could all get on with things. (Cries) I've got this terrible guilt.*
D: *Who do you need to tell this guilt to?*
P: *(Ignoring the director) I'm exhausted being around you. We'll have to take it in shifts. You fat, greedy pig eating all the time. You were 4 stones overweight. You knew! You knew!*
D: *Tell him.*
P: *I wish that stroke had killed you stone dead. You're a crazy-maker. You knew! You knew!*

In this interaction with Pia, the director did not have to do very much by way of interviewing to clarify what feelings were present. The clarity came by the protagonist being allowed, indeed actively encouraged, to express herself, so that her anger with her father-in-law and her sense of bitter injustice could emerge. At times, this type of ventilation alone can be helpful in changing perceptions and in altering a person's role structure. The so-called 'ventilation' is in fact a definition of the affective component of Pia's role system, and without it being recognized, it is unlikely that Pia could move on. Psychodrama is most successful at these types of primary definitions, which can be rich and useful for people.

Few writers, however, including those from the psychodramatic tradition itself (Moreno, 1964; Blatner, 1985; Kellerman, 1984) consider ventilation to be usually a sufficient condition for therapeutic change. Certainly the strategic position regards the desire for emotional expression within the whole context of the person's appeal for therapy, and looks carefully to see whether emotional expression may not be part of the problem rather than of the solution. Clients who seek therapy for ventilation purposes, and do it over and over, bind therapy itself into the problem. Emotional expression is an important part of a person or system's self-definition, but therapy needs to protect the client from this solution becoming a restrictive one.

A systemic psychodramatist also takes into consideration the function of feelings: feelings are social, as well as 'internal' to the person. As well as being an expression of the self, there is a certain politics to them, even if the political arena where they were spawned (the family of origin) is long gone. They are influenced by others, and attempt to influence them in their turn. One only has to observe a child who falls over and delays the tears until the mother is present to recognize this. Yet there is nothing false about the tears — they are simply a part of the child's complex interaction with others, part of the 'patterns which connect'.

71

A director might ask (before or during a psychodrama) some questions that reflect the connections between the protagonist's state and the other people in his or her life. The questions can be asked out loud to the protagonist, or they may simply be part of the director's thinking and formulation of the systemic hypothesis (see Chapter 5): What was the stimulus for the feelings? Towards whom are they directed? Who is most likely to be affected by them now? Who was most likely to have been affected by them in the family of origin? The audience of others is vitally relevant to feelings, even when this audience has long departed. Most psychodramatic enactments attempt to direct the expression of feelings to their relevant location, so these questions are by no means new. A systemic interview and enactment, however, may be more thorough in its investigation of the social origins and effects, and of the restraints on the protagonist taking any other course than the one he or she does take.

Feelings can certainly be a true compass pointing to the direction of spontaneous action; they are a genuine expression of being, a source of discovery, an agent for change, an action tendency, and for most of us, maybe even the reason for living. They are both the means and the barometer of contact with others. They are not the only indicator of whom the person really is, however, and can cloud as well as reveal a way for change. People can be restrained from feeling enough, or restrained from effective thinking and action because they feel too much.

Ideally, change or new learning makes a client feel better at the end of therapy. But the aim of therapy is not to feel better: one can feel better without change — by having a massage, or by taking a tablet. Strong feelings can even interrupt the course of therapy: if a person attempts to begin a psychodrama whilst 'flooded', for example, there will not be much chance of him or her hearing instructions, managing role reversals, etc. Directors then need to require early role reversals, and have the protagonist blow their nose, dry their eyes, and clean up a little as they go into the new role. Alternatively, they can concentrate on getting all the objects of the scene around. Focusing on the objects can serve as a warm-up to a scene if a person is flat, or can help the development of managerial and observer roles if the person is too flooded. The aim is to have protagonists reach a state where their network of presuppositions are loosened and restraints on possibility are relaxed. Strong expression of feeling can help or hinder such a task. Strong feeling can be as much a resistance as no feeling at all.

Let us consider the protagonist who appears to be experiencing strong emotions but cannot describe or even enact that experience to the director or audience. A wordless state often suggests that the person in the scene is very 'young' — possibly pre-language. The person may be in touch with deep feelings, but does not have 'the words to say it'. In such a regressed state, it is very difficult to make decisions, or even to establish a satisfactory scene and dialogue at first. Such protagonists will usually respond to a request for role reversal to another trustworthy, helpful person 'who knows all about little girls/boys'; in role as that person, they can set up the scene, or collaborate with the protagonist in doing so. If the protagonist had not developed childhood roles appropriate to girls or boys of that age, the director, using the necessary techniques, can work with the adult protagonist teaching his/her own child. The director actively works with him/ her at that time discussing what is happening and establishing double descriptions. There is no such thing as an 'adult' role — only roles that are adequate, spontaneous, and creative. Both children and adults need such roles.

In contrast with the flooded protagonist, other clients become stuck in therapy because there is insufficient feeling available to them. Far from not having 'the words to say it', they seem only to have the words and not the connections. With emotional data missing, they appear to have little idea of the wellsprings of their actions; they lack imaginative life and resonance with themselves. With such protagonists, it is preferable for directors to assume that the feelings are very strong, rather than to reprimand the person for being in some way impaired. Such a reprimand is, in any case, usually counterproductive, making the person dive for cover. Numbed people are often in an affectless state following unbearable pain or loss or deprivation, which may have taken place very early in their lives. They have learnt to cut off, and have forgotten who taught them the lesson. Gentle and persistent development of feeling states can be most productive for such people, who gain a sense of kin with suffering and laughing humanity.

D: *What stops you? Choose it.*
P: *I can't. Responsibility weighs me down and I can't see anything. I haven't cried for as long as I can remember. I feel so different from people here. They all seem so emotional, so open.*
D: *Choose someone to be 'responsibility'. (He does) Reverse roles and weigh Perry down.*
P: *Ouch. Owww!*
D: *Who are you saying that to?*
P: *I don't know.*
D: *If you did know, who would it be?*
P: *I don't know.*
D: *Is there a wise person in your life?*
P: *Yes, my cousin Emille.*
D: *Reverse roles. Emille, are you older or younger than Perry?*
E: *I'm older.*
D: *What do you do for a living?*
E: *I'm an accountant.*
D: *Really? Do you know all about figures?*
E: *Sure do, it's my living.*

D: And about living?
E: Yep, know something about that, too.
D: Emille, who does Perry want to say 'ouch' to?
E: His younger brother. He was always better than Perry at everything and his dad loved him more.
D: Thanks, Emille. Reverse roles. Choose your younger brother. (Perry does so with 'responsibility' still draped over his neck.) Address him.

Perry tries, but finds it difficult to speak. The auxiliary he has chosen as Responsibility is huge, and weighs him nearly to the ground. He tries to throw Responsibility off. It persists, and a wrestling match develops. No attempt has been made at this stage to develop the role of Responsibility, to find out where it came from, when it came, etc., although this would have been a legitimate course of action. Eventually Perry succeeds in his struggles, and stands up straight. He is flushed, his eyes sparkle for the first time.

P: I want to talk to my dad.
D: Get him here, then.

The auxiliary is chosen, and the father is interviewed in role. Perry begins to cry as soon as he sees his father psychodramatically represented. The drama begins. The 'what' (in Perry's case, responsibility) has become a 'who' (brother, father) and has led the way to interpersonal therapy.

This drama mostly reflects standard psychodramatic practice; the extended interview with Emille illustrates the long path that sometimes needs to be taken with a 'stuck' protagonist, who only in role as another person can nominate relevant figures from the social atom who provide the warm-up in the drama. An early focus on feeling can be exquisitely accurate, or can produce a flattened, narcissistic self-exploration in the protagonist, which is usually undesirable. The explosive emotion often released in psychodrama is used as a powerful vehicle for new learning, and as a memorable carrier for new roles. Usually it defines some system or other, often family-of-origin, and then redefines that system in a new pattern of organization. Human difficulties often arise when emotions are not recognized. Emotional need is thwarted, and because thwarted may become dominant, fixed, and rigid. Psychodrama can help people to experience intensely the subjective self and thereby recover the vitality needed for change. It helps people generate new ways of experiencing that have previously been restrained from awareness and possibility.

Consequences

Just as roles are born in a context, they are 'designed' to have an effect, even though the exact nature of this effect cannot be predicted. If I sulk with persons A and B, they may respond by queries as to my state of being. If I sulk with persons C and D, however, they may simply go off and leave me alone as 'bad company' or 'no fun'. Fortunately or unfortunately, in human systems, especially in close systems like families, the effects of a role can often be predicted with more certainty. So knowledge of the effect a role has can lead to a conclusion about the nature of the role itself — a nature that may otherwise have been obscure.

Because roles are interactive, those that we take up affect the roles that other people take up, and vice versa. Often the meaning or function of a role only becomes clear when one observes what the outcome of the role is, so far as an outcome is observable at all. The meaning of a person adopting the role of sick person may become apparent in the roles that other people take up around this sick person, such as solicitous helper, or guilty lackey, or frustrated lover. The role of sick person may indeed not have emanated from that person at all, as we would usually assume, but may have been created by a significant person in the social atom who needs to be a solicitous helper. For the system to be defined properly, several acts of double descriptions may be needed, even for such an apparently individual role as 'sick person'.

Let us return to Prue and her steel band. The complete system within which Prue enacts her roles is not yet apparent. A two-party family interaction usually presents an inadequate information-base for the director or protagonist to assess 'what is going on'. Prue's mother, and perhaps even other siblings are likely somehow to be involved in the reported interaction. For example, Prue's mother must be involved at least in her capacity as a role model: how is it that she does not influence her husband and son on their views about women? Does she agree with them? What is their marriage like that they have such views on the passivity of women? Perhaps she believes that women are weak and need rescuing by men. What happens if any member of the family changes their position? What would happen to Prue if she did not believe that she needed to sit still — what is that belief doing for her? What did it, or the contrary belief, do for her and the family when she was younger?

The whole point of Prue not being hitherto angry with her father, in the aforementioned case, may have been that she wished to protect her mother from change, because if she changed she might leave her husband. This is a consequence usually feared by children, and they will do a great deal to avoid it, even become ill, delinquent, or anorexic so that parents will stay together to look after them. While it is a feared consequence, however, it need not be an inevitable one. But Prue may be restrained from seeing reality in any other way. This is where the belief aspect of a role, the person's construct system, comes into play, and is perhaps the role element that most needs to change, as we have seen. In any case, Prue, by stopping being angry with her father in order to protect her mother from changing, which would have led to parental separation, takes the role of parentified child or protector of the marriage. This crucial role may not emerge in the natural course of the psychodrama, if the psychodrama is not systemically considered.

The following five questions are useful ones for directors to bear in mind when assessing the consequences of a role:

1. What function does the presenting difficulty (usually revealed in the initial interview) serve in stabilizing the social atom?
2. How does the social atom operate to stabilize the presenting difficulty?
3. What is the central theme around which the problem is organized?
4. What will be the consequences of change?
5. Therefore, what dilemmas does the protagonist face?

In the case of Prue, significantly, the scene is set at the age of 15, where questions of control and release are likely to be turbulent and important. Her blinding headaches served to stabilize the family just as she was entering early adolescence and her mother joined the workforce once more. Perhaps an outbreak of sexuality in the family would have been disruptive to the parents' marriage. Certainly, grandmother did not approve of mother working outside the home. The family operated to stabilize her difficulty by grandmother bringing pressure to bear on mother to be at home full-time. (Mother had just taken a job.) The central theme seems to be repression versus release — it is beautifully illustrated by the steel band. The consequence of change would have been that mother stayed in her job, learnt new things about herself, and became less dependent on father. The feared consequence is that they would separate as a result of mother's independence. The therapeutic dilemma is how to be free and to be loyal at the same time.

Circular questioning is one way of identifying significant others and reviewing the consequences of role relations. For example, these questions could be asked:

D: *What does your grandmother think of your father's relationship with your mother? (Prue answers)*
What does your mother think of your relationship with Andrew? (Prue answers)
What does your father think of Andrew's relationship with your mother?

This sort of questioning, based on the Milan associate's (Selvini Palazzolli *et al.*, 1980) practice, can save unnecessary role reversals, and accelerate the warm-up to the family system. The questions increase the protagonist's systems awareness, and can actually help prevent her undergoing another stuck psychodrama where she begins as the eternal victim of a misunderstanding father and emerges as a vindicated revenger. This routine is not so much a danger for a person's first two or three psychodramas, but can become so thereafter, a point that will be developed in the following chapters.

A director might even ask the protagonist (Prue) to predict the outcome of a struggle, and relate that prediction back into the system. For example:

D: *If you had a fight today with your father, who would be most likely to cheer you on?*
P: *My mum.*
D: *Who in the family would have to change the most if you really became angry?*
P: *My sister.*
D: *Who in this family here or in our extended family would be the most horrified to see you bringing them here in a psychodrama?*
P: *They all would be.*
D: *But who especially? Which two?*
P: *My mum and my sister.*

These questions should not be overdone, for reasons suggested earlier (of cooling the warming-up process). Relevant beliefs and reactions will emerge best of all in the actual enactment. In fact, any one of these questions can itself be made part of the psychodramatic enactment by the director suggesting that the answer be relayed directly to one of the other participants. For example, supposing Prue's answer to the question 'Who in the family would have to change the most if you really became angry?' was 'My mother', the director can then say, 'Express this directly to your mother' and after she has done so, have a role reversal with the mother and a mother/daughter dialogue. This interaction itself could become the point of the drama, or could be limited to one or two interchanges at the warming-up stage.

Chapter five

Strategic psychodrama

A change in epistemology means transforming
one's way of experiencing the world

Bradford Keeney

Psychodrama as revelation/psychodrama as therapy

Even though Moreno was conducting a type of systems therapy from the
1930s, it is fair to say that only in the last thirty years have therapists *en
masse* taken the once-revolutionary step of asking whole families to attend
sessions (Madanes, 1981). These days, it is common to conceptualize 'individual' therapy as one way to intervene in a family — the therapist simply
sees one person in the family and not the others when an individual client
presents for treatment. The individual is the arrowhead, the outermost
representative of the social atom. While such is not yet the majority view in
psychological and psychiatric circles, it is certainly one that now has
considerable prominence, to the degree that elaborate arguments are made
(Braverman *et al.* 1984; Fisch *et al.* 1984; Weakland, 1983) actually justi-
fying the times when an individual might be seen on his or her own — a far
cry from the days of individual-only treatment.

Psychodrama is a group process in which persons act out certain situations, usually stressful, as pointed out in Chapter 1. It is more of an interactional and systemic therapy than most traditional therapies, as has also
been seen, although its systemic potential has not yet been fully developed
or exploited. Most dramas are interactional or systemic at least to the
extent that other people take part in them and that the protagonist's difficulty is thought to be interpersonal. This conception is nevertheless short of
a thoroughgoing systemic view, though it does leave room for it: simply to
populate a therapy with characters does not necessarily imply a theory of a
system. In the dramas so far depicted, many of the scenes concern family-
of-origin, with the 'family' being present via auxiliaries. In enacting their
dramas, protagonists frequently find the new solutions that they seek by
entering a state of spontaneity and of new relationship with the depicted
others. When their lives are shown (defined) according to all their relevant
connections, they can move on. They retain the learning from the psychodrama, and somehow keep that state alive in the theatre of the outside
world. So far so good.

Some questions arise, however. Is the 'psychodramatic shock' given during the drama strong enough to propel, as it were, protagonists through the rest of their lives with the spontaneity garnered during that session? Clearly not — that is an impossible demand to put on any therapy, and Moreno himself engineered 'spontaneity training' and 'role training' precisely to maintain a new state that was functional and that would carry his patients through the humdrum and disappointments of daily life. For a therapy to be called 'therapy', the new code book introduced by the therapist must somehow outlast the dysfunctional code book that the client already uses.

Therapy can have many meanings: people can say that doing needle-work is therapeutic, or talking to friends, or meditating, or swimming, or understanding more about their inner processes, or becoming more 'aware', or 'individuating', or developing their spiritual self. These activities are indisputably beneficial and restorative: they contribute to richness, rest, and beauty in human living. To suggest that they are not therapy is in no way to indict or devalue them — it is simply to restrict that term to certain other processes. It is to attempt to tighten its range of convenience so that the term 'therapy' is not simply conterminous with 'everything that is good'.

A therapy is not a hit-and-miss affair, but a deliberate intervention in the client's life. It is a meeting between two systems — the family system and the therapeutic system, with the latter trying to influence the former around a problem: it triggers change but does not necessarily give solutions. What will be proposed here, under the name of 'strategic psychodrama' are certain ways of conducting psychodrama and group work that are based on providing a new definition, a new code book for clients, a systems-sound structure within which spontaneity can flourish.

Former protagonists, trainees, and members of the audience of psychodramas do not necessarily cherish the memories of their dramas specifically as therapy, although they may well believe that the drama had been good for them. Psychodrama is most loved for its epic qualities, its richness, for showing people the value and intentionality of their lives, for validating a viewpoint, or making sense of a crazy experience, for expression of pent-up emotion, for providing a spark, a moment of epiphany, intensity, or poetry. 'I try to give them courage to dream again. I teach people to play God', Moreno wrote (1972, p. 6). Psychodrama was Moreno's way to reunite mortals momentarily with an eternal world of all-spontaneity (Kraus, 1984).

Indeed, psychodrama may not even be at its best when it is applied as a therapy, when it is asked to 'do' something for someone apart from providing a setting for them to experience the spark of the divine. Just as paintings and plays and novels are not at their best when they become didactic or political, trying too hard to achieve some improvement in their audience, could it be that psychodrama should leave therapy alone, content with providing great moments, with celebration and revelation rather than change and reform? Is psychodrama to be of and for itself, then, just as art can be, endlessly self-delighting, sufficient in its own generativity?

Many of the intensive and 'deep' therapies also tap into the world of aesthetics and the world of the personal epic, which may account for their patients' devotion to the method and the therapist. Much of therapy is used for personal revelation and epiphany rather than 'cure', one suspects, although the treatment must parade as cure to legitimate the process (and attract the finance and health-insurance benefits). Therapy is not necessarily a higher-order procedure than personal revelation or theology — on the contrary. But although psychodrama's evocation of passion and revelation of meaning is not really in question, its status as a therapy is not so clear. Are all the methods and principles of 'a therapy for fallen gods' suitable for fallen humans in a busy clinic, or for a group that meets to overcome eating disorders, or for a child who wets the bed, or for people who have been in a psychodrama training group for many years and yet seem to be going backwards in their life rather than forwards? People who are lucky to make it to work, far less to heaven, may certainly be regarded as fallen gods, but the question becomes how to get them back to work.

If action methods or psychodrama are to be used as therapy rather than as revelation, theology, or epic representation (perfectly good uses for psychodrama, mind you, but not necessarily therapy), they may need to take into fuller account the systemic nature of the problem's maintenance, and the ways in which new solutions, including the intervention of therapy itself (Farson, 1978) can lead the client into more trouble than the original problem ever did. Strategic psychodrama's contribution to psychodramatic theory and practice is specifically as therapy, rather than as epiphany, as history, as literature, as theatre, as community with suffering humanity, or as a way of contacting the beauty of one's life. All of these things psychodrama does well — better than any other method, perhaps, given that most people do not (without help) have the capacity to enact plays about themselves in ways that move others to the heights of fellow-feeling, as psychodramas can.

To suggest some applications of psychodrama as a strategic therapy is not so much to advocate improvements to psychodrama's basic philosophy or practice as simply to add some kitchenware for everyday use: a few sturdy plates, a strainer, a sharp knife or two, a set of whisks, and a nice large mixing bowl. These serviceable implements may allow the fine dinner setting to be kept for best, since the best applications of psychodrama may well be as revelation of the inner spirit. In psychodrama as therapy, the aim is to keep the aesthetics of change — a type of respect, wonder, and appreciation — married to the pragmatics of change: the specific techniques to bring it about. Pragmatics without aesthetics can be ugly and instrumental;

aesthetics without pragmatics, as Keeney (1983) remarks, 'may lead to free-associative nonsense'.

Proposing a strategic form of psychodrama and group work, therefore, is not to advocate a process of blunt pragmatics. Bateson (1972) viewed communication as an aesthetic process, attempting to map patterns as revealed through metaphor. Allman (1982) alerts therapists to the dangers of an overpragmatic stance, a stance with technique that does not allow for passion. Systems concepts can be used as a way of keeping clients and families in place and avoiding the disruption, randomness, and spontaneity involved in the continual search for aesthetic unity. Both therapist and client/protagonist need to be open to the spontaneity of life itself.

Strategic psychodrama can be low-key and quiet, or high-powered, noisy, and enjoyable. The psychodramatic section of strategic psychodrama may often look very similar to conventional psychodrama: much of the strategic work takes place in the group prior to the enactment, especially in the refinement of what is a problem, what the minimal goals for change are, and how the protagonist or anyone else in their social atom would notice if they had changed. The strategic questioning may also take place weeks after the psychodrama, when the changes since the drama are highlighted.

Strategic group therapy differs from traditional group work and sociometry in that it has adopted techniques to examine the status of the problem, the co-evolution of the problem and its resolution, and the alliances and coalitions in the group around the problem. The method then takes various measures, both sociometric and psychodramatic, to resolve the problem. Strategic group therapy has as its premiss that current interaction between the group member and involved others, either inside or outside the group, is the most central factor in the shaping and maintenance of the problem behaviour, and that therefore its alteration gives the most leverage in resolution of the problem. Present situations, however difficult and distressing they may be, are constantly being remade in the course of present behaviour among the individual members of any system (Weakland, 1983). The persistence of the problem in a group or social atom, in terms of the alliances and coalitions that form around it, therefore become more a focus of interest than the origins of the problem. This formulation implies that strategic group workers carefully spend time on action methods such as group sociometry, and take very seriously an examination of the status of current problems and their attempted solutions, including the solution of therapy itself.

In the actual psychodrama, strategic psychodramatists propose that if interaction between members of a social system is the primary shaper of behaviour, it follows that alteration of the behaviour of one member of a system can lead to a related alteration of other members of the system. It is feasible, therefore, to influence the behaviour of other members of a system indirectly, by influencing the behaviour of the person with whom one has therapeutic contact. If this were not so, then individual therapy never would have had any success, which clearly is not so. Ideally, a therapist meets with all the relevant members of a system, and such is the usual practice of family therapy. Where such meetings are not possible, however, all is not lost provided a cybernetic rather than a linear perspective on the problem is kept, and the interactional nature of roles are paramount in the therapist's mind. Alternatively, therapists can *create* a system of significance, such as a therapy group, and then seek to influence people's behaviour within that system.

Strategic therapists believe that therapy should at least attempt to solve a problem that the client offers, and to which, perhaps after considerable negotiation, the therapist and client agree *is* the problem to be solved. There is no obvious incompatibility between this and psychodramatic practice at the central-concern, contracting, and interview stages. They may ask the protagonist what the 'minimal goal' for therapy is: 'What would allow you to look back on a day when you had this sort of problem and say: "I have had this and lots of other problems, but today was a good day".' The interview-in-role may take in particulars of everyday life in the social atom, highlighting the specific exchanges that are seen as problematic, the problem-maintaining solutions. In all of this, the director is structuring the protagonist's framing of the problem, preparing him or her for new definitions, and defining the nature of the therapist's own relationship to the protagonist (Coyne, 1986b). If protagonists are satisfactorily heading towards a definition of the problem that does not involve their failed attempted solutions, the warming-up process can be let go in a traditional way. Therapy is not violated by working on a real problem, but nor are clients well served if they are naively encouraged to dig deeper into their attempted solutions.

That is why directors at the interview stage might ask apparently odd questions such as: 'How is this problem a problem?' or 'If this problem remained the same, who in your family would be most pleased?' To a degree, strategic therapy must be regarded as having failed if the problem is not solved, no matter what other changes have taken place (Hayley, 1976; Rabkin, 1977; Watzlawick *et al.* 1974). The strategic interview not only elicits an account of the protagonist's or group member's beliefs, feelings, and actions, but therapist and client co-create those beliefs, feelings, and actions within a therapeutic frame. The meaning of a situation is framed not as something fixed and determined 'in the protagonist's head', but rather as in interactions with significant others. The linear question is: 'How long have you been depressed?' while the interactional question is: 'Who is making you so sad?' An important component of clients presenting their problems as insoluble is that they persist in describing their problems in abstract terms, such as 'I need to grow' or 'We don't relate'. Remedial action for such vague problems is almost impossible to take, except, perhaps, the remedial action of 'more therapy'.

Not all therapists agree that therapy should be concerned with problems, proposing instead that it is a form of general education and reorientation towards the whole of the life force and the inner spirit. A strategic therapist would not object to this opinion, provided that in the process of this reorientation the problem was resolved. The aesthetics and the pragmatics, the passion and the technique, must both be present. Strategic therapy, because focused on a problem, is not a narrowly behaviourist procedure — it recognizes that in the course of solving a problem many other changes might be necessitated, including people's maps of themselves and others, which consistently point to failure. But it does not take on more of a person's life than it has to in order to solve the problem. At least, that is the ideal — there is wastage in any method and therapy can suffer from false economy as much as from lack of economy. Strategic psychodrama is not free of rhetoric and blind spots, just as traditional psychodrama or any other therapy is also only partially sighted.

Given that strategic psychodrama is problem-oriented, it will tend to change its methods according to the problem presented, while still retaining the psychodramatic focus. This focus is essentially one of spontaneity. A systemic theory of spontaneity might read thus: there are major and minor, gradual or sudden shifts through which all social atoms, such as a family, must pass (see Carter and McGoldrick, 1980). Some of these shifts are in response to internally generated life transitions, such as courtship, marriage, the birth of a child, schooling, adolescence. Others are in response to incidental variations — loss of job, loss of relationship, accident, rape, failure in examination, etc. At these points of pattern change, existing social atom or personal constructs are put under duress.

Fraser (1986, pp. 73–4) suggests that members now need 'to construe these new pattern variations in ways which both adapt to their new directions while assimilating them under some broad enough umbrella construction so as to maintain the system's general definition of itself as an ongoing unit'. But if people are 'restrained' from these adaptations because their social-atom constructs are few, narrow, and rigid, the way they do adapt to the changed pattern can create even more serious problems. In this case, members try to force invariant 'templates of constancy' on a changed and changing system, and a vicious cycle may ensue in which their solutions become the problem. A change in constructs or patterns — spontaneity — is needed. The task of therapy is to inhibit the repetitive and ineffective use of a current solution in order that new constructs may develop.

The sorts of interventions, if any, at the surplus-reality level, the length and nature of the interview, the tightness of the contracting, and the amount of follow-up in subsequent sessions will all vary. But a core theme is that problems persist because the efforts of the client and others involved

— their attempted solutions — unwittingly serve to maintain or even exacerbate the problem behaviour. If marriage is assumed to be 'blissful', and turns out to be not quite so, clients may attempt to fix the situation, perhaps by getting drunk, or by having affairs, or by trying another marriage. When these solutions do not work, the client may then feel that their behaviour or that of the other person is mad or bad. The attempted solutions provide the clues to the 'network of presuppositions' that prevent spontaneity developing. People act in certain ways because they are restrained from seeing other ways in which to act — a focus that we will develop in Chapter 7. The goal of strategic psychodrama and group work is to prevent the repetition of dysfunctional sequences and to introduce into the client's system more complexity and alternatives — that is to say, spontaneity.

A strategic psychodramatist almost always thinks in terms of systems, even on occasion treating one person as a 'system' and setting up a dialectical structure between this person and an object 'outside' him or her so that difference may be created in a process called 'double description' (White, 1986a). A problem is a type of behaviour that is normally 'part of a sequence of acts between several people' (Hayley, 1976). It usually concerns people's maps or code books of reality, rather than reality itself. It is these maps, or objects, or roles, or internal representations that are interpersonal in their origin, and it is towards other persons that they are relevant and directed. So while it is very useful and even preferable to have the relevant others present, therapy can proceed without them. Indeed, no therapy is better at calling up the dead or absent than psychodrama — its methods were invented for just that purpose. The issue, then, is not so much how many people are actually involved in the problem, or how many are present in the psychodrama, but how many people are involved in the director's way of thinking about the problem.

Strategic psychodrama and group work focuses especially on the social context of human dilemmas. It attempts to shift the social-atom organization so that the dysfunctional pattern is no longer necessary. Strategic psychodramatists use the interview and the enactment to get and give information about behavioural sequences so that the ones that are maintaining the problem can be interrupted. In group work, they regard the complaints that group members make as representing a desire for spontaneity, but also involving themselves in a restricted set of behaviours, perceptions, and feelings. Any exceptions to the complaints (Lipchik and de Shazer, 1986) involve perceptions, beliefs, and feelings that lie outside the complainant's restraints, and can therefore be used as building blocks for double description (see Chapter 7).

A protagonist of the future: the little old man

To illustrate some of the points that have been made so far, let us take the rather unusual step of presenting a case that a family-therapy group saw in their clinical practice. The issues at the time are elaborated, some ways of hypothesis formation typical of strategic therapy are outlined, and the type of action methods that might be used at the time of family presentation are suggested. Then comes the leap — if this is the way that therapists would act at the time, should they act very differently if the identified patient, Ralph, presented himself in a psychodrama group twenty years on? That is, apart from some differences in techniques (because the whole family is no longer present), should one use nonsystemic principles when an adult client presents with family-of-origin issues, but systemic principles when the whole family presents with a current problem? Let us see in the case of Ralph.

The Biggles family consists of Jane Biggles, a thin, depressed, intelligent, and shabby woman of 40 who is employed as a social researcher. She is the widow of Simon Biggles, a specialist in tropical diseases, who had died two years before in Bali, where the two children Ralph, 13, and Theresa, 9, were born and grew up. After Simon's death, the family were left with only a small lump-sum insurance payout, and decided to return to their country of origin, Australia, so that the children could get a good education.

Ralph is highly intelligent, handsome, and sharp. He has an 'old-manish' air about him, and discusses the family problems and the results of his own behaviour with perfect ease. He distances himself from himself and from events within the family by using terms such as 'one' and 'any boy my age'. He has other roles, however, that appear to be the direct opposite of the rather superior person he portrays in the therapy room. He had been a manageable but rather unruly boy when his father was alive; but since his return to his parents' home country he had broken out in his behaviour, and in eighteen months had managed to get himself expelled from one school, and put on the warning list for expulsion at another. The local GP offered the mother an opportunity to have him certified and forcibly put into psychiatric care — a somewhat extreme measure, one would think.

At home, relationships also degenerated. Mrs Biggles had gone with the children to live with her brother in his large house. But there was no peace there, either. Ralph fought violently with his uncle, on one occasion, nearly biting his ear off in an argument when the uncle was admonishing Theresa. The uncle demanded that Ralph go elsewhere, and as a result he was sent to live with his grandparents. His behaviour there, too, became 'intolerable'. On one occasion he managed to start up a forklift truck in his grandparents' timber yard, and drove it through a fence. The grandparents are now anxious to be quit of him.

Mrs Biggles goes to the grandparents' house each evening to do Ralph's washing, to see to his homework, to put him to bed at night, and to sit with him until he goes to sleep. Theresa, of course, is somewhat neglected in these transactions, but she seems to be uncomplaining. Meantime, Mrs Biggles is searching for a house for them to live in. But she runs into dilemmas with this search. To move to the outer suburbs, where she could afford to buy or rent a house will mean that she must withdraw the children from their schools, and that she must spend most of her day on public transport going to and from her work. But the family cannot afford to rent or buy where they are currently living, which is close to her workplace and convenient to the family's childminding supports, and they cannot emotionally afford to go on living with the extended family. It is at this stage that the family seeks therapy.

Numerous problematic issues confront this family: grieving for the husband; grieving for the father; grieving for the country the three of them knew as 'home'; loss of family structure; loss of status and income; dislocation in a new country; depression and low self-esteem of the mother; overinvolvement of the mother and son; competition between siblings for mother's attention; rivalry of Ralph with any replacement father figures; Ralph's behaviour at school; mother's inability to be a spontaneous loving parent; and many more.

Whichever of these are settled on as the 'main' issues, the family's problems are clearly interconnected. Because of the stability of the difficulties, and their interconnection, the treatment of any member in isolation does not seem to be indicated. For example, although the mother may well benefit from the support offered by long-term therapy, such a therapy is almost a luxury in her present situation. She is at her wit's end; she needs to act quickly. Similarly, perhaps, some would say that Ralph could profit from 'working through' some of his issues, but this would be a slow process, and one that could be foiled by mother's or Theresa's actions if larger systemic matters are at stake. The family's interdependence of problems and attempted solutions (for example, to place Ralph in a succession of homes and a succession of schools) appear to rule out 'personal work' on the part of any one of them, even on the part of mother, who is unlikely to be referred as a client anyway — not, that is, until or unless she finally does collapse. The most logical type of treatment is a treatment of the whole system: their problems are too bound up with each other for individual work, and their needs are too basic and too urgent for long-term therapy based on insight.

The therapist needs an orienting concept, to link the data: 'How do the interacting roles serve the system as a whole?' or to put it another way, if Ralph is to be kept the focus: 'What do Ralph's roles allow the family to do?' For example, Ralph may believe that he needs to help his mother in her widowhood by distracting her with his own problems. Or his problems may stop her from meeting anyone else (the last thing on her mind!). Or they may keep the whole family on the move until they must return to Bali. The family role analysis involves five procedures.

1. *The therapist needs to understand the history of the problem, especially with respect to alliances and coalitions and any changes that may have taken place (context of a role). Perhaps it will be necessary to track the history of the problem in past generations and enquire as to what are the family traditions in relation to the problem. For example, what are the family traditions in terms of sons and mothers, in terms of sons succeeding at school, in terms of being nomadic?*

2. *The therapist spends time tracking sequences around the problem. This is a relentless process. When does the problem occur? When does it not occur? Are there any occasions when it is worse than at other times? (Behaviour).*

3. *The therapist identifies critical beliefs and behaviours that stabilize the system. For example, Jane's determination not to take pleasure in her life may express itself in her half-hearted limit-setting with Ralph. Her constant dilemmas where she always seems to lose, may actually become a form of stability. Ralph's shifting of schools stabilizes them as a nomadic family, stops them settling down, keeps Jane's attention hard on present problems, perhaps prevents her from getting too depressed. What are they attempting to achieve (Beliefs, consequences).*

4. *The therapist then conjectures what would actually be the consequences of change. Most importantly: what would be the negative consequences of change? As a result, that which was implicit becomes explicit. An exposure of the whole system at once is achieved, rather than exposing one person. The aim is not insight but 'outsight' — knowledge of relationships. (Feeling, beliefs).*

5. *Enquiries about the consequences of change lead to investigation of the attempted solutions. What has been tried so far? What are the restraints on change? The family is like it is, and events have taken the course they have taken, not so much because they have been 'made' to by a cause, but because they have been restrained from taking alternative courses. Restraints establish limitations on the amount and type of information that Ralph, Jane, or Theresa can manage. They are unready to respond to certain differences or distinctions, and so they are incapable of spontaneity, or seeing ways out of the dilemmas. They keep repeating their attempted solutions.*

What, then, are the possibilities for action methods as an adjunctive, family-therapy technique with this family at the time of presentation? Actually, the Biggles family offers more scope for psychodramatic work than is often the case. Further details of appropriate psychodramatic possibilities with live families are given more fully later (see Chapter 11). From the core outline, however, it is evident that clearing up 'unfinished business' between the individual family members and the deceased father and husband may be relevant, especially as a way of checking loyalty issues to Jane's husband and Ralph and Theresa's father. Were they enduring miserable lives as a way of showing him that they needed him, that they could not cope without him? What transgenerational injunctions are they enacting? Does Mrs Biggles think that she should have been consumed on the funeral pyre with her husband?

The deceased Simon Biggles could be represented by an empty chair, and family members could be asked to address him. The therapist may focus the dialogue with 'Simon' by suggesting issues such as 'the family then and the family now' or, 'What is it like now that you are not here?' thus drawing distinctions. Bali, which had once meant so much to the family, could also be represented and reacted to psychodramatically. The hypothesis that Ralph's difficulties are a way of keeping the family on the move until there is no choice but that they all return to Bali, can be acted, here and now in the therapy room, with Bali on one side and Australia on the other. This action can take sociometric form, with the family being asked to 'stand on a line' somewhere between Australia and Bali. Thus one of the restraints, operating outside of consciousness that prevents them doing anything other than what they do and limits their vision of reality and possibility, may be brought into the open. Another hypothesis, that Ralph's behaviour stems from his desire to 'save' his family and have them all return to where his father is buried (a positive frame for the family's behaviour), can also be suggested, if appropriate, by the psychodramatic representation of that grave. Jane's depression as a way of showing her late husband that she cares about him, or as a way of showing him that she, too, should be dead, can also be depicted, provided there are signs of warm-up to this idea, and that the timing is right.

It may be counterproductive to 'hot up' the interaction between mother and son by means of doubling, role reversal, or maximization — some of psychodrama's most celebrated techniques can be dysfunctional when a whole family is present. Better, at least at first, relentlessly to track the sequences of Ralph's behaviour via questions and sociometric procedures highlighting difference (see Chapter 11). A structural element enters, too. Mrs Biggles needs to understand some of these sequences and needs actual success in imposing actual limits on her son, while he needs the safety of her doing just that (see Chapter 6). Structural enactments intervene in actions that stabilize the symptom: a sequence of role-training exercises as 'assertive mother' can be instituted with her, first with Ralph out of the room, and then with him present. Even exercises in which Mrs Biggles physically holds and contains Ralph may be indicated — they can give her a sense of potency and assurance, and him a sense of limits — there is, after all, someone who can contain him, although Ralph is a little old for that sort of thing and his behaviour is not usually of the tantrum variety that requires a holding technique (see 'The tired mother').

If Mrs Biggles does manage to contain Ralph, either physically or analogically, what will Theresa's reactions be to her mother's new roles with Ralph? Will she be pleased or displeased at this disturbance of the status quo? What new alliances and coalitions are necessitated by such a change in the family dynamic of 'bad' Ralph becoming 'good' and 'weak' mother becoming 'strong'? Will Theresa now need to be 'bad'? The possibilities raised by these dilemmas (future enactment) can be acted out by the children, perhaps by establishing a 'bad' end of the room and a 'good' end, so that differences in time and state can be noticed. Later, these ends may be relabelled as 'frightened' and 'safe'. Again, 'news of difference' not only between frightened and bad, frightened and good, safe and bad, safe and good, etc., can be created.

An escalation of the conflict to break through to the 'feeling level' between Mrs Biggles and her children does not appear to be called for. There is usually plenty of affect already in a family; the task of therapy is to provide a structure where it will naturally emerge, rather than elicit it in the specific therapeutic context. Nor would 'more communication' seem to be helpful, if that communication already repeats the family's attempted solutions. The matter is not simply one of expression between mother and children about their relationship with each other, though expression in terms of grieving for the father or husband and the re-formation of the family unit is doubtless called for. Simple expression of 'feelings' between the present members, even if it could be achieved, would probably not answer or alter the complexity of interactions and alliances that have evolved in this family.

The strategic approach

If it is not helpful to 'treat' any individual member of the family now, what should be the status of treatment, let us say, twenty years later, when Ralph as an adult joins a psychodrama therapy group? Should the therapeutic thinking be very different? Needn't one be a systems therapist any more? Just as it would have been ludicrous to understand Ralph's problems then in isolation from the system that he was in, and fatuous to offer him individual child psychotherapy — far less to certify him as insane and lock him in an adolescent unit — does individual treatment within psychodrama make any more sense now that he is in his thirties and very unhappy?

Obviously, we do not know what Ralph's 'problem' would be in twenty years' time; directors would have to work strategically with that at the group level in terms of attempted solutions, restraints, negative explanation, and circular causality; they may initiate treatment by drawing distinctions, double descriptions, definition and re-definition of the problem (see Chapter 7) while Ralph is still in the group. If Ralph were then to enact a psychodrama about his family-of-origin, directors can legitimately conceptualize his circuit of interaction in the past in a similar way as they would if Ralph and his family presented for help at the time. They would take into account the five components of a role outlined in the previous chapter. Analysis of context, behaviour, affect, belief, and consequences automatically lead to a co-evolutionary view of the roles involved. Such an analysis leads to the five ways in which an orienting concept (already outlined in this chapter in the discussion on Ralph and his family) can be gained: tracking sequences, alliances and coalitions, the critical behaviours that stabilize the system, the consequences of change, and Ralph and his family's attempted solutions.

Like all psychodrama, strategic psychodrama works 'analogically'. Analogical communication has many referents, not all of which can be expressed 'digitally', by means of words representing exactly what the person wants to say. In digital communication, only one referent is possible. In the case of Ralph, his 'symptoms' would mean only one thing, and one thing exactly. In particular, relationships between people can be expressed only analogically, as there is no exact digital referent for them. The dramatic mode is essentially analogical — an action can have many meanings, and can only be understood in context; for example, crying may express joy, pain, relief, or many other emotions. A headache is always a pain in the head, but it may also be an expression of something towards someone else — reluctance, anger, or boredom, say.

A problem, therefore, is regarded analogically as a way in which one person communicates with another: Ralph's biting his uncle's ear may be a way of his communicating with his uncle, his mother, or even his dead father. Just as a symptom metaphorically expresses a problem, it is also a solution, albeit an unsatisfactory one, for the people involved. Action occurs mostly at an analogical level and so does an intervention at the level of enactment. Behaviour and its treatment becomes communication on many levels. A symptom considered at the analogical level becomes a communication about the person's life situation and therefore a referent to many other things outside itself. Analogical presentation and repair of problems is highlighted in the drama of 'The can-can dancer', to be presented in Chapter 6.

The essence of a strategic approach is that the clinician initiates what happens during treatment and designs a particular approach for each problem (Hayley, 1973). Strategic therapists take responsibility for directly influencing their clients. This does not mean that a rigid format is required, but merely that therapy is conceived as an interpersonal influence process in which therapists have the role of presenting the client with a set of circumstances within which spontaneity is likely to take place. Directors may or even must take deliberate action, since they influence the direction of the drama no matter what they do, as we saw in 'Dale's dilemma' (p. 40) and as could be pointed out in any drama in this book, or any piece of therapy in this or any other book. The most 'non-directive' of therapists cannot avoid influencing their clients, and are, in fact, paid to do so; it seems more practical and realistic for therapists to say that this is what they are doing, and to take on the responsibility for doing it well.

Since the most common types of interventions germane to psychodrama are structural, structural interventions at the level of surplus reality form the focus of the next chapter. Even the presentation of a wisdom figure into a conventional psychodrama, such as in 'Off the rails' (p. 40) or 'Dale's dilemma, (p. 40) is a structural intervention, though not of a family-systems kind. Structural therapy in family-systems terminology is usually concerned with hierarchies, boundaries, and subsystems. Because these concepts are, in essence, spatial metaphors, they lend themselves very easily to action methods, which are happiest when playing around with space, time, and geography. Structural interventions are not only compatible with the strategic approach (Stanton, 1981) — they are often identified with it. In fact Jay Hayley, perhaps *the* leading light in strategic therapy, left his colleagues at the Mental Research Institute (MRI), where he had been working since 1962, and in 1967 joined Minuchin at the Philadelphia Child Guidance Clinic. He went from there in 1976 with his wife, Cloe Madanes, to establish his own family-therapy institute in Washington, DC.

The overlaps of family-therapy schools are quite complex, and it will not serve the purpose of this book very well to provide yet another 'tour' of them. If they are known already, such a tour can be intolerably tedious. If they are not, a tour is insufficient — it takes many months of reading and working for the differences to sink in as 'real'. Rohrbaugh and Eron (1982) have suggested that the 'brief problem-focused therapy' (Bodin, 1981; Fisch *et al.* 1982), 'structural family therapy' (Minuchin and Fishman, 1981), 'strategic family therapy' (Hayley, 1976; Madanes, 1981), and 'systemic family therapy' (Selvini Palazzoli *et al.* 1980) are all 'strategic', 'systemic', and 'brief', and that at least two are 'structural'. Together they might be called the 'strategic systems therapies'. As this is rather a long title, and as Michael White (1983, 1984, 1986), the other author of note to influence the direction of strategic psychodrama, has also been identified as a 'strategic therapist' (Munro, 1987), 'strategic therapy' will be the title most frequently used to identify the type of work being advocated.

There seems to be sufficient broad-based similarity at the goal level (spontaneity) legitimately to adapt some of the methods from strategic therapy to psychodrama and the group work from which a protagonist is eventually chosen. Some of the methods will remain incompatible, while for some others there seems to be no real reason why, during the establishing of the therapeutic contract — the interview for a role — the surplus-reality phase of a psychodrama, and the group interview in group work, action methods, sociometry, psychodrama itself may not gain clinical leverage by adopting procedures from other systemic schools.

Applying a systemic hypothesis in psychodrama

Within a family system such as Ralph's, individuals are tied to one another by strong emotional attachments and loyalties. Psychodramatically, or in the course of family therapy itself, they can be revealed in even the most puritanical or culturally barren of families. These loyalties provide emotional richness and help the whole unit through maturational changes and unexpected crises. Even when the children have grown up and the parents are dead, these ties continue to influence family members over several generations. A dead father may be more demanding than a live one.

Strategic psychodrama focuses on these ties or the invisible loyalties generated by a family or other system; it attempts a more comprehensive definition of the system than had previously been possible, so that the system, once it has defined itself more fully, has room to move. The restraints on change that prevent new maps and spontaneous movement are at base interpersonal: the desire to help someone or the unwillingness to hurt someone or the compulsion to obey someone, even though the 'someone' be long dead. The new definition that allows spontaneity is attained chiefly by the director helping protagonists to draw distinctions that may unravel the net of invisible loyalties. When these are presented in their fullness, protagonists can take new paths.

The strategic view is that it is not less 'human' to see people in their connectedness, but more: people's connectedness with others is one of the most human and touching things about them. If anything is 'wrong', it usually means that this connectedness is felt to be wrong. Rather than reducing a person to a solitary being with unsatisfactory hydraulics, or unexpressed passion, or incomplete individuation, systems therapy regards people as social beings, the richness of whose lives must be seen in the round. Strategic psychodramatists tend to hold interactional and circular views of causality that free them from having to blame anybody — not the protagonist, and not the protagonist's mother, either. They attempt to identify the strivings and despair of the entire system and acknowledge the suffering and frustration that have been created by its failed attempts at change. In his foreword to Cloe Madanes' book on strategic family therapy, Salvador Minuchin remarks:

The members of a family may hurt each other in the process of living in a confined interpersonal space, but their basic motivation is to help each other. Indeed, they probably cannot do otherwise, since as members of a larger organism, the family, they respond to signals of pain in any part of this body.

(Madanes, 1981, p. xvii)

Psychodramatists are trained to detect the springs of true spirit in people, and to lead them into the warming-up process. In this process various psychodramatic techniques, such as concretization, scene-setting, and the interview-in-role are employed to produce and develop interactions with others, or with 'parts' of the self. From the production, the dramatic interchange, comes the essential role analysis that can lead to a systemic hypothesis; when directors observe what the protagonists say and how they behave towards other people in the scene portrayed, they gain an idea not only of the protagonists' roles, but other people's roles towards them. The systemic hypothesis, based on role analysis, comes as much from the production of the scene as from the interview-in-role; enactment is diagnosis and treatment at the analogical level.

The vibrancy of the psychodramatic process makes it easy to overconcentrate on the protagonist's own interactions with other key figures in the drama, as if the protagonist were the hub of a wheel, and all emotional energy within the system were directed at him or her. After all, protagonists are the tellers of the tale, and one's sympathies tend to lie with their subjective experience, so raw and sometimes so heroic. Acceptance of the protagonist's linear hypothesis about 'what went on', however, can lead to more unhelpful information being produced in the system, which may confirm the restrictive information upon which the protagonist already thinks, feels, and acts. If the protagonist feels 'hard done by', for example, that belief, while perhaps justified, may restrain him or her from taking certain courses of action that might otherwise be open. If they want to 'grow', even that belief (the complaint) is already part of the restrictive system, and therefore hinders rather than helps spontaneity — the very state they are seeking. Nevertheless, it is part of the protagonist's definition of self, and needs first to be confirmed as a belief belonging to the protagonist (rather than as 'true', of course). It provides the starting point of the group interview, protagonist interview, or drama that may then build to a place where perception of the network of presuppositions (the protagonist's and family's mutual construct system) becomes looser and spontaneity is possible.

A systemic hypothesis takes into account the interacting roles of all relevant members of the system, and attempts to determine what restraints on change are operating, and why it is unlikely that anyone in the system will act in any other way than the way in which they do act.

'Who do you think will first notice that you have grown? What will they notice? If you became an independent person and did not use drugs anymore, how would you be able to ensure that people still care about you? How would you know that you still care about your father if you gave up this habit?'

The protagonist's restraints are usually based on a form of love, fidelity, or loyalty to some other member in the family system. By maintaining a systemic, rather than a purely protagonist-centred hypothesis, directors do not attempt to persuade their protagonists of anything in particular, or to give them insight into the system that they are in. They set up a new code, side by side with the protagonist's code, so that protagonists can draw distinctions between the two, and thereby produce information for themselves upon which to act.

Protagonists need to be joined by the director in such a way that they can establish a dramatic system (and later, it is to be hoped, a 'real life' system) that is less restrictive than the one under which they currently operate. The restrictions, inadequate maps, take the form of restraints on their undertaking trial-and-error searches for new ideas that could lead to new solutions. The solution, however obvious to someone else who does not have the protagonist's restraints, cannot be seen and the appropriate action cannot be undertaken. To ease restraints implies much more than providing a 'free atmosphere', since an atmosphere is 'free' to a protagonist only if it can be perceived as that. There is a threshold even for seeing what freedom is. That is, the easing of restraints is a more skilful process than simply providing a liberal atmosphere where anything goes. It requires the creation of a context for adventure and discovery (White, 1986), not simply because such a context is fun, but because it contributes to the protagonist's skill in responding to new information.

Systemic hypotheses are generated from the interview-in-role and from role analysis made during the enactment. A role analysis does not necessarily rely on a formal interview-in-role, as we have repeatedly noted: sometimes the production alone throws open the system to a degree where satisfactory hypotheses may be constructed without the aid of prolonged verbal interviews. Different avenues for action are provided amidst a strategically designed context of adventure and discovery. These different ways of acting in the system will no doubt lead to different ways of thinking about it, but the thinking is done from the 'inside', as it were. We tend to think about our families or friends differently if one person behaves towards us differently, or we alter our behaviour towards them. At the simplest level, an action change can precede a 'thinking' change. Psychodrama usually proceeds by action change first, and lets the thinking catch up.

Let us attempt to summarize some of these beliefs about people-in-systems in actual working terms. A systemic hypothesis, rather than solely a protagonist-centred hypothesis, has the following advantages:

1. It helps one to 'read' the cycle. Instead of focusing on the agonizing or uncomfortable nature of the problem, the director is able to ask a different sort of question: What does this symptom allow each member of the system to do? How is this symptom a manifestation of love or loyalty within the system? These types of questions suggest a positive connotation that is not a device or a gimmick, but actually stems from the way the therapist understands the situation.

2. It reconstrues the problem from something being 'internal' to some-one, to something happening between people. Whatever the causes of a difficulty, its effects are almost always relational and interactive. The rules of the system, rather than an individual's needs, drives, or personality traits, are what most often determines behaviour between participants. The reconstruing of problems to derive their definitions from patterns of interaction is essentially a Batesonian notion.

    In 'live' work with families, this reconstruction is done by obtain-ing the description (for example, the reason why Tony steals cars) from multiple sources, such as the other family members. A similar process can take place in psychodrama, even though family members are represented by auxiliaries. A new set of descriptions is obtained on the behaviour by the protagonist role-reversing to each member of the social atom.

    D: *Father, what's your theory on why Ted gets expelled from school?*
    R: *(In role as father) He just wants to get out of school.*
    D: *How do you explain that he wants to get out of school?*
    R: *(As father) I ... dunno. He's frightened, I s'pose.*
    D: *(Reverse roles and be your mother) Do you agree with your husband? (Etc).*

3. A systemic hypothesis gives greater flexibility for further action and intervention, releasing therapists from the cage of working within one person's affective system. Holding the protagonist to be simply the victim of the system becomes no longer a tenable line of think-ing; repetitive therapy and coarse psychodramas that reinforce that belief are automatically avoided.

    (a) Directors can work elsewhere in the system rather than directly with the protagonist; for example, with Ralph Biggles' mother rather than only with Ralph, even though he is protagonist. The form of work can be applied to several points at once, given that the whole system is the focus, rather than merely one person's participation.

(b) The relevant time to go in the psychodrama is suggested by the hypothesis. It leads to the simple question: 'When did this problem begin and what was it like before?' In Ralph's case, the obvious time would be that of his father's death.

Protagonists, of course, will often go 'unconsciously' to the time of relevant warm-up to the role; but systemic hypotheses may help direct the drama to the time in the social atom when the system itself altered. The crucial change in roles may not necessarily have begun in the protagonist, nor even in one other person directly interacting with the protagonist. It may have begun between two or more other people in the system.

(c) Circular, rather than linear causality is suggested. Circular, rather than linear change is required. The burden is taken off the protagonist: change somewhere in the system will necessitate change in the whole system. Ralph can give up his 23-year-old habit of reform. A new 'reality' can be established, a proper set of family relationships within which protagonists can experiment with their being.

(d) The shape of the surplus reality might be suggested from the systemic hypothesis, although this shape might not even be considered by the protagonists, so embroiled are they in the system. That is, directors are able to formulate the pattern that is required in the current or original social atom, and can 'intervene' by producing that point and presenting it to the protagonist. In Ralph's case, this may be a mother that sets limits, or a mother who expresses her grief for her lost husband, or simply a bereaved family who now co-operate.

The importance of the systemic hypothesis is illustrated in the drama of 'The tired mother'. Polly's problem is reconstrued away from something happening within the protagonist to something happening between the protagonist and another person. The director work 'elsewhere' in the system (that is, between Polly and her husband) and the relevant time for the drama is suggested by the strategic interview. The shape of the surplus reality is influenced by a systemic understanding of the problem.

The tired mother

Polly, the protagonist of this drama, is a large, physically strong-looking woman of about 40. She had presented herself to Dot, the director, for a drama in the course of a one-day workshop on psychodrama conducted in a large country town. Neither she nor the other members of the group had had any prior experience of the method. Her theme was 'tiredness' — she seemed to be tired nearly all the time. The group, 90 per cent female, had had some experience of being tired themselves, and was most interested in her theme. They fully supported her being a protagonist.

'How long has being tired been a problem?' asked Dot in the initial interview. 'About nine weeks', replied Polly, in a weary voice. 'And what was going on nine weeks ago: anything unusual happening in your life about then?' Polly told Dot that at that time she had taken on a new job. Dot persisted with her questions, however. Something in Polly's voice, its flatness, perhaps, suggested that further strategic questioning might better illuminate the warm-up to the tiredness.

It would have been standard practice, and quite legitimate, to have gone immediately to the scene of Polly beginning work, and to have developed that scene, letting the action itself become the diagnosis. If the new job were not the most relevant factor, the scene would have soon petered out, with the protagonist warming up to a second and more relevant scene. Do all roads lead to Rome, then? Does one always arrive at the core scene no matter whether the procedure is by strategic interview or by having the protagonist act down through the 'layers' until the psychologically relevant place is arrived at? It is hard to say, but probably that sort of opinion is overly 'mystical', and does not sufficiently allow for the interactive effect of protagonist and director as together they create history and together create a map of the problem. In any case, Dot takes the strategic tack:

'So the tiredness started around then, and before that you weren't so tired.' Polly tells Dot that, actually, she was tired before she started the new job. 'How long before?' asks Dot. 'Oh, maybe about six weeks before', says Polly. 'And what was going on at that time — anything different in your life then?' 'Well, at that time I was having a bit of conflict with my daughter', Polly answers. 'Uh huh. Let's see you in a scene of conflict with your daughter. Where does it take place, and who is there?'

Polly has not been hedging: she herself has probably not associated 'tiredness' and conflict with her daughter. Only with Dot's help, perhaps, is she able to make the relevant distinctions. She sets up a kitchen scene in her farmhouse. Her daughter, Sarah, aged 14, is preparing for school. In role reversal, Polly as Sarah is very distressed and angry, banging plates about and thumping things down. She is angry with her mother for having been away for the weekend, her first absence in six years. Polly tries to comfort her and simultaneously maintain her rights to have a weekend away visiting friends in a neighbouring state. Her efforts are fruitless: Sarah has worked herself into a rejecting/rejected rage by this time. She says that Polly is 'just like my other two mothers — they let me down too'. Polly's sense of guilt and anguish increases during the interchange. Eventually Sarah leaves for school.

Dot interviews Polly about the circumstances of Sarah's adoption. She learns that Sarah was abandoned by her natural and then two other adoptive mothers. She asks about the relationship between Polly and Sarah over the years that Sarah has lived with Polly and her husband, Bill. She also enquires about Polly and Sarah's relationship since the incident in the kitchen. Polly tells Dot that it had 'settled down', but had broken out again after Polly was required to be away from home for a week, this time for a mature students' camp at the local higher education college that she was attending.

The second scene is brief: Polly is met by Bill and Sarah at the railway station upon her return from the camp. Bill carries Polly's bags to the car; Sarah has refused to leave the car, and is sitting on the back seat, scowling. Polly has been dreading this moment, and makes strenuous attempts to form a harmonious relationship with her. This fails, and the family drive home in strained silence. Relationships since then had been at very best 'cordial'.

The final and major scene of the drama takes place in Sarah's bedroom two days after Polly's return. It is a very long scene that involves coaching by the director, the introduction of a new auxiliary, a conference with the husband about parenting, and the demonstration of a limit-setting technique. Polly has brought in freshly ironed clothes to Sarah's bedroom. She looks around at the room, which is in a mess, and asks Sarah to tidy up. Sarah flies into a rage, and knocks the ironing out of Polly's hands. She screams at her, calling her a f . . . .g bitch, and just like all those c..ts of social workers, and all her other no-good mothers who have let her down. Polly at first tries to remonstrate with her, then to explain herself, but to little avail. She deflates and sags at the middle. Sarah renews her attack — she is screaming and out of control. Polly has no power with her, appears weak at the knees, and retreats before Sarah's accusations and physical assault.

Dot chooses an auxiliary from the group to act as an alternative opponent for Polly. She gets the auxiliary to push against Polly. Polly pushes back. Dot asks the auxiliary to escalate the pushing, but no matter how hard she pushes, Polly is much stronger. In ordinary circumstances, Polly certainly seems not to be lacking in fight or strength. When called on to manifest these qualities with Sarah, however, there is no transfer. As soon as Sarah begins her guilt-inducing diatribe, Polly collapses. Dot coaches her in breathing through the belly, and in taking a bent-kneed 'samurai' stance so

that she can feel her power. The procedures are to no avail, however —
Sarah's accusations make Polly go 'tired', and she gives up the fight.

There are numerous paths that Dot could follow at this point. A time-honoured psychotherapeutic reasoning process would be to conjecture that Sarah could not attract Polly's guilt unless there was a predisposition, possibly from her own family-of-origin, to be guilty in the first place. By this logic, a family-of-origin psychodrama should have taken place between Polly and her own mother or father. In fact, Dot did make an enquiry to this effect, asking Polly whether this feeling of guilty helplessness reminded her of any other scene from her life, perhaps when she was a child. Polly said that it did not.

Another obvious path would have been to interview Sarah-in-role with great thoroughness. The 'multiple mothers', after all, was a heart-rending revelation in the drama. Maybe Dot could have developed Sarah's role more fully, deepening Polly's understanding of her rejection and disappointments in life by means of extended role reversal. It seemed, however, that Polly was already too well aware of what Sarah had been through, and was already overcompensating for it. Dot was cognizant of the danger of she herself overjoining the absent Sarah, and becoming influenced by the pathos of Sarah's life. She believed that there were possibly more fruitful lines to pursue concerning the here-and-now maintenance of the problem.

She decides to extend her understanding of the difficulty further into the system, and questions Polly on what Bill's attitude to the dispute had been. Polly replies that Bill could 'see both sides' of the conflict. From her systemic questioning, Dot receives no evidence that Sarah's acting-out is in response to marital disharmony, or in order to deflect any tensions from the marriage on to her. Nor did it seem that Polly or Bill were triangulating Sarah, attempting to detour their own unease with conflict away from themselves, as we shall see may be the case in 'Priscilla and the porridge' (Chapter 6). The acting-out child as a means to unite warring parents is a classic first hypothesis amongst family therapists, but it is not one that is always validated. Often it is too simple; often not simple enough. Nevertheless, in this instance, Sarah had managed to split her parents on a basic parenting issue — that of containment — in such a way as to render them impotent and herself out of control.

Dot sets up a psychodramatic meeting 'as parents' between Bill and Polly, just as she would if she were conducting therapy in a family clinic with all members available. Her language acts as an embedded command for the couple to work together exclusively in their parenting roles for the care and protection of a young human being.

The couple discuss Sarah. Bill is supportive of Polly, but somewhat ambivalent in his attitude to Sarah. With coaching from Dot, Polly is able to shed some of her own ambivalence and guilt about even wanting to contain Polly and about needing Bill's help to do this. Eventually, she clearly states that she needs Bill's help, as a parent, to manage Sarah's behaviour. This is promised, via role reversal. She then goes back to the scene in the bedroom. Sarah is as before, spitting, cursing, fighting, accusing, and frightened. This time Polly wrestles her with full strength. In role reversal as Sarah she puts up a full-blooded resistance, and continues her taunts and accusations of Polly being a noncaring, abandoning mother. Back as herself, Polly overcomes her daughter, and after much struggle, brings her to the ground. She pins her by the shoulders. Sarah kicks mightily with her trunk and legs. Polly calls for Bill to come and sit on her daughter's legs. He does so. They both hold Sarah, who goes through stages of rage, crying, pleas, promises of reform, etc., so long as they will let her up. They do not. Eventually, in role reversal, Sarah relaxes and apparently enters a state of deep peace. She and her parents begin talking.

This final scene provides a rather striking comment on the ability of psychodrama to tap into people's 'psychological truth', since the effect of the holding technique in the drama was remarkably similar to the effect of a holding technique in family therapy with a 'live' family. The drama was also remarkable in that the point of the fight is not the usual psychodramatic one of expressing rage, or coming to a spontaneity state via evoked emotion, but actually one of control and limit-setting. In this case, the limits are physical. Jay Hayley reports a similar case in *Uncommon therapy* (Hayley, 1973) where Milton Erikson instructs the mother of an outrageous child actually to sit on the child for a whole day. Since that book was published, various 'holds' have been devised in family therapy for a father or mother physically to contain a terrified child who fears that there are no limits and therefore there is no safety. The child acts out more and more, and becomes more and more fearful if it is not contained. The scene is also unusual in that a mother, so often the persecutory or blamed figure in psychodramas, is 'in the right' for once. Her stand with her child is supported by the weight of the psychodrama (and her own not inconsiderable weight) rather than being subtly eroded with hints of psychopathology about guilt and her own family-of-origin.

Dot chose dramatically to expand the definition of the problem from the Polly-Sarah overinvolvement by introducing the father's unwitting participation in maintaining the problem. The problem itself is not seen as Polly's, nor as Sarah's, but as a recursive problem in the whole family. The 'solution' consists in developing Polly's roles, not so much as an individual, but as a wife and parent. That is, only after she has been able clearly to state her needs to Bill can she begin to deal with Sarah. After that, she herself was able to overcome Sarah and bring her to the ground, whereas before she had been powerless. Bill was involved only when the battle was nearly over. The point may have been that at least he now was not acting against her as a parent. His former ambivalence does not necessarily betoken 'trouble in the marriage' — an old therapy favourite — so much as trouble in family rules and function. The focus is kept on the child, but the father's participation in the parental subsystem is increased so as to separate the overinvolved mother/daughter dyad (Minuchin and Fishman, 1981). By supporting the parental subsystem, the psychological distance between the mother and child is increased, and the distance between the spouses is decreased, by giving them common tasks as parents.

Throughout the drama, Dot has challenged Polly's epistemology in several ways. There is no longer one 'identified patient' in the family — herself — but at least two, and possibly three. That is, all the interactions in the family need to change if the problem is to change. Secondly, Polly can now only with difficulty believe that one family member — herself or Sarah — is controlling the system, rather than each of them serving as a context for the other. Sarah's role of accusing, rejected waif can only be maintained if Polly adopts the role of guilty, abandoning parent, and vice versa, Polly can only adopt such a role if Sarah 'agrees' to be an abandoned waif. Moreover, Bill can help Polly develop her guilty-parent roles by being himself split between the two. If he had adopted another role towards either of the others, their roles, too, would have had to change.

The family's role system is not a classic persecutor/rescuer/victim one, however, but a complicated system where 'pathology' occurs almost by accident and by neglect of each person's sense of responsibility for self. In becoming overresponsible to others, the two adults actually shirk that responsibility. They are by no means sick — they simply do not know what to do. It was sufficient for Polly to develop the collaborative, determined parent role for her to drop the guilty role, indicating that it is not always necessary to work directly on a so-called intrapsychic process such as guilt. Guilt is interpersonal, and is called up by specific contexts and by other people inviting it or providing suitable environments for it. The drama took the course it did because of a systemic rather than a 'linear' reading of the cycle of interaction. It was a co-creation, a new map, jointly produced by Polly and Dot.

Chapter six

Structural interventions in psychodrama

Marriage is a horrible state and the only
thing that's any worse is being single.

Whitaker

In the 1970s structural therapy emerged as one of the best-known approaches in the family-therapy field. Even people relatively unfamiliar with family therapy may nevertheless have heard the name Minuchin, and may identify family therapy with that particular Argentinian-born psychiatrist. Structural therapy's claim to popularity might also arise from its clear framework that brings order to the powerful but unpredictable ways in which members of a family affect each other. It describes families as having an underlying organization in terms that provide intelligible guidelines for diagnosis and treatment.

The boundaries and coalitions, systems and subsystems, that are said to make up family structure are abstractions, just as roles in psychodrama are abstractions. They are distinctions that help one notice difference, however; for example, using the concept of family structure brings news of difference to therapists, and enables them to intervene in a systematic and organized fashion. Structural distinctions are also helpful in psychodramatic interventions: making a structural intervention at the surplus–reality level is a way of organizing the data that the protagonist has presented, and co-creating a new reality in which spontaneity is possible. Structural family therapy is designed to unfreeze families from rigid habits, creating opportunities for new structures to emerge; structural interventions in psychodrama aim at a similar goal, though this time the 'family' is an internalized one, present only in the personal constructs of the protagonist.

Any system is defined by its boundaries — that is how we know it is this system and not that. Your skin is a boundary. You also have a boundary around your spouse and children that you call 'family' to distinguish it from 'non-family'. Within that family, there is a boundary around your spouse and yourself — the 'spouse subsystem', and another one around the children — the 'sibling subsystem'. Likewise, when therapists see clients, another boundary is drawn, which they agree upon as the 'therapeutic system'. These are examples of the myriads of boundaries in our lives, invisible barriers that surround individuals and subsystems, regulating the amount and type of contact with others.

'Boundaries' represent the perimeter of the system, holding together the components that make up the system, and controlling the flow of matter, energy, and information to and from the system. They protect and regulate; they keep the elements within the system intact and cohesive, but they also need to be permeable and allow the system appropriate exchanges with the outside. If boundaries are too permeable, the system loses its integrity and identity, but if they are too closed, the system 'starves' for information and 'food'. Rigid boundaries are overly restrictive, and permit little contact with outside systems, resulting in disengagement, say, between parents and children. 'Enmeshed' subsystems, on the other hand, while giving the parties considerable mutual support, can reduce independence and autonomy for all concerned.

Family structure is determined partly by universal factors and partly by factors specific to that particular family. For example, all families have some kind of hierarchical structure in which parents and children have different amounts of authority. Within the family structure, each person may have set roles — provider, comforter, helpless one, organizer, etc., which have been born out of transactional patterns so ingrained that their origin is forgotten and they are now regarded as necessary rather than as optional. The perpetuated patterns of interaction form a structure that becomes resistant to change — the roles become rigid.

Most families operate by 'rules', which are usually unstated and out of awareness. These rules make life easy in terms of economy of decision-making, but also prevent members from utilizing a full range of behaviours that might otherwise be available, especially when members are confronted with a developmental crisis such as a new baby, the children leaving home, or the mother taking paid employment outside the home. Some rules are necessary, and some needlessly restrict spontaneity. An understanding of the rules organizing the interactions helps an understanding of how the family defines its interactions. Family structure is the organized pattern in which family members interact; it describes sequences that are predictable, repeated, and have established enduring patterns. Structural family therapy is directed at altering family structure so that the family can solve its problems. Since the goal of therapy is structural change, problem-solving becomes a by-product of that change.

As we have observed, family structure involves a set of covert rules governing transactions in the family. Changing these rules may or may not affect the structure, but changing the structure will almost certainly affect the rules. Changing the structure in surplus reality is one of the easiest concepts both to do and to understand, and hence this chapter is presented ahead of the more difficult systemic concepts to be described in the next chapter. Most psychodramas, in fact, involve a change of structure of some sort in surplus reality — for example, Peta changed the family structure in 'The lady of Spain', p. 28, and Polly changed hers in 'The tired mother', p. 96. In the drama to be presented next, the change in structure occurs in terms of family boundaries. By altering boundaries and realigning subsystems, the director changes the behaviour and experience of each of the family members.

Structural interventions are particularly suited to the psychodramatic method in that both forms use enactments within the actual session to reframe the problem and its solution. All psychotherapies use reframing — clients or group members come with their own view of the problem, and the therapist offers a different and potentially constructive view. The *sine qua non* of structural therapy is to observe and modify the structure of family transactions within the immediate context of the session (Nichols, 1984). Seeman and Weiner (1985) quite accurately point out some of the differences between enactment in family therapy and enactment in psychodrama. The acted-out perceptions that form the basis of psychodrama are indeed not an imitation or reflection of reality, as we discussed in 'Dale's dilemma', p. 42. From a second-order cybernetic point of view, they are a playing out of the feelings and perceptions of the protagonist when united with the feelings and perceptions of the therapeutic system — that is, the director and group. Where these feelings and perceptions do concern the structure of the family, however, they can be altered or satisfied by a psychodramatic alteration of the family structures so long as the new definition fits.

The woman who couldn't get in

The warm-up for this drama was Pat's persistent feelings of being excluded from groups of people on the grounds of 'incompetence'. When asked towards whom she experienced these feelings 'most', she replied that it was towards her mother-in-law. The first scene involved a telephone conversation between Pat and her sister-in-law, Anna. In the call, Anna tells Pat that her mother is a 'bit put out' at the moment because of Pat's neglect in not having asked her to a special occasion. There seems little further 'mileage' in this scene, even though Pat is quite angry with Anna for her sneaky insinuations. Simply to escalate the anger would be to produce a tiresome, melodramatic psychodrama and little change in Pat's overall functioning.

Scene two takes place in the kitchen of Pat's house, and concerns an attempted confrontation between Pat and Andrea, the mother-in-law. Pat accuses Andrea of making her 'nervous and clumsy', that nothing she does 'is ever good enough'. This scene, too, seems to have nowhere to go. Vital information about the social structure of the family is missing, even though Pat's direct warm-up is to Andrea.

Duane asks Pat to 'show us what it's like to be in this family'. Pat rather half-heartedly begins a family map, using auxiliaries. Duane realizes that greater life seems to come to the drama when Pat is in role as Andrea, so he suggests that Pat role-reverse with Andrea and set up the family as she sees it. Andrea does this with a kind of twirling energy. She has no doubts. Right next to her, she places Anna, her daughter. On her other side, but at a greater distance, she places her husband, Ern. Further out from her daughter comes Peter, her son, and Pat's husband. At a little distance from him is Louise, Peter's first wife. Pat and her children are placed outside this circle.

During the interview-in-role, Andrea's beliefs received the most attention. She firmly believed that she had set up the essential family unit, and that Pat was not truly 'family', even though she had borne Peter's two children. Family was first family, and that was that: the issue for her was structural: it did not really matter how nice Pat was, how obliging, how attractive, how competent. She was out, and would always be out. Peter, no matter what his sins in divorcing and then marrying out, was 'in', and so was Louise, Peter's first wife.

After progressing further in a conventional manner, the drama became deadlocked. Lengthy interactions had taken place (not reported here fully) that had involved confrontations between Andrea and her own husband, and Andrea and Pat. There did not seem to be much point in Pat further railing against this woman or her fate, or tipping the whole lot of them into the sea, or some other grisly psychodramatic fate to which one consigns one's relatives and other persecutors. To be sure, Pat now 'understood' what was happening much more clearly. But her acceptance of her own version of the family myth also implied an acceptance of rigid family boundaries, and acceptance of Peter's essential links with his mother, rather than with her and their children.

The director asks Pat to set up the family map once more, but this time to do it in terms of the generations, rather than in terms of who is in and who is out. She does so, placing Andrea and her husband at one end, herself and Peter together on one plane, and then further out Anna, and then Louise, Peter's first wife. Behind them, on the next 'generation', are the children. Pat appears to be quite startled by this new configuration.

Further confrontation with Andrea occurs. The director suggests that Pat actually does have someone to help her, namely her husband Peter. She draws closer to him, and takes his hand as she speaks with his mother. After a few roles reversals, it is established that she and Peter are a unit, and that if family boundaries have to be established, they can be in the family of the two of them and their children. Acceptance by Andrea would be 'nice', but she realizes that Peter in fact has made new alliances, and that they are with her. The drama ends with her appreciating this re-formed family map. At follow-up several weeks, and then several months, later, the picture of that line through time, rather than the circle that excludes her, remains powerfully with her. Family relationships are reported to be excellent.

In this low-key drama, Duane's procedures represent an extension of, rather than a radical departure from, traditional psychodramatic exercises. The main point of the drama became an explicit redrawing of the family boundaries, a procedure overtly introduced by the director. Part of the problem seemed to have been the overrigid drawing of boundaries around 'family' by Andrea, and Pat's inability to mark adequate boundaries between her and her husband's family-of-origin. When she had a clearer idea of the appropriate boundaries around her own family, the point of the warm-up — 'exclusion' — is resolved.

If protagonists are asked to set up a family scene, not as how it was, but as how they would like it to be, they often do establish a family structure that looks sound — they achieve their own form of structural family therapy. Sometimes, however, protagonists cannot even envisage adequate structures. They may be too taken up with their own role within the system to be able to bring new thought, that is, spontaneity, into their interactions. It can then be legitimate for directors to suggest a new family structure alongside the 'old family' and see how the protagonist reacts to the difference. If the action flattens out and becomes lifeless, directors need to take that as evidence that the intervention was mistimed or inappropriate. Structural interventions work by opening alternative patterns of family interaction that can modify family structure. They do not usually create new structures, but activate dormant ones. If, once activated, the dormant sequences are functional, the appropriateness of the intervention will be reflected in the vibrancy and clarity of the drama's resolution.

A system is better thought of as a circle than as a wheel with a hub, the hub being the protagonist; protagonists feel like hubs, but in fact they are not. A psychodrama that concentrates on structure emphasizes wholeness, boundaries, and organization as unifying principles. 'Wholeness' in systemic literature means that no system can adequately be understood once it has been broken down into its component elements. In the case of 'The woman who couldn't get in', therefore, neither Pat's, nor Anna's, nor Andrea's, nor Peter's behaviour can be understood separately. Elements cannot be understood in isolation since they never function independently — 'the state of each is constrained by the state of all the others' (Goldenberg and Goldenberg, 1985, p. 29).

In working structurally, directors help differentiate the subsystems of various member's boundaries if they are enmeshed or to form them more tightly if they are too rigid. They can emphasize children's differences from each other and from parents. They can help parents to make age-appropriate demands. They can draw protective boundaries around spouse subsystems and sibling subsystems. They can help parents separate emotionally from children (and vice versa) when the child has been induced to take an inappropriate role as spouse or lover to a parent. A structural intervention at surplus reality allows protagonists to experience what a family (their family) would be like if it functioned appropriately, and what freedoms and boundaries would exist within such a structure. They can re-do their own child development, as it were.

Analogic versus digital therapy

As producers, psychodramatic directors have to ensure that the enactment is appropriately dramatic: it needs to be aesthetically pleasing and to follow basic principles of staging. The analogic forms of communication — the 'feeling' of relationships — take precedence over digital (content) forms, or the actual words that one puts on relationships (Watzlawick *et al.*, 1967). Tele is the Morenian term covering part but not all of this concept. A structural intervention in a psychodrama, therefore, needs also to take place at this relational or analogic level, just as interventions in family therapy operate chiefly at this level, though the investigation may have been at the digital (content) level. In a drama, individuals do not so much 'communicate' as become part of communication. They see, hear, smell, taste, feel, act, as well as talk about and 'gossip in the presence of'. They do not describe communication, but participate in it.

Every communication has a content and a relationship aspect. These two modes of communication complement each other in every message. When directors act as social investigators, they tap into verbal (digital) expression of, until then, vague knowledge of relationship. Digital message material, although of a much higher degree of complexity, visibility, and abstraction than analogic material, ultimately lacks an adequate vocabulary for the contingencies of relationship. 'Talking about' relationship requires adequate translation from the analogic into the digital mode of communication. In drama, the relationship is expressed directly. That is why sometimes all that is needed for a satisfactory family psychodrama is for the director to extend the production as far as it will go, and the structure tends to right itself. The 'can-can dancer' illustrates this point.

The can-can dancer

Pauline is an attractive and vivacious 28-year-old woman who still lives at home. She is the only child of the family. Her warm-up to this current drama is her despair at ever being able to form satisfactory relationships with men.

In the initial interview with the director, she tells Dot that she thinks that it is because of the 'rotten relations' her father and mother have: she has never been successful and happy with men because father relates to mother badly. The mother has 'been unhappy for thirty-two years'.

Dot is unprepared for a drama, and sees Pauline's warm-up as probably being best enacted in the format of a vignette. Pauline is invited to have a dialogue with her father and mother, which takes place with two auxiliaries, but without a scene being set. The essence of this dialogue is her accusation to father: 'In not loving her (Pauline's mother), you don't love me, because I am part of her'.

What steps should Dot now take, following such a startling statement? Should the next intervention be directed to the mother or to the father? The questions are actually misleading: although Pauline is claiming an identification with her mother that could be, to say the least, problematic, and although she may have formed a coalition with mother of blaming victim towards her father (it is too early to be sure), the interaction at this stage is best conducted with the whole family system in itself.

Dot's role of producer can be the primary one, since it appears that the social investigation and systems theorizing will be well looked after in the course of the drama itself. It is too early to be therapist. Dot therefore asks Pauline if she recalls a particular scene that vividly evokes those feelings she has towards her parents. The scene that Pauline creates occurs at the end of a family meal (how many major scenes in psychodrama and life occur around the dinner table!) when she was 'about 4 years old'. (Again, how many dramas, with various directors and with protagonists from all kinds of settings, have their core scene when the protagonist is 3 or 4 years old. These developmental-stage cues will be elaborated later in this chapter.)

From the way that Pauline places the auxiliaries, it appears that father and mother are a frozen, alienated couple. In the actual time of the drama, they have a row, during which father in a rage sweeps the teapot off the table, scalding mother: Mother begins to cry, and so does Pauline. The action develops with Pauline attacking her father, and the father trying to get her to sit down. To the observer, he may seem to be acting 'reasonably' enough, given the fraught nature of the situation. He pushes her, not too roughly, into her chair. She cries out to mother, who intervenes, placing herself between Pauline and father.

There is obviously room here for a fine piece of structural family therapy. After all, generational boundaries are being blurred, the daughter seems to be part of a triangulated battle; and parental authority is being eroded by a successful appeal by a child to one parent against another. A structural intervention at this stage of the drama could have been (in surplus reality) to have father and mother confer on Pauline's upbringing, and for them both to have set limits. Another type of structural intervention might have been to carry the fight further between father and mother, leaving Pauline out of it altogether; this would have been a way of marking the generational boundaries, and making clear to Pauline that what father did to mother, he did not do to her.

Although these would have been legitimate possibilities, Dot did not choose them. As the demands of the drama to be produced fully were not yet met, it was quite possible that intergenerational boundaries might still look after themselves, without explicit intervention from the director. If a structural intervention to a problem is given too early, the 'lesson' may merely be intellectualized. The information released into the system by the enactment in surplus reality will be redundant; the system cannot absorb it because it is not ready for it. Or, to put it in another way, there is plenty more analogic information yet to come, and it is unnecessary to translate what is happening digitally. By encouraging the dramatization of the events in Pauline's family, Dot is hoping for an analogic resolution — a resolution at the mysterious level of relationship itself, for which there are no adequate words.

Dot suggests that Pauline take the matter further with her father. She needs little prompting, and flies into a tempestuous rage with him. She dances from side to side, and back and forth in front of him. This rage is escalated more and more; she lays into him (a thick cushion is placed in front of the auxiliary playing father), flailing with her fists and feet. This goes on for quite some time, until she is exhausted. Each time that she stops, however, she keeps up a strange movement on her feet in front of him. When she talks to him, she moves from foot to foot.

Dot finds it difficult to understand what the movements represent: perhaps she is dancing in front of him; perhaps she still has more kicking left in her; or maybe it is some strange kind of approach–avoidance procedure being symbolized. Dot decides to plump for the first hypothesis, being fairly confident that it will be rejected outright if it is not accurate or appropriate.

As so often in psychodrama, it becomes difficult to know exactly when the protagonist is suggesting something to the director, or when the suggestion is the other way round. Perhaps it is better to construe them both as being in a system of mutual influence, where their active imaginations become fused, as it were. Moreno speaks of a 'co-unconscious', and that kind of terminology seems as accurate as any description of the ways directors and protagonists work together. Psychodrama is highly 'directed' therapy, and yet the amount of freedom that the protagonists enjoy to set out their worlds and live and act in them seems to be unparalleled elsewhere. A paradox, perhaps.

Pauline's to-and-fro movements suggest a kind of dance. This suggestion is reinforced by the material from the initial interview: that she still lives at home; that her father has 'ruined' her relationships with other men; that by not loving her mother appropriately he did not love her (Pauline) appropriately. These are only hints, suggestions from the data, rather than clinical 'conclusions' (which, when one thinks of it, can also only ever be hints and suggestions from the data). The 'hypothesis' of Pauline being her father's 'dancer' can be confirmed or denied if it is adequately produced.

Dot now needs to build an appropriate environment for this further stage in the production. She asks the group to hum the music from the can-can. *Slowly, Pauline begins to dance in a more formal fashion, escalating the to-and-fro movements she had been doing before. She looks extremely distressed as she builds up. In front of her seated father, she does a version of the can-can, with high kicking. In role reversal as father, she 'conducts' the music to louder and more giddy heights (the group had been beginning to flag). The scene has a tragic and hysterical air to it. Finally, after an almost unbearable amount of this, Pauline begins to weep; this time she really does confront her father, who is still acting as a conductor in an orchestra pit. She is not as violent as in the early kicking scenes, but on the other hand, there is not much play in it now either. At the end, she tells her father that her dancing days for him are over. In her final confrontation, she is no longer moving from foot to foot. The beginnings of her separation from him seem convincing to director and audience alike, who breathe a sigh of relief.*

Protagonists have long been used to a particular family script. They need assistance in transforming that script — to change its significance and to introduce other elements that modify the original framework. With the director's help, they grasp the distribution and characteristics of the reciprocal functions, that is, the interacting roles, of the family. In the staging of a scene, the protagonist supplies many verbal and nonverbal components that can lead to an understanding of interacting roles. These elements are perceived by the director in the form of a comprehensive gestalt on which to base efforts to have the protagonist redefine the situation. A director always does this, of course; but in the postulated case of directors using a structural family-therapy orientation, they look with special intensity at the position that each person takes in the family, and may seek to manipulate that.

Even though Dot escalated the production elements of the drama, she did so on the basis of an early assessment of the relative positions of the protagonists. She actively organized the elements supplied by the family to construct a new framework that was gradually built on during the course of the drama. At the outset of the drama it appeared as if Pauline's relationship with her mother was paramount. As the drama developed, however, there was evidence to suggest that the 'individuation' that Pauline needed to achieve might better come about, at this stage anyway, if she understood her separateness from father.

A systems theory of psychodrama not only views the protagonist in his or her system, but also takes account of the interaction of the director and protagonist. This drama was not just Pauline's, therefore, but a co-production of Pauline/Dot. Pauline and Dennis, or Pauline and Duane, Duke, Dean, Di, or any of the other directors mentioned in these pages would have produced quite a different drama. It was not at all inevitable that Pauline would end up as a can-can dancer before her father; the drama of the system is itself part of a system in which even the audience is influential.

As producers, directors need to be wary about reinforcing the protagonist's view of the family as it was, or even as it ought to be. Thus, they might reproduce the protagonist's family map, or influence the production at an early stage by refusing to move to scenes that star the family members the protagonist has viewed as being central to the problem. By being held back from their routine view of reality, protagonists are enabled to gain a new affective and cognitive appreciation of the family experience. Guldner (1983) suggests that protagonists are thrust into new perceptions, that is, into spontaneity.

Directors do not so much introduce 'extraneous' elements into the family script, as base the production on material that actually emerges from the transactions of family members with each other, the protagonist, and the director. They may restructure the elements that are offered, bringing to the fore unnoticed factors, and relegating apparently prominent elements to the background. Images that are buried within the drama might be emphasized, and the family invited to comment on them, or interact with them. The director is seeking not only a catharsis, but new learning, new structures, and a change in the family's rules. Even these new rules and new structure need to be unstable and provisory — otherwise the cultural conserve lives again. Protagonists are encouraged to make choices free from rigid models, including the models that they have set up for themselves in previous psychodramas.

Very often the production itself, and its carry-over into surplus reality, has its own momentum and carries its own therapeutic messages. A new configuration of the family pattern frequently emerges at these times as part and parcel of the drama. Overt restructuralizing then becomes unnecessary; the therapy, as it were, looks after itself.

At other times, extra input does seem necessary. The active stance advocated in the following pages is offered as a set of alternatives rather than prescriptively. Therapists are like tuning forks: they learn to resonate to the protagonist's system differently, at different stages of the therapeutic course. Based on a systemic or structural assessment, directors may propose different versions of the family script in the surplus-reality stage of the drama, which is one of the principal therapeutic stages. These interventions can be carried out in ways that are fully within the 'traditional' psychodrama repertoire, since most psychodrama is interactional and therefore, to a degree, structural and systemic.

Function and development

Psychodramas emphasizing structure investigate the function and development of the social system being depicted, rather than intrapsychic conflicts only. Let us now see what scope there is for focusing on the developmental stage at which the drama is being enacted: what developmental tasks must be mastered that are not being mastered, perhaps, and what new adaptational strategies are required? A family-of-origin drama that takes place at a particular age of the protagonist may indicate that the whole family is stuck, experiencing difficulty in moving to the next phase of its life cycle. Thus the 'can-can dancer's' family is confronted by a particular phase in Pauline's development and in the development of the whole family; later we shall encounter certain psychodramas such as 'The clockmaker's son', where the developmental stage at which the psychodrama is set is critical to understanding its central dynamic.

One of the goals of strategic family therapy is to help people past a crisis to the next stage of family life (Hayley, 1973; Madanes, 1981). In the strategic view, inadequate spontaneity (dysfunctional behaviour) is regarded more as a product of a struggle between persons than the result of conflicted forces within a single individual. Faulty dyadic or triadic relationships, therefore, tend to become the focus of the director's attention, and the intervention of the psychodrama may be to help the entire system alter its transactional pattern. The therapeutic endeavour revolves around producing (defining) the entire system's characteristic patterns of interacting with one another in both digital and analogic form. Directors working structurally have different rules that they use to make sense out of what they are experiencing, and different language to conceptualize and interpret information — the ways they go about obtaining information and drawing conclusions about the world; in other words, their epistemology is different from the epistemology of a traditional therapist or even a psychodramatist.

The narrative of the following drama, 'Priscilla and the porridge', in fact follows rather conventional lines. It is yet again from childhood, and is presented alongside some speculations of what might have been some of the developmental, structural, and functional elements at the time, and how that or further dramas might have been conducted from a systemic viewpoint. Priscilla's drama, therefore, provides an introduction to some of the possibilities of psychodrama where structural therapy may be emphasized, and does the spadework, as it were, of familiarizing us with some of the possibilities of this type of intervention within psychodrama. An attempt is made to link the protagonist's behaviour in the group with the narrative and structure of the drama.

Priscilla and the porridge

Priscilla is a 35-year-old, highly intelligent member of a training group. She is married, and has three children. She is a very able theoretician and case conceptualizer, so long as the conceptualizing is not about her. She is also an excellent double, liking to bond with people and to 'become' them. In her work as a psychologist, she is strongest on basic empathy, but her ability to manage a case is limited, and her cases tend to become 'endless'.

Priscilla makes many tearful demands on the group for time and understanding. The time she requires is to explain or have explained to her an event or remark. It is as if she does not understand quite where she 'ends' and other people 'begin'. In conversation, she appears to have difficulty in role-reversing, in seeing herself from the outside, as it were. She does not seem quite to know when people are letting her in, and when they want to move on to other things.

As a consequence, she becomes anxious and unresponsive to others' spontaneity when they do move on. This starts a stronger move away in the other person, which makes Priscilla even more anxious. An unhappy cycle eventuates. In her early days in the group she polarized other people's responses: acceptance means their total and unending acceptance of her. The smallest rejection is also total, and gives rise to many complaints. Most of her discourse with the group concerns anecdotes about how someone outside (usually her husband or the woman who supervises her at work) or inside the group has been unfair to her.

The group commonly give Priscilla the time that she asks, although in doing so they become increasingly angry with her. When a member expresses this anger, Priscilla becomes more and more tearful. At this point the group usually polarizes into those who wish that she would keep quiet, and those who react to her with compassion, or loyalty, or genuine interest. At least one of Priscilla's friends takes a lead role in comforting Priscilla and confronting the angry person for his or her 'insensitivity' if Priscilla is criticized.

On the occasion of Priscilla's psychodrama, she has gone to a scene where she is 4 years old. In the scene, she has been sent, by her mother, out of the dining room into her bedroom. Her crime is that she has thrown her porridge all over the kitchen floor. Anxiously, she waits in her bedroom for her father to return at lunchtime. When he does, she hears raised voices from the kitchen, and then her father's tread along the hall. He has been commissioned by the mother to punish her. He enters the room, takes off his belt, and begins to thrash her. The mother remains in the kitchen listening to Priscilla's cries. The beating is quite severe, and the group reacts with horror. In fact, they are more horrified than Priscilla is.

Child abuse in its mild or severe forms is frequently the subject of psychodrama. Reactions to beatings or even disciplining as a child lodge vividly within people's memories and when psychodramatically re-enacted produce extreme states of panic, anger, and revulsion in protagonist and audience alike. Beatings at boarding school or cruelty experienced from teachers, including members of religious orders, are not infrequently a focus of warm-up, reflecting in part the strong impression that such experiences of violence have on people. It also reflects, let us hope, the age group of people who enact psychodramas in the 1980s and who have been at school in the 1950s and 1960s when such forms of discipline were more common than they are today. Perhaps there will not be as many such dramas in the 1990s. Or perhaps they are archetypal, and represent *any* experience of intrusion and violence, whether verbal or physical, that everyone inevitably suffers at some stage of their life.

Let us halt this drama for a moment in order to speculate on what may be the relevant issues in Priscilla's presentation so far, aside from the feelings of rage or revulsion that violence towards young people restimulates. A drama can be conducted on several levels, and examined on even more. Let us start developmentally. Priscilla's ambivalence towards her father (which will be suggested later in the drama) and hatred of her mother at the age of 4 is suggestive of Oedipal issues in the family at that stage. In systemic terms, Oedipal issues are more likely to be concerned with alliances and ultimately with love than with sex as such. At the age of 4, Priscilla may love her father too much; she may fear that her mother does not love her father or herself enough; she may wish to draw away from mother a little and enter father's world more. Her mother may not appreciate or understand her defiance and drawing away, and may seek to form an alliance with her husband over the issue.

'Developmentally', then, we might say that this family is having difficulties with individuation when Priscilla is aged 4, and that these difficulties manifest themselves in certain alliances. It is even possible that Priscilla's parents are having trouble individuating from their parents. Carter and McGoldrick (1980) suggest that dysfunctional behaviour in individuals is related to 'vertical' and 'horizontal' stressors within a family system. The vertical stressors include patterns of relating and functioning that are transmitted down through generations, and the horizontal stressors are the anxiety-producing events experienced as the family moves through its life cycle — maturational crises as well as unexpected, traumatic ones. Even a small amount of horizontal stress, for example, a child throwing her food around the room, can cause great disruption to a family in which the vertical axis already contains intense stress. Carter and McGoldrick suggest that the greater the anxiety experienced by previous generations at any transitional point, such as the birth of a first child, the more difficult that point will be for the current generation.

We can also note that the conflict is about food, eating, and mess. Difficulties about food and eating are often indicative of battles for control, which raises the individuation issue once again. So far, therefore, the theme of the drama could be enacted at the level of sexual feelings, lost love, alliances, control, individuation, or of rejecting that which is stuffed down one's throat. Violence, rage, indignation, thwarted love, and powerlessness are all present too. As the family faces new tasks and learns new adaptational techniques, it also faces new risks of family dysfunction.

Or maybe Priscilla just did not like porridge and her mother was in a defeated mood that day, tired of remonstrating with her, and thinking she might get her husband to do a little strong-arm work for a change. Possibly so, but in that case why would Priscilla remember this scene so vividly, and act it out thirty years later in her first-ever psychodrama? The 'ho-hum' hypothesis does not fit with the intensity of the warm-up and the tension between the three people depicted in the drama.

We could also examine Priscilla's drama from the somewhat more uncommon angle of function: how the family organizes itself to care for, protect, and educate children. If we focus on limits and authority within the family, the drama reveals that the parental authority in Priscilla's family is random, unpredictable; violence seems to come from nowhere. Although father carries out mother's wishes, he does so somewhat unwillingly. At a simple level, there appears to be a lack of consensus between the two parents about child-rearing issues. This absence of consensus can result in damaging 'triangulation' or in total confusion for the child. In structural family-therapy terms, the conflict is suggestive of an inadequately formed parental 'holon'. A holon is a separate little whole within a big whole. So within a family that is a whole, there is a parental holon and a sibling holon. In Priscilla's family there seems to be a weak-spouse subsystem with inadequate boundaries (in this case, the boundaries appear too diffuse, though in other families, inadequate boundaries may be too rigid) to the sibling subsystem, represented by Priscilla.

Bowen (1966; 1972) has developed the notion of 'triangles' as a useful concept in discussing relationship. He maintains that the smallest stable-relationship format is a triangular one that contains three persons who are closely associated. The most available or most vulnerable third person is called in to lower the anxiety level and tension in a dyad. Once the third person is in, individuals may feel anxious and tense, but the system itself is maintained. In a family, of course, there may be not just one triangle, but many that interlock. His method of 'detriangling' reflects a structural and psychodynamic approach to family therapy that would be very difficult to attain in a psychodrama. The therapist excludes the most vulnerable individual from further sessions, and meets with the remaining family members. Once this member is excluded, the therapist would expect triangling moves from the family, which would then be resisted and explored by the therapist.

Priscilla's solution in the psychodrama was to seek immediate retribution. This solution seemed right at the time to the director, especially as it was Priscilla's first psychodrama. In a burst of vibrant liberation, she first beat up, and then reconciled with her father. Psychodramatic audiences are familiar with this cycle of cathartic rage leading to expressions of unity and tenderness. Priscilla's real quarry in the drama, however, was her mother, against whom she raged and spat at for some time. This rage was colder, and did not lead to a reconciliation. The drama eventually ended with Priscilla going for a long walk on her own, talking to various animals in the forest, who were represented psychodramatically. From a psychodramatic point of view, this ending was quite satisfactory, especially for a first drama.

Her solution in the drama is somewhat similar to the solutions she adopts in the group, that is, blame–retreat. Her 'fighting' in the group, however, was usually more covert, and involved a hostile coalition where she and her partner become co-victims. In the drama, at least, her fighting is overt, and she becomes spirited and clear. It is not a real failure of the drama or of therapy, at this stage, that Priscilla's solutions in the drama and in her group behaviour contain similarities, since her psychodramatic persona was more vigorous, 'honest', and lucid than the one she presented to the group. Repeated psychodramas of this nature, however, may be more dysfunctional in terms of the problem–solution cycle.

Let us now examine other directorial initiatives that may be possible. An obvious 'new solution' is a functional one. For example, the director might suggest that grown-up Priscilla coach the parents of her 4-year-old self on basic agreement between them about child-rearing issues, and a balance of control and authority proper to her age at that time. The total removal of limits is never a satisfactory psychodramatic solution, though for a time the protagonist may need to act in the godlike role of one who transcends limits, vanquishes her enemies, and is reconciled with her true loves. Usually the protagonist's 'enemies' and 'true loves' are the same people, of course: the parents.

In countless psychodramas involving parents, the resolution presented seems to be that the protagonist is struggling for liberation. The struggle might involve 'fighting off the forces' of personified parental injunctions that have become somatized as heavy weights, pains in the shoulders, back-aches, or the like. Sometimes the struggle involves actually wrestling with, setting free, carving up, pissing on, gagging, or telling off psychodramatic parents. The immediate result is a rush of spontaneity in the protagonist and a feeling of exhilaration. Such bloody victories are usually applauded by the group, and well should they be. The enemy is most often one rather than both of the parents, who has misapplied, underapplied, or overapplied their parental force. The spontaneity released by the battle usually results in a heart-to-heart talk with the now reformed and docile parent; once the layers of anger and fear have become known and expressed with true spontaneity, then the layer of love can emerge. The psychodrama might end in surplus reality with the formerly 'bad' parent having become a 'good' parent, who now manages the role as father or mother with love and good sense.

Boszormenyi-Nagy and Spark (1973) introduced to the therapy literature new terms such as 'legacy' and 'loyalty' to emphasize that family members inevitably acquire a set of expectations and a code of responsibility towards each other. Families maintain a kind of 'family ledger', a multigenerational account system of who, psychologically speaking, owes what to whom. Whenever injustices occur, there is an expectation of some later repayment or restitution. Problems in relationships occur when justice comes too slowly or in an amount too small to satisfy the other person. From this perspective, dysfunctional behaviour in any individual cannot be understood without looking at the history of the problem, and examining unsettled or unredressed accounts. The theme of Priscilla's drama, then, may simply be one of justice and 'balancing the books'.

Effective therapeutic interventions, argue Boszormenyi-Nagy and Krasner (1981), must be grounded on the therapist's conviction that trustworthiness is a necessary condition for reworking legacy assessments and allowing family members to feel that they are entitled to more satisfactory relationships. This is what all our psychodramatic heroines and heroes have done, in different contexts, and for different reasons. The authors suggest that families are best understood in terms of loyalty — who is bound to whom, what is expected of family members, how loyalty is expressed, and what happens when loyalty accounts are uneven. Their 'contextual therapy' helps rebalance the accounts kept in the invisible family ledgers. Peta's 'The lady of Spain' (p. 28) transgenerational drama illustrated this point as far back as her grandparents. Each family member is viewed as someone who is part of a multigenerational pattern where the ledgers need to be balanced by reassessment, expression, and forgiveness. So Portia is able to get back on the rails (p. 1), Phyllis no longer needs to keep wiping the sink

(p. 19), and Pansy need not be afraid of seeing snakes anymore (p. 24). Perhaps 'justice' is after all the keynote of family-of-origin psychodramas.

What are some other possibilities, though, apart from balancing the transgenerational books? Psychodrama is concerned to say something about the vitality and pulse of life in people. This intent is not vitiated, rather it can be intensified, by attending to the structures that actually prevent that vitality from emerging and sustaining itself. So let us take yet another tack. Let us suppose that the interactions with Priscilla being psychodramatically re-enacted stem from unresolved issues between the parents. Priscilla may actually even be incidental to this more major conflict, but in her efforts to survive may contribute to its escalation or to distracting the parents from fully dealing with each other. We know nothing about Priscilla's parents' intimate and sexual life; but it is probable that her family contains a 'malfunctioning hierarchy' (Hayley, 1976) where father and mother do not relate as peers and each retains executive capacity in the family.

Priscilla's behaviour may therefore play a major role in the poor conflict resolution between the parents by 'detouring' (use of the child by parents in avoiding marital strain), or by triangulation, where each parent demands the child side with them against the other. Supporting one parent is labelled as attack by the other, leading to paralysis, or to a 'stable coalition', where one of the parents joins the child in a rigidly bounded cross-generation coalition against the other parent (Minuchin, 1974). By 'coalition', Hayley (1976, p. 109) means a process of joint action against a third person. Priscilla, in fact, formed such a coalition with her father, a coalition that the mother did her best to break. Perhaps it is for this reason that mother gets father to deliver the thrashing to Priscilla. In any case, the parental exercise of authority in Priscilla's family is haphazard, alternating between beatings and hugs. Although the parents seem overpotent, and Priscilla the helpless victim, it is equally legitimate to view Priscilla as somehow controlling the family from her victimlike role. This role, of course, gives neither Priscilla nor her parents a great deal of pleasure, nor is it a very satisfactory way to lead one's life.

The issue in Priscilla's psychodrama, then, is not necessarily Priscilla's being a powerless victim of her mother's hatred or her father's compliance. If Priscilla repeatedly 'triumphs' in psychodramas, she may repeat her feelings of being vindicated as the injured party. Her active aggression towards her mother, which emerged during the physical battle with her, is indeed a new role, and a valuable one for her, since she gives outward expression to her own power and aggression, two very much denied facets of her personality. She also gets rid of some 'destructive entitlement' that may have been dogging the family for generations, as we saw in our discussion of Boszormenyi-Nagy and his co-workers. But possibly the learning can be taken a little further in functional terms: Priscilla needs to grow towards independence without excessive interference from the parents, but with adequate limits to ensure her feelings of safety and the actual physical safety that she requires as a small child. Further psychodramatic intervention in certain cases, then, may be at the parent-to-parent level, rather than at the parent-to-child level. The director could spend time with Priscilla in role reversal first as one parent, then as the other, discussing parenting issues as Polly and Bill do in 'The tired mother' (p. 96).

Distinctions are drawn that identify the troubled system's social hierarchy, at least in terms of different generations. Priscilla's warm-up and her problem begin to be seen as part of a broader sequence of action in a social context. The aim of a drama borrowing from structural family therapy may be to effect repair work between the parents first as spouses, then as parents. Surplus reality can include Priscilla witnessing adequate spouse and parental subsystems in her family, and observing what it is like to be in a family where the parental holon is repaired. She experiences appropriate interactions as a child, rather than simply the euphoria of psychodramatic victory. Priscilla's drama mostly concerned itself with the recovery of spontaneity and getting rid of her destructive entitlement. If subsequent dramas endlessly repeated this theme, they would run the risk of becoming stuck, and new interventions in surplus reality, as suggested above, may be called for.

Chapter seven

The systemic nature of roles

The use of an epistemology of billiard balls
to approach human phenomena is an indication of madness

Bradford Keeney

The psychodramatic stage simplifies and reduces the complexities of life down to its raw essentials. Protagonists warm up to an experience, intensify it, and toss out what is not pertinent to their enlivened perception. The process is one of selection, not dissimilar to that of the artist, who paints not the landscape, but a selection from the landscape; not the nude, but a version and selection of the nude. In psychodrama, the dramatic protocol ensures that events and reactions begin and end within the time allotted to them — the edges are clipped off neatly, unlike in life. Periods of years are passed over in an instant, while a significant moment might be isolated and take two hours to re-enact. Time is reduced or intensified, collapsed or expanded. This removal of complexities and shadings that normally beset a life produces a liberating effect, as the protagonists' perceptions become uncluttered and lucid. Intuitions and emotions normally experienced as fragmentary and dissociated become psychologically and dramatically linked, and the significant moments of life are categorically illuminated.

In strategic psychodrama, as in conventional psychodrama, reality is reduced to proportions in which protagonists are able to express the essential experience of their existence. Within the therapeutic frame, their lives at last gain unity and completeness, an intelligibility that replaces incoherence, and a validity that replaces cynicism and despair. Strategic psychodramas put to work the immediacy and vibrancy of the psychodramatic method, but enlarge its systems orientation. The dysfunctional behaviour of any one member of the social atom is regarded as a 'spy' about the family's difficulty in evolving. A problem is identified, the attempted solutions in the social atom are enacted, and the protagonist works towards new solutions by means of new information.

To be sure, the psychodramatic tradition already does possess a systems orientation, but it is embryonic and underused. Psychodramatic theory and practice, which has done so much to enrich other therapies, may now need to assimilate certain sorts of theory for itself to survive even minimally as a systems therapy. In this book, a new synthesis is attempted in which clinical 'leverage' is given to psychodrama and group work. In a psychodrama itself, this leverage applies mostly at the level of the interview-in-role and in the surplus-reality section of the psychodrama. In group work, the subject of the companion volume to this, *Forbidden agendas*, considerable attention is given to the recursiveness of interaction between leader and group, and to analysis of alliances and coalitions around a problem as being a good solvent for those problems. Prior to a psychodrama, the director focuses on the status of the problem as a problem, the minimal goals for problem resolution, and so on, as outlined in Chapter 5. Some time after a psychodrama, differences in the protagonist's functioning are highlighted, and 'The improvement routine' (Brennan and Williams, 1988) may be gone through. The aim of strategic psychodrama, like the aim of psychodrama itself, remains that of spontaneity, but the spontaneity involved is more systems-sound and systems-responsive. The 'complaint' in the group is treated as a message about relationships.

Since the theory and practice of family therapy spans many philosophies and many schools, there is no one process called family therapy, as we have already noted. The major influences that have been used to evolve a strategic form of psychodrama may now be apparent by the author citations appearing throughout the book: Gregory Bateson; the staff of the Mental Research Institute (MRI) such as Watzlawick, Fisch, etc.; an Australian family therapist called Michael White (1986a,b) who is himself highly influenced by Bateson; and the Milan group of family therapists — Selvini Palazzoli, Boscolo, Cecchin, and Prata. Bateson's and White's thinking will be particularly noticeable in the present chapter.

As dramatic and artistic experiences, well-conducted psychodramas are valuable for themselves; they do not need any 'extra'. Protagonists remember and cherish them as having been some of the richest moments in their lives — times when they have been truly filled with spirit, and in contact with the greatness of their own and others' humanity; times when the connectedness of all people and all reality becomes apparent; times of intense beauty and nobility even amid intense suffering; times when the perspective of the true heart is validated. I have earlier described the merits of this process and called it 'psychodrama as revelation'.

These sorts of epiphanic experiences are rightly to be venerated, and belong among the best that life can offer us. The world of aesthetics and the rule of the liberated spirit belong in the highest areas of our being. Contact with that world can be 'therapeutic' in the broad sense, but that world is not in itself therapy, and nor, perhaps, should it be reduced to function, 'for' the sake of something else. It is absolute, categorical, and exists in its own right, rather than as an instrument to make us feel better, or to cure us. As a clinical modality involving this sort of world, however, psychodrama can act for good or ill. Reiterative psychodramas chasing cure in places where cure does not belong can become part of the problem rather than part of the solution, as we shall elaborate in the following chapter.

Strategic psychodramas are problem-focused: they recover spontaneity within the system by helping to redefine the system according to all its relevant connections, its 'invisible loyalties'. Like the therapy of the strategic/systemic schools, such a method attempts to prevent a repetition of dysfunctional sequences in which a person or family is involved, and to open out their system to more complexity and alternatives. It uses psychodrama's ability to collapse time, evoke space, and produce an intense reduction of complexity so that a person's life data is suitable for the therapeutic frame. Psychodrama's capacity to direct emotional experience to its essence is combined with systemic thinking in order to open out new domains; the emotional experience becomes enacted in all its relevant connections with other people. It employs the systemic-role analysis that was introduced in Chapter 4, to focus on the interpersonal context of roles, and the recursiveness of people's interaction with one another.

Cl: *I have anorexia nervosa.*
Th: *What does it mean for you?*
Cl: *(No answer)*
Th: *What does it mean for your mother? What sort of problem is it for your sister?*

The therapist finds that the client thinks mother is unhappy because of her, father is unhappy because of her, and her sister purports to be unhappy because of her. This kind of power, while in one way pleasing, always has paradoxical consequences: one is powerful, but one does not get what one wants.

The client is then asked whether mother may be unhappy because of any other problem; whether she thinks she will ever look as good as her sister; whether, if she were not anorexic, her parents would enjoy their own relationship more or less, and whether they would like her more or less than her sister; whether her sister would 'fall apart' if she gained weight. In these questions, the therapist is not only potentially getting information, but also giving information by means of indirect suggestions concerning looking good, enjoying relationships, looking after others, disastrous consequences for someone else if she became normal size, and so on.

Moreno started with the idea that the spontaneous/creative matrix could be made the central focus of people's worlds, not only as an underlying source, but on the very surface of their actual living. Strategic psychodrama suggests a further approach to spontaneity — one based on cybernetics. Spontaneity is the capacity to take up adequate new roles within a system; it is made possible when the person or whole system has access to certain sorts of information, certain definitions of itself that become 'news of difference'. Sometimes a 'standard' psychodrama will be adequate to provide this new information, as we have seen in Chapters 1 and 2. At others, the therapist needs strategically to create more unusual contexts for adventure and discovery so that the new definition can be arrived at.

Since psychodrama with one protagonist is essentially systemic therapy with an individual, directors work with individuals to help them make use of their own energy and entity in interacting with others. The question becomes one of finding ways to release the energy so that, if necessary, individuals can utilize themselves as potential therapists within the family system, or within their immediate social atom. A social atom, you may recall, comprises the people who are essential to the protagonist in the here-and-now. Family members would usually, but not always, be included, but so could workmates, friends, and even organizations. To be change agents within their own system, protagonists may need a new form of thinking and being; to 'see the difference' that has been created in the psychodrama.

In the previous example of Anna, the anorexic, the therapist believes that the hidden rules in Anna's social system form a network of pre-suppositions that prevent or restrain her from seeing reality in any way other than that in which she currently does see it. These restraints, largely acting out of conscious awareness, help form Anna's consciousness and tend to dictate her behaviour in terms of making it more likely that she will do some things and less likely she will do others because of the way she 'sees' reality. A systems therapist sets about unravelling the cultural and social rules with which clients are complying or defying, and the restraints that prevent them from acting in other ways, or appreciating different alternatives. These social 'rules' are comprised of sets of meaning that are for the most part hidden. In removing some of the restraints, the way is cleared for spontaneity and the discovery of new solutions.

The therapist's questions to Anna have mostly concerned difference, especially difference within relationships. In very pathological families, news of difference is dangerous. The nonresponse to difference may take the form of character and of action: if one sister is intelligent and the other very mediocre, the mediocre will become bright and the bright less clever so that there will be no difference. They all become stuck on doing something for each other: the anorexic in a family is often an excellent cook, feeding the other family members while starving herself. Anna *is* closer to mother than the other sister, but she asks herself whether she is closer because mother really loves her or because she is sick. The therapist reflects such inner questions and makes them overt:

You are very strong, very stubborn, but your mother does not trust you. When she does trust you, maybe you can stop your anorexic behaviour. But even if your mother does trust you, you can still go downhill. Perhaps your stubbornness is stronger than you.

The therapist implicitly conveys a systemic epistemology by the form of the questions: 'You do this *and* what does mother do when you do this?' All of us nearly always function in circular patterns of causality — the form of the question or of the therapy is designed to bring that circularity out. The direction of the therapy is to bring news of difference to the client, not only about relationships in the family, but even between the person and her stubbornness, which is externalized. An artificial distinction is therefore made, and becomes the basis of a double description between the person and her stubbornness. This form of working in the group and in psycho-drama will be illustrated in the drama of 'The relative influence of Peggy's Monster' (p. 129); but first we need to discuss what a 'cause' might be in human interaction.

Causality in living systems

Negative explanation

Therapists attempt to help their clients effect change in their lives. Some therapists believe that if they simply provide the 'necessary and sufficient' conditions, clients will simply change by themselves. Others hope to 'cause' change by adopting particular strategies. The notion of causality in living systems, however, is rather complex. Most of us have a billiard-ball idea of causality: strike the billiard ball accurately, and it will go into the pocket. This is a 'positive explanation'. According to positive explanation, events take their course because they are driven or propelled to do so; one can predict what will happen if one knows enough of the conditions — the force of the cue, the angle on which the ball is hit, and so on. Positive explanations are quite satisfactory for the world of the nonliving, such as billiard balls or piles of bricks.

A different type of explanation is called for, however, in living systems, and particularly in human systems. Try this for an experiment: take a chair, and push it around the room. It goes more or less where you push it, does it not? You can roughly predict where the chair will go by your strength, its weight, the surface of the floor, and so on. You are a cause, it is an effect. Now try pushing three other persons around the room, one after another. Person no. 1 falls on the floor, person no. 2 goes along with you, and becomes a chu-chu train. Then she becomes the engine and you the carriage. You circle the room, making noises. Person no. 3 does not like to be pushed. He pushes back, harder than you pushed him. The three act very differently to each other, and this difference has not been dependent solely on whether they are fat or thin, or on whether there is a carpet or polished boards under your feet.

Let us consider the person who falls on the floor: it is a man. You bend over him and ask if he is alright. A dialogue begins. You feel guilty for having pushed him over, and tell him this. He becomes accusatory and a little triumphant. You become even more guilty, and so on. Did you 'cause' him to fall on the floor? No, or at least not in the way that you 'caused' the chair to move. If you had caused the fall, why didn't the other two people fall? Yet it was the same strength of push you gave to each. After he fell over, did person no. 1 'cause' you to bend over and express guilt? Again, not quite, since another person may not have bent over at all, but may have gone about their business, or trodden on the man once he was down, or thrown confetti over him, or fallen down too, or whatever.

So if billiard-ball causality does not apply in human events, how do we then explain that anything happens at all? We cannot have a 'positive explanation' (I push/chair moves) and so are forced to a 'negative explanation'. When I push, the other person selects from a range of possible behaviours, and enacts one — he falls on the floor. The other two people selected and enacted different roles — one went with the pushing, and became a little train, while the other pushed back. We might say that the person who fell on the floor acted almost as if he were restrained from selecting other behaviours. The restraint is not absolute — he could have done differently; it is a matter of probability or tendency. Now here is where the notion is a useful one for therapy (not that falling on the floor is particularly dysfunctional behaviour that needs to be changed, but we will stick to the example for the moment). If ways can be found of lifting the restraints, opportunities for spontaneity can be created. If the man were not restrained from seeing that other types of response were possible and legitimate, if he were not blinkered by these restraints, he would be able to select other sets of responses that may be thought to be more enhancing of his being.

Let us go back over this for a moment, since although the example is simple, the ideas elude many people and do not quite fit our normal styles of thinking. A person is like he or she is, and a social atom is like it is, and events have taken the course that they have taken, not so much because they have been 'made' to by a cause, but because they have been 'restrained' from taking alternative courses (Bateson, 1972, pp. 399–400). Becoming aware that behaviour is as it is by the analysis of restraint, or negative explanation, provides a different kind of thinking on the problem to direct analysis of cause. Restraints establish limitations on the amount and type of information a person or system can manage — thus everyone has a threshold of perception of news of difference dictated by restraints that are largely out of consciousness. Restraints render people (us) unready to respond to certain differences or distinctions. People are restrained from the trial-and-error searching that is necessary for the discovery of new ideas and the triggering of new responses (White, 1986a, p. 171). Relatively speaking, they cannot think or act in any other way. They cannot even see that there are any other ways. Old ideas endure; new information becomes blurred; spontaneity is lost.

News of difference

We need another concept — that of information. Billiard-ball causality in living systems is not appropriate not only because of the cycle of an effect becoming a cause becoming an effect becoming a cause, etc. (I push/he falls/I become guilty/he becomes triumphant/I become more guilty/he becomes depressed/I become triumphant, I push/he ...) and not only because of negative rather than positive explanation, but because events among living beings, including animals and even plants, are determined more by information than by gross physical forces. The pusher and the faller are both reacting to information rather than to simple physics. They have information about the pushing, but also information (from their own personal-construct system) about what they 'should do' if someone pushes. That is, they make sense of the event as best they can. The way they make sense of data and turn it into 'information' is by making distinctions.

We only know 'hot' by distinction from 'cold' or 'cool', or even 'warm'. We know 'red' because it is different from blue or yellow or brown. We know 'kind' by distinction from cruel or indifferent. Even physically, our body acts on information, for example, by sweating when we are hot, and by producing scabs when we bleed. If our body acts on wrong information, or makes the wrong distinctions, for example by producing scab cells when we are not injured, we are in deep trouble. Systems, including the system of our own bodies, work by information.

Clearly there are millions upon millions of distinctions that we make daily. They are the basis for all action, for the smallest gesture, the tiniest step. Only a few are transformed into enduring ideas, and only a few are the subject of therapy. A person's map of reality or network of presuppositions provides a context for the restraints that will be operating when there is a need for new information and new distinctions. Information about events in the world (for example, I push/the man falls down) is transformed into descriptions in the form of words, figures, or pictures. The information becomes a 'story' via the explanation I give it, and this explanation depends on my own network of presuppositions. That is 'why' I bend over the man who has fallen, rather than throw confetti on him, or fall over with him. I have made up my own story about what that event means; his falling has acted as information to me. How the 'news' comes (of the falling) is dependent on how it fits in with my network of presuppositions.

Most of my network of presuppositions are shaped by others, particularly by my family of origin. This is where I gain my basic beliefs about the world — for example, that I should lean over when someone falls to the floor. For change to occur, these old ideas need to be replaced by new ideas. But the old ideas are very enduring, and so the new ideas must be equally enduring. A helpful new network must be such that it endures longer than the alternatives. People in trouble come to therapy having already attempted some solutions to their difficulties; but these solutions, and even previous therapy, may have served to perpetuate or even re-inforce the very problems for which a solution was sought. Even though the solutions may not have been helpful, they are resorted to time and again. The individual or family keep resorting to solutions as if they were restrained from discovering alternative solutions. If one examines the solution, information usually becomes available about the restraints. The task of therapy is to establish conditions where new distinctions can be drawn, and new ideas can survive longer than the old ideas (White, 1986a). Strategic psychodrama not only allows the system to define itself (by the very process of setting out the action in a drama) but takes steps to ensure the survival of new ideas.

Strategic psychodrama's path, ideally, is to effect transformation in the whole system so that the creative energy that has been 'locked up' by over-restrictive networks of presuppositions is released. Individuals are then liberated from some of the particular restraints of these networks; they become open to new information, and have more access to their own energy and the spontaneity that will enhance their way of being. The restraints-based interview focuses on what blocks the protagonist at a given moment or on a given problem from a course of adventure and discovery that is required for new solutions (spontaneity). For a procedure to be called therapy it may not be enough that a domain of adventure and discovery is merely provided. A therapy establishes a context that con-tributes to the client's skill to respond to new information, to make discoveries that endure as long as they are enhancing. More than the evo-cation of spontaneity is at stake, therefore. Its endurance is also crucial. At a literal and analogic level, protagonists are the most available and com-petent part of the system from which they come. By putting the weight of a psychodrama behind the protagonist, directors are responsible for co-creat-ing new roles in the system that are no longer so restrained by dys-functional presuppositions.

Redefinition

Any psychodrama, or indeed any events of one's life, are capable of creat-ing a context for adventure and discovery wherein new ideas may emerge. But there is little in the protocol of the psychodrama method that ensures the endurance of these new ideas. Sometimes it seems that directors hope to establish enough of a 'big bang' to keep the stars endlessly expanding outwards ... the more powerful the blast-off, the further into orbit the client may go. When this procedure is not successful, directors may join protagonists in a solution of more psychodrama or more therapy. The 'therapy of the moment' can be very valuable, but such therapy runs the

127

risk of becoming part of a person's dysfunctional system if the only 'moments' that a person can have are in therapy itself.

We have noted that living systems react within themselves (within their own reality) to what they perceive in order to maintain their own autonomous organization: they will 'take in' from the outside only if it seems that this action does not threaten their identify or autonomy (their 'reality'). A 'disturbance' from another system such as a therapist, however, might actually enhance the autonomy or identity of the system. Such a disturbance is regarded as enhancing if it recognizes the system as it is — if the disturbance is not perceived as 'foreign'. These sorts of disturbances are welcomed with open arms, as it were, and can be incorporated into a new reality, a new definition.

A direct proposal for 'change' that comes from a source external to the system may be perceived by the system as a threat to its autonomy. But a change that takes place after the system has simply been allowed to re-define itself makes internal sense to the changed person or system. Possibly the most effective way of influencing a system is actually to give it scope to enhance its own autonomy by allowing it first to see what that autonomy is. Here lies the advantage of psychodrama: in a psychodrama, protagonists are invited to share their *Eigenwelt*, or private inner world, no matter how bizzare or idiosyncratic. By this process, their sense of the system's autonomy is validated; they are then open to new distinctions and new information.

Behaviour of organisms, according to Maturana and Varela (1980), is not an accommodation to environment, but a manifestation of internal structure. Maturana's observations provide a useful chance to re-think our notions of change and causality. There may, after all, be little point in people trying directly to change other people; at best, one might be able to trigger an internal disturbance, a change in the internal logic of the system. If a system can be helped to reorganize itself as it is, and according to all its connections, it may then be able to change its internal structure. In therapy one can provide a 'domain' that is wider than the domain within which the system could roam previously. Successful therapy, therefore, offers a context that recognizes a system's unique way of being itself: the system is the only possible provider of the resources needed to deal with disturbances that do not enhance its wellbeing.

A psychodrama that helps define and then redefine the system can be a way of extending the domain, and of providing a more vivid definition of the individual or system for itself, as it exists now. The system receives an assurance, as it were, that it will not be bothered from the 'outside' when directors simply help the protagonist set their system out. But there is an extra element: the director assists the protagonist to set out the system according to all its relevant connections. Only then is the system properly defined. This is where skilful questioning from the director comes into play: the protagonist may not know what these relevant connections are — what 'invisible loyalties' are moving him or her, what networks and coalitions are working within the social atom to shape what is regarded as information and what is not so regarded. Perhaps Maturana is right: perhaps it is actually impossible to change anyone.

People change in relation to their interaction with the therapist only if it makes sense to do so in their own terms (Kelly, 1955). A therapist who confirms this essential 'fact' can actually expand clients' sense of themselves; a therapist who does not is likely to complain to colleagues and even hint to clients about the unusual amount of resistance they are encountering. By helping the protagonist set out their system according to its relevant connections, directors are not making an intervention — the interview is in itself an intervention (Tomm, 1987). They do not suggest anything at this stage, but rather say, 'What more? Who else is relevant? What is X's relationship with Y? What does Z think?'

With luck, the produced definition may allow the system first to recognize, and then perhaps to 'argue' with its own internal logic. Family therapists are familiar with this process: for example, if a daughter's behaviour in running away from home is described as a way of being 'loving' to her parents, and she is urged to consider the 'risks' in changing that behaviour, a second definition has effectively been given to the protagonist. The daughter may then say to herself, 'I'm not going to sacrifice my education and later life just to give my folks something to worry about now.' Her 'logic' has changed, and so does the 'internal truth' of the family members, who may also need to argue with their own former logic.

Strategic therapists can go one step further from simply defining a protagonist's system according to all its connections: they can add a new definition once the protagonist has made up his or hers. That is, the protagonist supplies one description, and the therapist another. The two are then coded side by side so that a difference is evident. By validating the two types of logic within the system, the system is allowed to argue with itself, rather than with the director. A drama becomes an orthogonal intervention, an internal logic changer, a massive bit of communication with the system that the system 'allows in'. It can become a confirmation, *par excellence*, of the system's autonomy, and at the same time extend the system's information about its internal relationships. It adds to the system's reality by recognizing that all change is a change in internal structure, and that only the system itself can accomplish such a change.

The relative influence of Peggy's monster

Some people are dominated by their presuppositions of being 'damaged' to the extent that they have little opportunity to live satisfactorily in the everyday world. Their fear, rage, or hurt overwhelms them so that their inner processing of these states disastrously interferes with their perception of daily events. They may be so 'shaky' and preoccupied that they cannot go to work, or if there, cannot function adequately. When with friends, the slightest remark may evoke an emotional response that seems out of all proportion to the content of the remark. When alone, they are excessively given to introspection and gloom.

Peggy was a person in such a state, almost permanently. A member of a training group that met weekly, she had also been attending another psychodrama group, for a couple of years. That is, she had had plenty of 'therapy'. Peggy is 30 years old, a slim and attractive woman with large eyes that frequently filled with tears. She was competent as an auxiliary and as a trainee psychodrama director, as was well liked by other group members. Indeed, some of the men in the group idealized her as the 'wounded woman', and compared their own apparently stoical barriers to emotional experience with her volatility and lability. It could almost be said that they had a stake in her remaining flooded and oversensitive. The women in the group were not so envious, perhaps being less prone than the men idealistically to confuse Peggy's out-of-control, flooded experience with emotional flexibility.

The case reported here represents a two-session intervention, separated by several weeks. It illustrates the potency of the interview-in-role as an intervention in itself when relevant distinctions are made that allow the protagonist news of difference. An essential feature was to externalize and personify one of Peggy's major and overdeveloped roles. This role is artificially separated from her, and a new role is developed 'in' her to ward off the threatening 'outsider'.

Peggy, who had been in Di's group for about three weeks, reported that after the groups she was scarcely able to function: 'I come here to get support, and I get it. But it only seems to make things worse.'

Di: *It seems as if you're presenting us with something of a paradox.*
P: *How come?*
Di: *Well, you attend the group and you become very warmed up. Then you get support for being so warmed up. That's a nice feeling and it makes you want to come back, but the process begins all over again. . . . How long are you upset after a group?*
P: *Oh ages — it takes days to calm down. I work as a consultant you know. I have to be on the ball.*
Di: *Are you still upset by Friday? (The group meets on Monday evenings)*
P: *No, I'm generally over it by Friday.*

Peggy and Di begin to work down from Peggy's global notion of being upset 'pretty well all the time' to an understanding (a revelation to Peggy) that she is most upset on a Tuesday. In fact, Tuesday is the only day her work as a consultant is really affected by her overwhelming negative feelings. She has already drawn a distinction that has enabled her to notice differences between a general state of 'being overwhelmed', and being overwhelmed on a particular day. Di encourages Peggy to draw distinctions between her state at one point in time, and her state at another point. It might have been equally effective to have drawn distinctions between types of 'being overwhelmed', and then to ask which type was the worst, next worst, etc. As it was, the over-developed role of 'flooded incompetent' was now seen as chiefly operating at certain times, rather than all the time.

Di next enquires whether, given the extent of her upset, she may not need more than one day to give herself up to it. She makes these enquiries not to be clever or 'paradoxical', but to help Peggy to make further distinctions between the present state of affairs and a future state of affairs if 'being overwhelmed' were to be extended more fully into a problem life style. Peggy replies that one day is quite enough. Di then suggests that since one day is enough, and more than one day is 'too much', whether she could possibly fit her upset into half a day — perhaps Tuesday morning — leaving the rest of the day 'free for work and pleasure'. Peggy replies that to do that would be to cut herself off from her feelings, and that her 'demon' would come back with renewed force.

Di has introduced the notion that there might be time in Peggy's life 'free for pleasure'. Peggy has countered with the notion of a 'demon' — one of her own roles that she can picture as being outside herself. She has given Di an opening to establish relative influence between herself and the demon, herself and her 'flooded' self that seems to take her over. Relative influence (White, 1986a) requires the establishment of two differently coded descriptions. In one of those descriptions, events are coded according to the protagonist's network of pre-existing presuppositions, and in the other, events are coded according to the premises contributed by the therapist.

We need at this stage to digress from Peggy and her monster to consider another important process — that of double description. Double description is a cybernetic concept that lends itself admirably to psychodrama and to action methods. First let us consider the hypothetical problem of the zealous father, Fred, who punishes his son, Sam. A single description of what is going on in the family from the viewpoint of the son might be: 'He punishes, I rebel.' And from the father, a therapist might glean the description of the situation as: 'He rebels, I punish.' If an observer combines the views of both parties, a sense of the father–son system will begin to emerge.

Keeney (1983) points out that there are several ways in which such a holistic description can be conceptualized. First, the construct generated by each person can be prescribed in a sequential fashion, with the whole series seen as a representative of the dyadic system. For example, when the two descriptions 'He punishes, I rebel' and 'He rebels, I punish' are collectively viewed, they provide a first landing stage for understanding the interactive system.

When these different constructs (or 'punctuations' in cybernetic terms) are placed side by side in a sequential fashion, the pattern that connects them may start to be discernible: the simultaneous combination of their constructs yields a glimpse of their whole relationship. This glimpse of the whole relationship — the role of the son and the role of the father combined at the same time — is called by Bateson (1979) 'double description'.

> Relationship is always a product of double description. He wanted two
> parties to any interaction to be regarded as two eyes, each giving a
> monocular view of what goes on and, together, giving a binocular view
> in depth. This double view *is* the relationship.
>
> (Bateson, 1979, p. 133)

In the case of 'He punishes, I rebel — He rebels, I punish', the double description would be that of what Bateson called a 'complementary relationship' — the actions of father and son are different, but mutually fit each other. Sam and his father are locked into a vicious cycle, a 'deviation-amplifying process' (Hoffman, 1981). The more the tension grows, the more each party resorts to his solution — more discipline or more rebellion.

Roles cannot fully be understood except in the context of the other. A role is 'an interpersonal experience and needs usually two or more individuals to be actualized' (Moreno, 1964, p. 184). Roles give a sense of the lives all around us — the lives that had passed before we were born, the lives that are still continuing; and the lives whose coming we would intersect. The concept of role is already systemic. It opens out the interpersonal construction of the self to the ebb and flow of the other, so that the definition of self must always be mutually constructed.

To understand the action of a role, a double description is almost always required. A follower requires a leader — a leader requires a follower, otherwise the terms leader and follower have little or no meaning. 'Leadership' is an extracted half of the double description 'leader–follower relationship'. Most descriptions of so-called personality characteristics actually consist of extracted halves of larger relationship patterns. It is possible to work directly with Fred or directly with Sam, but even in such an instance it is preferable to work on the Fred/Sam double description. It is possible to work on leaders, or on followers in an industrial consultancy, say, but it is preferable to work on leader and follower as two halves of a description.

In the case of Peggy and her monster, Di is establishing a double description between Peggy and one of her roles. In the example of Sam and Fred, above, the double description is between two or more people. Double descriptions can be established between a person at one time or another, between two or more persons, between a person in one state and another, and so on. Di has first mapped out, by drawing distinctions, the extent of the problem's influence on the protagonist, at least in terms of how long the problem is influential. She now invites Peggy to supply any information that may assist her to reach an understanding of Peggy's experience of the problem. She stresses that she needs information about the extent to which the protagonist is being 'influenced' by the problem that is now construed as 'outside' her. She has created a dialectic between Peggy and the problem. In her attempt to map out the extent of influence of the problem, she listens especially to Peggy's ideas of being out of control, of not being competent.

She also gains information on the protagonist's own 'influence' in the life of the problem, ascertaining to what extent she has been able to stand up to the problem's oppression. That is, the protagonist is invited also to select out ideas of competence and ability, as well as non-competence and difficulty. Protagonists may find it extremely hard to find areas of competence and ability with respect to the problem; with help, however, usually they can access one or two areas. This procedure, of course, is in no way intended to 'jolly along' the protagonist by pointing out that things aren't so bad after all. Rather it is to establish understandings of difference, and the relative influence of the problem.

After protagonists have nominated such a large area when their lives have been ruled by the problem, the director may then be able genuinely to express surprise that, under the circumstances, the protagonist has been able to maintain some influence in her life and ward off a total surrender to the problem (White, 1986a). This is why Di asked Peggy whether she might not have needed more than one day for her collapse. The influence of the monster (now externalized) has been fixed as lasting one day, not more and not less. As they interact, Peggy is developing a different set of roles towards Di during this interview; she seems brighter, more forceful and alert as she discusses her problem. She has moved from the role of tearful incompetent and warmed up to her alert, problem-solver role.

She has also developed a markedly different orientation towards her problem, which has changed from the paradoxical one of being completely out of control and therefore needing the group to support her, and yet becoming completely out of control because of her attendance at the group. That is, therapy had become part of the problem, rather than part of the solution. The problem's 'influence' is now seen as extensive, but by no means overarching. What has taken place is not simply a logical correction of vague or loose talk, but a new way of seeing and being. If the problem is construed as huge, permanent, and out of control, then it actually becomes so. (That, generally speaking, is why a problem is a problem in psychology.)

Di's next approach was to ask Peggy whether she thought that if the monster was 'kept out' for too long it would build up its strength and become unmanageable. Peggy thought that it would. Di has tapped into a repression hypothesis held by Peggy and by many people who attend groups or are involved in individual therapy. This implicit hypothesis maintains that most psychological difficulties are caused by repression and that the answer to these difficulties is expression. The worse one feels, therefore, the more the need to express hidden pain, hurt, or anger.

Peggy fears that if she does not give herself over to being overwhelmed and feeling all the pain, confusion, and despair she must feel, at least on a Tuesday, that the monster will grow in size because it has been locked away. Who knows what psychological damage might result if she is not completely open to all her negative impulses and sentiments: she may end up being defensive, and in real trouble.

D: *It's as if it goes off and pumps iron. And if you leave it too long in the gym, it becomes enormously strong.*

P: *Yes, just like that.*

D: *Stand up. Reverse roles and be the monster. (She does) Who are you?*

M: *I'm her fear.*

D: *How long have you been around?*

M: *Oh ages.*

D: *Is it true that she should encounter you all the time, so that at least you're kept busy and can't get any bigger?*

M: *That's just it. Only if she stays completely open to me has she got any chance. If she ignores me, I'll just grow.*

D: *Thank you, monster. Reverse roles (to Peggy).*

D: *Have you ever thought that you could pump iron?*

P: *What?*

D: *Well, while it's off exercising, are there any exercises that you can do? Sort of build up your own strength.*

P: *Well, I've never really thought of that.*

D: *Think about it now for a minute. What are your weak points, here in this group?*

Di and Peggy discuss Peggy's 'weak points' — the situations in which she most becomes upset and most feels out of control. They mostly concern her losing boundaries, and becoming 'flooded' with the material that anyone in the group is presenting. She loses capacity to differentiate and to think, and then goes into an 'I'm worthless spiral', feels isolated, begins to cry, receives comfort, and the whole cycle begins again. Peggy and Di then discuss how she can recognize these occasions as they emerge, and what sort of 'exercises' she can do. Peggy says that she can 'mentally pump iron' when anything happens in the group that triggers her old cycle. Di encourages her in this, and they go through a routine of mental push-ups and barbells. Di does not challenge Peggy's belief that the monster will only get bigger if she ignores it. Rather, she enters the metaphor but creates a different set of descriptions around her own behaviour. The 'drama', which in fact, had been rather like an extended interview-in-role, finishes for the time being.

In the following three months, Peggy only cries in the group twice, in completely appropriate circumstances, and acts as a skilled auxiliary and able group member. She challenges others, supports them, and speaks her mind to Di on occasion. She ridicules the men in the group who lament the loss of her wounded-woman role, so voyeuristically fascinating for them, so uncomfortable for her. She also reports that she is not missing any days at work now 'not even Tuesday', and is surprised by the pleasure she now takes in little things.

A few weeks later Peggy enacted a lighthearted drama, a vignette showing herself at her training gym. The instructor at the gym, Leola, was very beautiful and wore 'beautiful leotards'. In the interview-in-role Leola said that she had to 'keep an eye on her ladies so they don't strain themselves — keep to their programmes'. When asked her opinion of Peggy, she said 'She has a few problems — she's not very strong. I'll have to make sure she continues — she needs encouragement.'

The vignette was quite humorous, with Peggy baulking at the more for-midable machines, and role-reversing as various 'macho men' and 'macho women'. In one interaction with Leola she says; 'I think I'll skip having a body like yours. I'll stick with these lower weights for a while.' When Leola inquires about Peggy's progress, she replies; 'I ache a lot — does that count?' Leola tells her that to 'ache' is not necessarily a valid criterion for success or progress.

Leola and Peggy continue to talk about her fitness programme in a fashion that is, to the onlooker, fairly clearly analogical with Peggy's progress and her difficulties in the last few weeks. Peggy has chosen an unlikely but in actual fact satisfactory wisdom figure — a gym instructress — with whom to have dialogue.

Chapter eight

The problem–solution cycle

Mock on, mock on, Voltaire, Rousseau,
Mock on, mock on, 'tis all in vain!
You throw the sand against the wind,
And the wind throws it back again

William Blake

When therapists evoke a social atom in psychodrama or in therapy, they are not outside that system; they inevitably form part of a new system with the protagonist. If this new system is managed successfully, it becomes a 'therapeutic' system in which new possibilities can be generated, and different roles can become available. But if directors over-identify with any part of the family system, protagonists may use the psychodrama to reinforce, once again, their original dysfunctional structure, despite the added psychodramatic expressionism and fireworks. It looks good, it seems therapeutic, but the system takes up once more its familiar rigidity, and little important learning (change) has eventuated. In fact, the system might be even more rigid, since now a therapist is validating it.

It is easy for directors to prop up a person's notion of being the victim of an evil social atom, oblivious to his or her own roles in perpetuating the interaction. The drama becomes a cops and robbers chase, or worse, a family soap. The group and protagonist can combine in a thorough blaming session, while the director acts as a stabilizing agent for the blaming dynamic, and reinforces the system's homeostasis. Since the original role of the protagonist in the system does not change, his or her horizons actually become narrowed by therapy rather than expanded. The new definitions are not very different from the old, and the original network of presuppositions is stengthened. Sometimes therapy gets stuck in its own philosophy and its own solutions, and emerges with a pseudo-solution — more! The therapy becomes hectoring and overbearing, raucous and repetitive. Strategic psychodramas themselves are not exempt from this trap, which is one of epistemology. Strategic therapists attempt to build-in the safeguard, however, of being ready to consider therapy itself as part of the problem–solution cycle.

Andolfi and Angelo (1982) draw an analogy between Pirandello's play *Six characters in search of an author* and the wishes of people coming to therapy. Each character, they remark, appears to be imprisoned by his role, but paradoxically wants the director to help him play it better. Similarly, protagonists in family dramas seem to want the director to help them recite their parts better, but without altering the preconceived script. It is only 'natural' for the protagonist psychodramatically to act out the family script once more, and to get the other family members to do so; there may also be pressure towards having the director and the group play archaic roles within that script. If directors passively accept the functions that the protagonist assigns to them (such as fifth columnist, mother, rescuer, therapist, shining knight) the play will not be very different from the one already played many times in the family. Or if, unlike Priscilla (see p. 113), the protagonist is 'experienced' as a therapeutic client, at least the play will not be very different from the solutions previously adopted in other psychodramas. Watzlawick *et al.* (1974) define stuckness as 'those moments in a session where the counsellor makes a predictable response to a repeatedly expressed situation, thus more of the same problem being recovered'.

When a car is stuck on a muddy hill, the driver might keep trying the same solution — to use more power. But the more the accelerator is pressed, the more the wheels spin. The more the wheels spin, the deeper the hole that is created under them. The deeper the hole, the less chance of getting out. In a stuck system, such as a family or a group, repetitive attempted solutions can prevent more successful sequences from occurring. No matter how hard they 'press the accelerator', the members cannot seem to deal differently with each other, and thereby confirm their belief that they have failed, probably through not pressing the accelerator hard enough. They press it more, but the solution is beginning to cause further problems, as the wheels spin deeper into the mud.

An altogether new solution is called for — a 'sideways thinking'. This sort of thinking requires the whole context of the problem to be viewed: the driver, the car, the hill, the mud, and the solutions that have already been tried. Likewise, in a systematic view, people's difficulties are best seen in a context of gender, family, job, or even culture itself, together with the solutions — including therapeutic solutions — they have already tried. I have suggested in earlier chapters that a double description of a problem already begins to suggest pathways to spontaneity. A double description of the car on the hill and its frantic driver pressing the accelerator as a system bound up with its dysfunctional solutions can begin a process leading to spontaneity.

Systematic descriptions and double descriptions do not come naturally to any of us. Linear thinking is more instinctive and easier than circular thinking; linear 'solutions' spring more readily to mind than cybernetic or ecological stances. When we think in a linear fashion, we tend to think in opposites; so, if people are angry, we might tell them to calm down; if depressed, to cheer up. Even therapists tend to take the linear path: they somehow regard the solution as the opposite of the problem. A strongly held therapeutic belief, for example, is that most difficulties are due to repression, and that therefore the solution is to encourage people to open up. But the therapeutic solution (to open up) may actually exacerbate the original problem, rather than solve it. In fact, the drive to open up may become the problem itself.

Vigorous activity, shouting, fighting, tears, and embracing are part and parcel of psychodrama. They help to raise the protagonist's spontaneity, and suggest that new thinking may be on its way. They can also be repeats, not only of the dynamic in the original social atom, but even of other psychodramas that this protagonist has enacted. Within any form of therapy, participants quickly learn the language of the therapy and begin to speak it. A psychodynamic client will become psychodynamically conscious; a gestalt client begins to talk the language of awareness; and a psychodramatic client becomes spontaneous as a learnt function. In psychodramatic circles there is a real possibility of a false spontaneity, a spontaneity that is not true to the moment, but is only an acting-out and impulsive expression shaped by the psychodramatic culture itself. The repetitions are now dressed in the garb of novelty.

Moreno's notion of spontaneity is of something operating in the present, 'now and here; it propels an individual towards an adequate response to a new situation or a new response to an old situation' (Moreno, 1953, p. 42). Sometimes surplus-reality resolutions of family psychodramas are only apparently spontaneous; in reality they may repetitively act out family scripts, and are still dictated by the family structure. 'Adequate' is the operative word in Moreno's definition. The mere release of pent-up emotion, though quite helpful at times, is not necessarily an adequate solution to a family-of-origin problem — or a current problem. When repeated over and over, the drama can become megalomanic, rather than a way out of megalomania.

What we accept as spontaneous, because it is emotional, may not be spontaneous at all, but a replay of the family pathology. In such a case the director can be a stabilizing element in a system in which the protagonist is, for example, the eternal victim. The director has become a linear thinker, applying the techniques of scene-setting, maximization, concretization, etc., to produce vivid 'results', but they are the same results as last time. In repeated psychodramas of this kind, we are not seeing reality differently, but reinforcing our maladaptive constructs. The director must be the destabilizing agent within the system, disturbing the rigidity of the family, enabling a redistribution of the functions and capacities of each individual.

Members of most systems adapt themselves to a view of reality complementary to other members' views: crazy member, sane member, persecutor and victim, heater and cooler, sage and fool, rescuer and helpless person. They may apply rigid specifications about when and where each function will be enacted and whether it shall be done fully or toned down. A neurotic system constantly reorganizes itself so that it will not have to change. Roles, functions, and interactive space become rigid. To counteract the stress involved in developmental change, the system may select an individual member to represent its symptomatic behaviour. This member becomes the identified patient (IP), and around him or her the anxieties of all the other members revolve. The designation of 'patient' may fluctuate from one person to another within the system, as it so often does within a psychodrama, where the parent is now labelled 'crazy' instead of the child. This flipping of labels may be useful in the short term, if the protagonist has long suffered the title of 'crazy one' and has lived up to that title. A short blaming session may not go amiss, and is in many cases quite appropriate — a sign of something 'healthy' happening within protagonists as they contact their life force in a drama. The process becomes problematic, however, when it is part of the protagonist's stuck thinking.

When protagonists play out their dramas on the stage, it is useful to remember that they have been in a continuous drama within their social atom long before the roles of that system are enacted psychodramatically. The script has been replayed over and over again, until the systemic myth about the exact roles of each member is enacted automatically. To live according to the myth is then the only way to live, even if individual members, or all the members, profess utter misery. Attempts to act outside the myth, that is, to differentiate oneself, usually fail, and lead to guilt and self-reproach. Dysfunctional families lose their capacity for true creativity and spontaneity, diverting their creative energies to simple improvisations on a theme. For example, the children might find various ways of helping the parents avoid intimacy with each other by manifesting such distracting problems as asthma, vandalism, school refusal, or anorexia. But whatever the symptom, the main plot unfolds in predictable interrelated sequences leading to a persistently unsatisfactory conclusion.

Like us all, protagonists want to change without change. To change does indeed require spontaneity — a leap into thinking and behaviour with unpredictable consequences. We act as amateur scientists, says Kelly (1955), attempting to predict and control our world, as we must do to survive. This very attempt cuts us off from seeing any other sorts of worlds — we go on the way we do because we are restrained from seeing possibilities as truly possible. Most change-seeking behaviour has thus a paradoxical element to it — a resistance. A protagonist in a psychodrama serves simultaneously as the guardian of the system's stability, and an agent for systematic disruption: the problem is how to move while standing still.

Psychodramas can even become iactogenic when they reinforce rather than loosen the protagonist's network of presuppositions. They may narrow possibility down to one definition: 'I have been hard done by' and one solution: more therapy. Regardless of the validity of psychodrama as a medium, if in the short term it fails to have any influence, in the long term it is likely to become part of the stuckness that is repeatedly expressed through the protagonist's responses to the situation. Directors' own inputs play major parts in the process; their own ways of thinking can also become focused repeatedly and unproductively on the situation, or repeatedly and unproductively on one type of solution — more. A stuck psychodrama in this context does not mean a drama that gets a little bogged down, or one that lacks energy and vitality; it means a drama that is stuck in psychodrama itself — where therapy is part of the problem. The change brought about in stuck psychodramas is often that protagonists use their dysfunctional patterns with more sophistication. The effort of a strategic psychodrama is to break up those patterns.

Projected roles of either persecutory or helpful members of the social atom often do have historical validity, be it said. To hold views of circular causality does not imply that the therapist sees sadistic behaviour as just wonderful, or that all parents, no matter how beastly their portrayal in the drama have nevertheless done a superb job in parenting. Far from it. It is necessary to understand, however, that at an individual level the protagonist is attempting to separate into parts (split) those contradictions that he or she so far finds too painful to experience at a personal level. Members of the original social atom may have been incapable of 'owning' their own conflicts and contradictions concerning change and immobility, dependence and separation. They may have split various welcome or unwelcome roles into one member of the system group, perhaps the protagonist, so that they do not have to bear the contradictions involved. The protagonist may reverse this split in therapy, and can propose a plan for therapy that does not essentially alter existing equilibriums.

All this may sound a little like blaming the protagonist for not changing. On the contrary; the therapist is the person who needs to change, to alter his or her own network of presuppositions that prevent him or her from seeing the problem in a new way. The director needs to keep in mind the premiss of circularity that 'whenever a loop is drawn, there is the potential for everything to change, or restructure itself when information is introduced' (Penn, 1982, p. 271). The loop includes the director, the protagonist, the protagonist's symptom, and the protagonist's social atom. If directors can free themselves from their own stuck thinking, they can then create conditions of double description for the protagonist whereby distinctions can be made that allow a new definition. The therapist's spontaneity is required lest psychodrama, or any type of therapy for that matter, becomes part of the problem-maintaining cycle.

Paul's pain

Paul, the protagonist of this drama, is a vigorous man in his thirties. He was chosen as representing the group central concern (see the section on central concern, p. 35–8) on the theme of his being caught in no-win interactions, and on the underlying theme of valuing the self. Paul declared during the contracting section of the drama that these unsatisfactory inter-actions occurred with his girlfriend, Kerry, but that the details were intimate and that he did not wish to disclose or portray them to the group.

Paul's unwillingness to portray intimate details of his life with Kerry was welcomed by the director, Duke, who took it as a sign of progress for Paul, since one of Paul's difficulties was that he made inadequate distinctions between his public and private domains. That is, his personal and social boundaries were blurred. This affliction plagues many people, particularly men, who are involved in the psychology/personal growth fields. Very often the working hypothesis for 'cure' in such psychologies, including, alas, bad psychodrama, is a simple one based on defences and repression. Thus people set themselves the unenviable task of not being defensive any more, and enter a state of restrained mania. Such an undertaking does not pass unnoticed by their loved ones, nor even by people who may not necessarily have their best interests at heart.

As a result, the poor growth-seeker is sometimes confronted with a downward spiral. More and more, they bare their soul. 'Not good enough', says the other — 'more!' Their dedicated fervour becomes dysfunctional in itself, and leads not to the compelling encounters that they desire, but to pain, despair, and the insight that they cannot really have been trying hard enough. The solution, echoed by others in their social atom, is once again 'more'.

This spiral can also occur when the goal is 'to be more spontaneous'. The growth-seeker is on the hope/despondency treadmill again. Quite often the new roles that need to be learned need to be learned precisely around those very interactions that involve these very goals. That is, the person may need to learn not to have the goal, rather than how to achieve the goal. A useful question to pose to the growth-seeker is 'How is not being spontaneous a problem?' This question introduces a conceptual shock, and ironically enough, can actually lead to spontaneity. The spontaneity involved can be a fresh vision of the whole endeavour to become spontaneous, and the dropping of its pursuit as an ideal. Maybe another ideal would do as well, such as 'to be sensible' or even 'to defend oneself adequately'. Order, care, and deliberation around the problem at the contracting stage of a drama do not exclude unpredictability and useful extravagance later on. But the original meticulousness concerning whether the problem *is* the problem can prevent the drama being a reinforcement of the problem, rather than a discovery of new solutions.

After a brief discussion with the director, Paul recalls a scene in the school yard when he is 12 years old. Another boy, Ernie, is bowling a cricket ball to him. Ernie, a big, tough, strapping lad, the son of a local fisherman, is described as 'a bit of a misfit'; he also happens to be a very formidable

141

athlete. Paul, in role reversal as Ernie, presents as a figure of malevolent vitality, almost an archetype of male power.

He bowls Paul out first ball, and jeers at him. Paul, his hands clenched over an imaginary bat, makes a jerky movement backwards. His hands go into his belly. Duke asks Paul to repeat the movement. He does. The director decides to personify or 'concretize' the hand movements, using a person from the group to represent each hand. Separate auxiliaries are chosen to be the left hand, which flies towards his belly, and the right, that vainly tries to keep it out. As the left hand, Paul moans 'Oh, oh!' After a little more of this, Paul falls to the ground, crying.

These procedures are quite standard to psychodrama, being ordinary examples of the use of concretization and maximization. Small but involuntary movements of the body, especially when there seems to be a dichotomy between them, such as the left side of the body doing something different from the right, are personified (concretized) and expanded (maximized). The motif then becomes one of conflict. In this particular case, the theme of conflict is a repeated one: it is mentioned in the original contract — of Paul being in a no-win dialogue with his girlfriend. It is repeated in Paul's encounter with Ernie — of being 'bowled out' by him. And finally, it is repeated intrapsychically in the conflict between the two sides. Any one of these manifestations is good enough to work with psychodramatically: the intrapsychic manifestation is simply another way to help Paul surprise himself, and eventually to discover-by-being a new role state.

In the contracting section of the drama, Paul had been asked what 'work' he had done on this difficulty before, with what results, and what had most helped him learn. Paul said that he had done 'a few angry numbers' in the past. They had been helpful enough at the time, but that he 'did not want to travel that road again'. Duke had replied that although it was good to do things differently sometimes, anger was a 'tried and true' way for Paul, and that it would be a pity to change 'too soon' a method that had served him so well in the past. Paul's puzzlement at these remarks was most understandable, given that designated 'change agents', such as directors, are expected to manifest endless enthusiasm for change.

In this instance, however, Duke is emphasizing the restraints on change, rather than change itself (Bateson, 1972; White, 1986a, b). These restraints are always present — otherwise the person would spontaneously change and not need any help. But they are seldom legitimated in therapeutic interactions. As a result, only the 'disturbing motive' (Whitaker and Lieberman, 1964; Whitaker, 1985) is expressed, leaving the 'reactive motive' — fear or guilt that is in conflict with the disturbing motive — always lurking at the back of the protagonist's mind. Both the disturbing motive (the desire for something) and the reactive motive (the opposition to that desire) can be 'in' protagonists themselves, and also 'in' the social atom. Other intimates of the person can have stakes in the disturbing or reactive motives, which are then mediated interpersonally — the inner dialectic is reflected outward.

Paul had become habituated to a particular solution (doing 'angry numbers') and attempting to become more and more expressive about his difficulties. He was probably working on a repression hypothesis — one has difficulties because of repressed and unacceptable feelings (see 'Peggy's monster', p. 129, for example). The solution to repression becomes the antidote — expression. At the same time Paul was becoming suspicious of his habitual solutions because he did not seem to be getting anywhere.

To express the reactive motive for the protagonist is not to dabble in paradox. Rather, it is simply to enunciate what is: that there are many restraints on change (otherwise the person would change) and that it makes sense, in some way, to stay the same. Duke, then, stresses how it must seem sensible for Paul to adopt the solutions that he had formerly adopted. But Paul is already suspicious of these solutions, and Duke's taking the no-change position actually strengthens Paul's resolve to change his methods and possibly his constructs. It is easier to push something downhill than to push it up, certainly, and this alone would provide a good reason for Duke saying what he did. But his actual motive was to help Paul define himself as he was, so that he would then be able to move to a new definition if he so wished. In the section that follows, he insists on Paul experiencing fully his own definitions, even though Paul wants to move rapidly to change.

P: *I don't want to get angry and blast the place apart. I've done that before. But I feel like I've got a machete in my hand.*

D: *Go ahead and use it.*

P: *I don't want to — that's not the way any more. But this is awful. I'm in a hole. I hate it.*

D: *Be the right hand. (Paul reverses roles) Say to the left, 'I love this.'*

P: *But I hate it.*

D: *Just try.*

P: *I love this. I love it down here. It's familiar.*

D: *Who is relevant to you right now?*

P: *My mom. (An auxiliary is chosen to play the role of mother)*

D: *Tell your mother why you're not going to change.*

P: *But I want to change.*

D: *Possibly so. But what about just practising telling her some reasons why it's good to be as you are.*

P: *(To mother) It's comfortable here.*

D: *Louder.*

P: *(Shouts) It's comfortable here. I like it.*

D: *Tell her what you'd lose if things were any different.*

P:　　*I'd lose you washing my two pullovers.*
D:　　*Select two people to be the pullovers.*

Paul watches his mother washing the pullovers. He is fascinated, and so is the group, at the emergence of this memory, so apparently trivial and unserious. Somehow the pullovers have the function simultaneously of conveying the meaning of an intentional train of thought and 'repressed' train of thought. The duality, which has been a theme throughout, is in some way continued by there being two pullovers, rather than 'a' pullover. The ambiguity of the scene makes it difficult to tell whether there is a single primary reference here, or a multiplicity of references that the pullovers take up.

While he is watching, the director gives various suggestions to the effect that he may not know 'right now' what those two pullovers mean, their meaning may become clear to him later, perhaps in a dream, perhaps with a sudden flash of insight. These instructions, of course, constitute a kind of posthypnotic suggestion. Psychodrama is arguably a trance state (with scenes being constructed of chairs, and near strangers being addressed as if they are mothers, fathers, etc.). Hypnotic phenomena, such as negative hallucination (not seeing something that is there, such as the group), or positive hallucination (seeing something that is not there, such as our mother in an empty chair) are part and parcel of the psychodramatic repertoire. To tell Paul that he may be 'surprised' by what he learns and when he learns it, is to follow a classic Eriksonian strategic-therapy tack.

Paul is next asked to select from the group someone to represent what his mother 'would have to give up' if he became different. He does so, without questioning at all this rather strange concept. He is then asked to select someone to represent what his girlfriend 'would have to give up' if he became different. This he also does, though he says, 'they're the same.' He is told not to name specifically what these two figures represent. He takes up his position on the floor, looks at them, and says, 'I know what they represent.' He seems quite 'clear' in his face; there is a calm gravity about him — the sort of look protagonists usually get when they have finished a drama. Finally, he is asked to stand up and move around, breathing smoothly and deeply.

The figures of what the mother and the girlfriend would have to give up may well have represented the systemic restraints on change. The restraints on Paul's own side have already been explored. But there are also restraints within the system — that is, other people's stake in our remaining the same. Unless these forces are at least recognized, there will be a tendency to pull the person back into the system as it is. By acknowledging as many of these forces as possible, by acting them out, by selecting various group members to represent them, the systemic nature of the difficulty becomes more defined. Once having been defined, it is freer to change.

Paul had very little recall of his drama. At follow-up, some weeks later, he reported that things with his girlfriend were 'going well', and that they were getting married soon. It would be quite foolish, of course, to attribute this result to the drama; but perhaps the drama may have cleared the way a little. Paul reported having had 'some amazing dreams'. He was curious to know what had happened in the drama, but what with one thing and another, the processing of the session was always put off, at his request, because he wanted 'to think about things for a bit first'. He never did get around to processing the drama, and it remains as mysterious to him now as it was then. Some of the changes in his life, however, do seem to have persisted.

The seductive power of the family myth

When directors 'enter' a family via a psychodrama, they experience strong pressure to be part of its thinking via the thinking of one of its members — the protagonist. A protagonist whose major role is that of victim, for example, may enact reiterative psychodramas where he or she is crushed by a persecuting parent, spouse, or friend. Sometimes the spontaneity induced by the drama is not sufficient to produce a new framework of understanding and responding to the family reality, and in such cases directors are responsible for not replacing one faulty system with another.

In the original event depicted in a drama, the people concerned are somehow restrained from acting in any way other than the way they did act. They habitually applied certain solutions as if there were a force forbidding them from discovering alternative solutions. How to get at the nature of these restraints? An examination of the attempted solution is one path that could lead to hypotheses about the restraints. It is useful to know, therefore, what has been tried in the past, and what the person or persons is/are doing now to get over their difficulties.

Psychodrama directors conduct a restraints-based examination in the interview for a role, especially where the 'belief' aspects of the role are drawn out. An individual or a family in trouble usually has reified frameworks for defining and responding to reality. In psychodramatic terms, they lack spontaneity. If directors become part of this reification, they will recover more of the same responses. Hence directors need to be able to change themselves and the position they take. New images have to be recovered from a background that has almost limitless possibilities for restructuring reality. An individual may lack it, or a whole system can be struck, just as a whole system, and therefore everyone in it, can become spontaneous. No-one, in particular, has the answer, or alternatively, every-one has it.

A very simple model of systemic 'pathology' is Karpman's drama triangle. It is a more interactive model than Satir's famous categories of 'computer', 'blamer', 'placator', and so better illustrates the point being made. The drama 'triangle' family have the roles of victim, persecutor, or rescuer. The triangle may be represented thus:

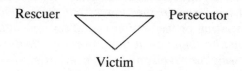

Rescuer   Persecutor

Victim

If the members of the family attempt to solve the problem of being locked into their various roles, which in any case is rare, they merely find them-selves changing roles within the triangle. The persecutor, for example, may decide to reform, but will tend to pitch her reform attempts at bailing out or defending the victim, and so becomes a rescuer. He or she may single out another member of the family as the persecutor, so that member then becomes the victim of the persecutor-turned-rescuer. Or the victim may refuse to be helped by the rescuer, resulting in anger and frustration for the rescuer, which may manifest itself towards the victim once more in a perse-cuting fashion. One's head spins with all this. But not any faster than the heads of the members of the triangle family!

Of these three stock roles, the one most often played out in a psycho-drama is that of victim. Often the victim in a family will be the child, which makes the situation more poignant. The child, as we have seen, may have been relatively powerless as compared to a persecutor or rescuer, and at the time there may have been apparently no other response possible than to take the one-down position. In the context of human suffering portrayed, the director's own highly developed roles as 'protector of the weak, and 'scourge of the bully' are likely to be drawn into the drama. After all, this is why many therapists take on the profession in the first place.

But a systemic-thinking director will be also alert to the possibility that the victim is not as powerless as might first be imagined, and that there can be a great deal of power in powerlessness. For example, adult victims, such as many people who are labelled as 'hysterics' are very skilled at drawing on other people's (rescuer's) time (for example, group time or psycho-dramatic time), work (mercy dashes, fixing mucked-up arrangements, bail-ings out), love (reassurances and promises), and even money (loans, guilt money, or overcompensatory presents). While the powerlessness of the victim is overt, that of the rescuer or persecutor is much less obvious. Their apparent strength, however, is as unfree as the victim's apparent weakness. All are bound in their triangle, helpless to behave in more enjoyable and constructive ways.

Both psychodramatists and family-systems therapists would similarly analyse dysfunctional systems as lacking in spontaneity, and would regard the recovery of creativity within the family as a prime goal. In the drama to be reported next, the director does not attempt structural interventions; she does not attempt to change the organization of the family in surplus reality, thereby enabling the protagonist's experience of the family to become different. She works systemically, rather than structurally, emphasizing differences, and attempting not to fall into the predictable solutions of therapy itself.

The apocalyptic sister

When a protagonist is likely to be 'flooded' by an actual enactment of a scene, a kind of notional psychodrama can be performed simply by a systemic interview. Ideally in the systemic interview when the family presents 'live' for therapy, a description of the problem and the patterns of interaction are derived by obtaining the discussion through multiple sources. Milan therapists (Selvini Palazzoli, Boscolo, Cecchin, and Prata, 1980) are interested in differences between family members in terms of particular beliefs, behaviours, relationships, and also differences between an individual at one time and then at another time. In the following drama, Di will pitch her questioning at these differences, although she is limited by the fact that only one family member, the protagonist, is present. The differences in perceptions and the differences over time all have to come from the phenomenal world of one person, the protagonist, just as they must when one is conducting an individual therapy within a systemic framework (see Weakland, 1983).

The context of a problem includes its pattern through time (Bateson, 1979). Patterns and sequences of experience are built into one's map of the world, and also help build one's map of the world. The 'map' then becomes the context from which further experience is experienced. In the next psychodrama to be outlined, the director attempts to track the evolution of the 'symptom' as it co-evolved with patterns of relationships and beliefs over time within the protagonist's family of origin. She aims to focus on the point in the history of the system 'when important coalitions underwent a shift and the consequent adaptation to that change became problematic' (Penn, 1982, p. 272).

The next case to be outlined is the most extreme form of enactmentless psychodrama to be presented in this book. It is not offered as a model for strategic psychodrama, but rather as a representation of working with an individual in a group on a family-of-origin warm-up that uses procedures more verbal than action-based. Di even does some direct teaching within the process, using blackboard figures as visual analogues of the family members. There is bound to be some question in the reader's, and indeed the writer's mind, whether 'The apocalyptic sister' is a psychodrama at all.

Paula is a woman aged 30 who complains in the group that she has fantasies of 'apocalyptic rage'. When asked if she wishes to enact a drama on this issue, Paula replies that she does not, because she fears that she will be overwhelmed by her feelings. When she has enacted dramas in the past, she says, they have only made the images stronger and more lurid and left her more out of control of her life than ever. Di begins the interview with Paula. Although she does not directly challenge the problem as stated ('How is this problem a problem?'), her later directions will begin to point away from the problem as something 'inside' Paula to an interaction that is bred of a certain context and affects that context.

Instead of asking Paula to come out on to the stage, as is usual for the beginning of a psychodrama, Di asks Paula to remain seated where she is. In fact, until the last section, the whole drama is enacted while Paula remains in her seat with the other group members. Di's interviewing style, at the outset, is a traditional psychodramatic one in so far as she hints that the key lies in the past, instead of enquiring what circumstances are maintaining the problem in the present, and whom the problem most affects in the social atom. She gains an overview, however, in a way that is apparently detached, thus keeping Paula away from an overheated warm-up according to her own request.

D: *Can you think of a scene where you experienced this rage?*
P: *Yes, it was in the dining room.*
D: *How old are you?*
P: *About 7.*
D: *And who is there?*
P: *My brother Michael, who is one year older, and Sam who's three years older.*
D: *And what are you doing?*
P: *I was stabbing Michael in the back with a biro. I stabbed him again and again, so hard that he had to go to the doctor for lacerations.*
D: *What did you all do to get the fighting started? How did Michael get you to do that?*

Di's last questions, 'What did you all do to get the fighting started?', and 'How did Michael get you to do that?' is her first simple challenge to Paula's reality — 'I am the world, and I am the problem' (Minuchin, 1974, p. 159). Uncertainty is introduced, and Paula's construct system is loosened. Paula is nonplussed by the question, which suggests that the new version of reality being introduced is not quite acceptable yet. But it is needed to wean her away from the persecutor/victim polarity that seems central to her construct system.

Di questions Paula further on what led up to that scene. She finds that the context had been Michael and Sam teasing Paula and colluding to exclude her. She had become enraged, grabbed a ballpoint pen, and had run after them both. Michael had tripped and fallen, and Paula had sat on top of him, stabbing him repeatedly in the back. Sam, although much older, was terrified and had hidden. Di asked how the stabbing had stopped, and Paula replied that her mother had rushed in and pulled her off Michael.

Di's questions here have the effect of producing connections as well as merely getting the narrative out. Her demeanour is of a person who is interested but neutral, as is conveyed in the question, 'How did the stabbing stop?' She is formulating hypotheses while she is working, and testing them as she goes. But Paula is making her own links. Di first uses the information presented thus far to illustrate the triangular nature of her relations with her brothers, suggesting that for simplicity's sake, their roles might be described as fitting into those of persecutor, victim, and rescuer.

She tells Paula that these descriptions are 'only shorthand' and do not take in much of the complexity of the situation. Nevertheless, even these simple roles tend to rotate, so that it is hard to know whether the victim invites the persecutor to persecute, or whether the persecutor begins it all, or even whether the rescuer sets something up between the other two so that he or she will be able to take up a role that is familiar. She draws little diagrams on the blackboard to illustrate the circularity of the role-taking. She sets out three chairs in a triangle, and without asking Paula or auxiliaries to sit in them, she herself speaks directly to the persecutor, victim, and rescuer. She asks Pauls to identify which is which at any given stage of the action. Paula appears to get a great deal out of this explanation, and offers several examples where she played in each of the three roles towards the other two. She offers the notion that a new triangle was formed when her mother came in as the rescuer, while Michael is a victim to her own persecutor.

Paula's response to herself as an autonomous but venomous entity has begun to be shaken. She does not control the family system; rather each person is the context of the other. While Paula's rage may be her own, its context is systemic by definition: it is one of mutuality. Although these insights are not necessarily accompanied by high levels of emotion, they do begin to place this terrifying event within some framework where it can begin to be understood. Di has invited Paula to draw distinctions about the family members' participation with each other around the problem at the time of the incident. Her problem is beginning to be seen in terms of how people act, and are activated in a system.

Di next moves to the future. She questions Paula on the immediate and long-term aftermath of the incident. It appears that after Paula's mother had dragged her off her brother, her father had come in from the garage where he was working on his old car, and given her the hiding of her life. This thrashing, needless to say, was not re-enacted. Paula was then sent up to her room, and was locked in overnight. What scope for a scene of loneliness and pain is here! Ordinarily, an enactment here would be legitimate and helpful. But Paula is still in her chair, in the middle of the group, telling her drama from afar. There is nothing 'easy' about this process, though. No doubt Paula would have found it easier to act out the drama in the rough 'n' tough ways to which she was accustomed rather than be dealing with her family dynamics in such a fashion.

Di, however, makes very little empathic comment that might serve to reinforce the already horrific mental image that Paula has of the event, and of her own rage about the punishment she received as a result. Paula is far from lacking in readiness to be emotionally aroused. But it is precisely her capacity for remanufacturing images, and becoming warmed up to them over and over through repeated expressive psychodramas, that is so debilitating to Paula. True enough, to enact a psychodrama and replace the images with others from the surplus-reality section is often a successful device, and one that may lessen the destructive entitlement through several generations, as we have already noted. But in Paula's history, such procedures have only served to increase her emotional lability.

Di begins to ask Paula about differences in family relationships before and after the incident, using a simple sociometric 'Who was closer to whom?' format: 'What did the event mean for you? What did it mean for your mother? What problem is your anger for your father? What did it mean for your brother?' She is again asking questions that produce connections. She is helping Paula treat the symptom as a message, asking her what the message means for the whole family. Paula's answers to the questions are not as important as the fact that the questions are provoking different possibilities.

According to Paula, who naturally enough had never before thought in such terms, Michael had moved close to his mother, but further away from his father, after the stabbing. Sam had moved further away from both mother and father, while Paula herself had moved further from mother — or rather, mother had moved further away from her, despite her desperately needing and wanting her mother after that period. In a paradoxical fashion, she was somehow closer to her father, at least through the

*contact of constant misbehaviour and constant beatings. After the stabbing,
her father, who had periodically bashed her mother, ceased forthwith.*

By the way in which the drama is conducted, with explanation of the
various contributing roles of family members, blackboard diagrams, etc.,
the protagonist is helped to select new ideas, and locate the problem
within the context of circumstances and conditions, including the beliefs
and feelings of each family member. Thus Paula's 'characterological' explanation of her problem ('I am a woman filled with dangerous hate and
rage'), is contradicted. Di's construction of the problem is that it is a solution to a previous problem, the onset of which correlated with a change in
important relationships within the family. The problem remains unresolved
because while it remains a problem, another problem involving a
relationship dilemma does not have to be addressed. The problem creates a
system, however, that is not confined to the family — it goes on and on in
Paula herself, for example, long after she has left her family.

*Di poses to Paula the dilemma of whether she thought it had all been
worthwhile, choosing to sacrifice her relationship with her mother for the
sake of her mother's relationship with her father. At first Paula did not
understand the drift of Di's thinking. She still locates causality within
herself. Di repeated her reframing of the incident, this time asking Paula
whether she thought she had been 'too generous' in helping her mother not
get beaten up any more.*

Raising dilemmas is a common practice in family therapy, often for the
sake of creating a therapeutic bind. A preferable understanding of the
value of raising dilemmas, however, is that they establish conditions for
double description. Di's retrospective description of Paula's 'generosity'
towards her parents allows her a new vision — should she go on being
generous by being the apocalyptic sister, or should she strike out for a life
style that suits 'her sort of person best'? These descriptions are placed side
by side, enabling Paula to draw her distinctions. Should she have continued
to participate in the family in habitual ways, or should she have made a
departure and worked on a new formula for the family members' participation with each other? Such questions, of course, would be best asked at
the time and with all the family members present, but one deals with what
one has — in this case a sole protagonist examining a current problem that
seems to relate to the past.

*Paula becomes very thoughtful, then tearful. Her brother Sam had died of
a brain tumour two years previously in another state, she explained, and
her father had died of heart attack about three years before that. She had
'never felt much' at his death, though her brother's death had meant a great*

151

deal to her. Di asks her what she wants to do 'right now'. 'I want to dance with my father', she says, 'I want to go to a bush dance with him.'

For the first time, Paula becomes an actor on stage. Prior to this, the whole drama has been enacted conceptually, as it were. The room is set up, with a band, caller, children, adolescents, and adults at a country-style dance. All the group members, save those in the band, participate as dancers, while father and daughter dance around exuberantly. When everyone is exhausted, the drama ends.

Was this drama a travesty of the psychodramatic method, and was the resolution a manic defence, a flight into hysteria? Almost certainly not. Paula's problems had always seemed to be not so much avoiding emotion but too much exposure to it through other expressive therapists and groups, so that she was scarcely functional. She had avoided no questions during the hour-long interview about family reactions to her rage. Neither did she 'avoid' intellectually or emotionally — she answered all questions very thoughtfully, and sometimes would commence crying or start being overtly angry, and then calm herself down again. Her dancing with her father at the end did not appear to be a denial of the pain, anger, and loss in their relationship, but rather a resolution and transcendence of those emotions.

The early scenes of a psychodrama usually involve the action of the environment (for example, the parents) on the individual, and in its later play, the individual heroically acts on the environment (surplus reality). This latter action produces a change in the protagonist, and some change in the beliefs, feelings, and behaviour of other members of the system. A systems-oriented director, however, may see the protagonist's distress less as a system-maintained device (the usual view) than as a system-maintaining device (not such a usual view, and certainly not one that the protagonist will hold). Sometimes, of course, direct systemic intervention is unnecessary, as the system becomes unbalanced in the course of a psychodrama itself, via the protagonist's new-found spontaneity.

In group psychotherapy, the relationships between group members, and between them and the therapist, are only gradually built; the system, therefore, is not so powerful before the therapist enters it, but evolves over the life of the group. But in family therapy, the relationships within the 'group' have been operating for many years and are deeply invested with affect. That is, the system is immensely powerful before the therapist enters it. Interactions within the 'group' have become systematized and have withstood pressures for change from divers sources such as neighbours, physicians, relatives, friends, barmen, taxi drivers, hairdressers, and other community psychologists. A family-of-origin psychodrama is at one remove from the force of the actual family dynamic. But even at this remove, directors who 'enter' a family by way of the protagonist's projections may quickly find themselves part of the systematization of the family's own construct system — their defences, if you like.

A therapist somewhat perilously enters the immense power of a family system. Once there, it is relatively easy to 'buy' the family myth about what is wrong. Paula herself 'bought' this myth that she was ultimately a destructive individual. And in 'live' family therapy too, such myths most clearly operate when one particular member becomes the 'identified patient' and in some way acts out or symbolizes the family pathology: an anorexic teenager, a school-refusing child, an alcoholic mother, a pathetic or absent father.

The family develops an unwritten set of rules and beliefs about itself for the purpose of making its reality less difficult to understand. All members of the system have adapted to it: it has its own internal logic, and does not seem quite so strange from the 'inside' as it may from the 'outside'. The system gets settled, and develops ways to prevent itself from being disturbed. Family members bold enough to question this defined reality will generally have pressure put on them to question their own perceptions instead — to feel crazy, or at least a little silly. They may indeed 'go crazy'. Even the therapist is as susceptible to being isolated or rejected for 'breaking the rules' as is any one of the family members. The family acts quite rapidly to talk the therapist (and at one remove, the director) into its reality, and can even attempt to isolate or reject the therapist who insists on a different reality. With Di and Paula it was touch and go, until Paula accepted a new therapeutic code book that was not only different from her old one, but was even different from her old code books about therapy itself.

Chapter nine

Transference aroused

What seas what shores what grey rocks and what islands
What water lapping the bow
And scent of pine and woodthrush singing through the fog
What images return
O my daughter

T.S. Eliot

Introduction

In intensive psychotherapy, a therapist's role as designated authority on the psyche leads to deep and puzzling emotions in those who have come for help. Strange reactions are stirred up, eddies and swirls of feeling, apparently from the therapist's slightest remark or smallest action. To the clients of this ultra-intimate process, therapists appear to know, without being known, to move without being moved. The lesson the client learns is ultimately that of frustration: they are aroused to reach out for what they want, but they cannot get it. The person with whom they are seeking union in fact becomes 'the mother of separation' (Stone, 1961).

As experts who seem to know more about their clients' lives than the clients do, therapists reach deep into memories and fantasies. They are automatically invested with power to show a new way, to enlighten, to make clients better, happier, and stronger. The intensive therapeutic process, when based on transference, causes clients to 'regress', to go back to being little, while the therapist takes on archetypal roles of primary care-giver.

When we were little, our crying in the night was calmed by a person who miraculously appeared to assure us that we were no longer alone. For clients in individual or group therapy, the therapist can seem to be that person, wonderfully resurrected. We all started out as helpless recipients, simultaneously luxuriating and despairing of our dependency. Contact with a pivotal social figure such as a therapist can tap into our childlike patterns, and disarm us.

The intensive therapist also taps a longing for someone who is at once an ideal and a comforter. Someone to establish justice in the world, to right wrongs, and fill the hollows in one's being. These more-or-less universal longings are harmless enough; they do a disservice, however, when they prevent people from taking pleasure in whatever happiness they can grasp: from enjoying the human contact that is available right now, and the limited love that is within reach, rather than the perfect joining that we took for granted as part of reality in the first few months of life.

Living well seems to require the skills of a tightrope artist: to leave room for hope, imagination, and magic, and yet to abandon childishly idealized versions of how things should work. People who give up all hope, trust, and belief in adult fulfilment are half dead; but if they cling too desperately to fantasies of total fulfilment, they are condemned to live their lives in hurt disillusionment. The messiah may not be born, but they can learn to enjoy now, with themselves and others, some of the pleasure that they thought would come from his (or her) hands.

For clients, the therapist as messiah takes on many forms: the one who blocks them, who stands between them and their private apotheosis (negative transference); or the saviour who needs to be possessed in order to reach that miraculous union and happiness that they have been seeking (positive transference). Certain types of therapeutic procedures can lead to the wish that the therapist and the therapy will become the means whereby they are transformed from the pathetic victims of their past and present into the magnificent masters of their future.

But the real aim of therapy, even a 'therapy for fallen gods' such as psychodrama, cannot be this. More modestly, it tries to help us to be creative, to have adequate roles for the situations we find ourselves in, to be flexible, and to live more comfortably and pleasurably with our fellows. In so far as it sets up a structure involving intimacy, it does so temporarily, accidentally even, and with the goal of appropriate structures where intimacy may occur within our own social atom. To accept these limited goals entails a loss of innocence, but also brings a diminution of needless suffering that our illusions of being special and our impossible demands on life have brought us.

Transference is not a 'thing' but a particular set of role relationships that are determined by the therapeutic context as well as by personal constructs about authority as such. An ecosystemic (Keeney, 1979; de Shazer, 1982), rather than observer, epistemology is required — a way of thinking that takes into account all the elements, including those provided by the therapist, and which emphasizes the systemic nature of transference reactions, including 'real-life-based' as much as 'transference-based' attitudes. It will be suggested in the following two chapters that neither psychodramatic nor systemic methods necessarily hinge on 'transference resolution': some people's improvement in therapy may indeed revolve around gaining new roles towards dispensers of power and comfort, but for others these issues are more or less irrelevant. Transference resolution is no omnibus solution.

The reader might wonder what place transference may have in a code of therapy that purports to call itself 'strategic'. After all, Jackson and Hayley's (1963) article seems to have put paid to the topic in strategic literature once and for all. Not quite. Transference is such an important topic in the history of group and individual therapy that it deserves some space.

Secondly, even in a group run on strategic principles, puzzling phenomena do occur that concern the leader. It seems important, since psychodrama is a group method, to go into definitions and a short history of the concept.

Description and history of the transference method

Transference is the term used for an emotional reaction 'brought across' from an old relationship towards an authority. When that sort of reaction occurs between peers, it is usually called displacement — the irrational aspects of any relationship between two people. All transference, therefore, is displacement, but not all displacement is called transference. It is convenient to define transference as displacement that occurs in a hierarchical relationship.

Projection is another term in the trilogy: projection refers to aspects of the self that are displaced onto others. For example, we may project onto the other person that he or she is angry or uneasy, whereas it is we ourselves who are angry or uneasy. If we say the boss is angry with us, when really we are angry with the boss, our attitude might be defined as projection. But when we come home from work and kick the table instead of the boss, we are displacing from one relationship to another. The way transference and displacement is used in therapy is roughly this: if I do kick the children, or my spouse instead of the boss or even the table, an escalation is likely to occur with uncomfortable results for all. But if I 'kick' my therapist (verbally, let's say), it is hoped that he or she will not buy into my game the way my family might have to. I will get a new type of response, and in the long run, will learn to separate therapists, tables, bosses, and children.

Definitions such as transference or projection are not 'things', but merely distinctions to enable us to talk more clearly about interactions that are hard to account for. By means of language we hope to order experience and have a way of communicating it to others. And so it is better to have the terms as clear as possible, short of making a fetish of them, or believing that they contain secrets that have power over those who do not know what they mean. Transference, or 'transference processes', to use Kubie's (1968) less reifying term, is a label for a type of interaction that is said to occur in particular contexts, usually therapeutic. It is not a 'thing' in itself. And indeed, the label indicates the stable — the origin of this particular set of beliefs about the way the world works is of course a psychodynamic one. The question can never be whether transference is 'true' — it is created by certain contexts and therefore it assuredly does exist. Plenty of clinical demonstrations of 'its' existence can be made once it has been created. The question, therefore, is not about the existence of transference phenomena, but whether transference is a useful thinking-tool for one's work.

Transference is commonly understood as a displacement from one time to another, and one person to another. The individual is said unconsciously to displace on to a current 'object' the attitudes, feelings, and responses that were developed towards earlier 'objects' in that person's original social atom. The prototype of all object relationships are the earliest relationships with caregivers, usually one's parents: they are regarded as the ultimate core of the emotions being transferred to the therapist or other person in authority. But the analytic literature also suggests that transference can involve displacement of later experiences and relationships with people (or even institutions) other than the parents. Since displacement occurs unconsciously, so the theory runs, it thereby leads the individual unwittingly to experience reactions towards the current object that are not proper to it. The reactions come not from the 'reality' of the relationship in the present situation, but are brought across from the person's unfinished business in the past. They are a new edition or facsimile of impulses and fantasies that belong to the past, but are 'revived' and offered to the analyst in the present.

At least until 1912, Freud viewed transference as a 'regrettable' phenomenon, a nuisance that interfered with the process of therapy. Although he saw transferences as inevitable, they were regarded simply as one more creation of the patient's 'disease' to be combatted like the neurosis itself. But over time, Freud's view changed. At first transference reactions were a necessary evil to be confronted and overcome by the patient once the analyst brought their existence to consciousness. Later, however, Freud came to regard transference as a 'powerful ally', provided its presence is detected and explained to the patient. It becomes a sort of go-between, an intermediary between the illness and real life. Luckily, the intermediary is more easy to get at than the original illness, and presents the therapist with a convenient way of working.

> The transference thus creates an intermediate region between the illness and real life through which transaction from one to the other is made. The new condition has taken over all the features of the illness; but it represents an artificial illness which is at every point accessible to our intervention.
>
> (Freud, 1914, p. 154)

The phenomenon of transference is regarded as so important in the analytic tradition that it is actually nurtured like a scientist nurtures a culture, or a gardener nurtures an orchid in a hothouse. Once the intermediate status of the transference neurosis is accepted, the relationship between the patient and analyst becomes pre-eminent. Instead of attacking the genetic origin of the 'illness' in the past, one can approach the present relationship as repeating everything it needs to repeat of past relationships. Perhaps that is why it might be claimed that Freudians are as much 'here-

and-now' therapists as Rogers; despite their preoccupation with the past, all therapeutic matters are worked out in the present, and in the encounter between therapist and client. The attainment of a transference relationship is believed to signal maximum involvement with the unconscious, and its eventual resolution leads to a new edition of the client's script originally received from the family.

Yet the reality of their relationship, no matter how intense, is separated from everyday life. The expression of transference drives or fantasies by the client does not actually result in a response by the therapist at the level of reality. The 'Can I have you?'/'No you can't' dialogue appears to be endless, as the therapist applies the 'rule of abstinence'. The aim is to allow the patient to express drives and wishes that would normally be withheld. The patient's reactions to the therapist are said to encapsulate all the ways that a person misinterprets, misresponds, and misperceives the present in terms of the past; yet its artificial nature is said to allow patients to evaluate the unrealistic nature of their impulses and anxieties.

Freud compared the behaviour of the therapist to a nontransparent blank screen. The therapist reflects back only what the patient has manifested. This opacity was intended to prevent therapists from transferring back feelings that patients had transferred on them. Thus, whatever distortions the patient presents can be demonstrated as just that. Granted that the therapist gives the patient very little data upon which to base his or her attitudes, those attitudes must, then, by definition be distortions emanating from the patient.

The therapist's apparent neutrality goes even further: if he or she only analyses, then the analyst cannot act as a teacher or model of any sort, thereby enhancing the patient's autonomy and complete responsibility for self. Rogers, of course, was similarly interested in client autonomy; in the therapist providing only the conditions but not the direction for growth. It was an impossible dream in both cases — the therapeutic method itself is ideological, and its very structure shapes its message. A second-order cybernetic view, on the other hand, does take into account therapist, client, and context in analysing any interaction.

Just as transference reactions are carefully nurtured, so they are equally carefully dissolved, and the treatment is over. In fact, that is the treatment. The development and final resolution of the transference is regarded as being able to 'mop up' all the neurosis that was around; all 'madness' becomes focused in the transference madness, so when the transference madness is resolved, away go one's other irrational and destructive habits.

The patient is said to have a 'repetition compulsion' to repeat crucial previous experiences in terms of satisfaction of infantile drives and defences with the therapist as the object of such gratifications. The 'opaqueness' and lack of responsiveness of the therapist become a huge source of frustration. He or she just will not come to the party, and so the patient must learn other ways of satisfying infantile drives or erecting infantile defences. The therapist, meantime, is merely silent, or merely interprets. Patients do not so much deal with a real figure who reacts to them, but with an opaque and mysterious personality, upon whom they are said to 'displace' their own affect-laden personal constructs. Just as the wishes for the therapist become conscious and are magnified by the fantasy nature of the relationship, so the possibility of their satisfaction becomes ever more consciously remote, as the therapist interprets every move.

Freud regarded transference simultaneously as 'an instrument of irreparable value' and 'a source of serious danger' (Freud, 1940, pp. 174–5). Even the transference of positive feelings functions as a *resistance*, in that the patient pushes aside his or her aim to become healthy, and chooses instead to win the applause of the therapist. Since transference reactions are regarded as repetitions of the patients' early relations with parents, they reproduce the ambivalences of those relationships. Thus, it 'almost inevitably happens that one day his positive attitude to the analyst changes over into a negative, hostile one' (Freud, 1940, p. 176). The hostile transference, too, is regarded as a form of resistance: in misunderstanding the present in terms of the past, patients defend themselves against remembering their infantile conflicts by reliving them.

Already we can note some important differences here between the analytic form of working and the psychodramatic form: at a most basic level, psychodramatic directors actually encourage the person to relive the past, rather than to discuss it. In analysis, the reliving is interpreted; in psychodrama, it is re-enacted. Or rather, the director's interpretations are expressed through the directing interventions themselves — role reversals, scene changes, suggestions for various auxiliary egos, the use of the double, and so on. Reliving is not regarded in psychodrama as a form of avoidance; rather it is the core of the work. The trick is to have the reliving done not only very openly, but very fully; to take the impulse or fantasy to its *nth* degree, so that a state of spontaneity results and the person learns adequate roles. In psychodrama, the protagonist is encouraged to return to the haunted house, to stamp around the rooms, and to meet the ghosts head on, rather than via the therapist/director. The focus usually goes away from the direct relationship between protagonist and director. Analytic therapy relies on the therapist to represent the client's social reality symbolically; psychodrama takes the symbolic representation a different route through auxiliaries and scene-setting. It lays out fantasy in three dimensions, and relieves the therapist of the task of becoming everything to the protagonist. Transference reactions, and their resolution, therefore, are not central to psychodramatic 'treatment'. Nevertheless, from time to time, directors may use protagonist's reactions to them in a strategic manner.

Enactment of a superficial transference reaction

The drama of 'The clockmaker's son' illustrates some of the processes by which relevant material from the past is evoked by the therapist's presence. Apart from the numerous psychodynamic and systems-theory implications of this drama, it illuminates the simultaneous importance and superficiality of certain reactions that go under the label of transference. In this case, the person upon whom the emotions are initially displaced (the director) is in real life almost completely unimportant to the protagonist, who had only known the director for one day. What is important, however, is the director's role as a stimulus for significant interactions that are debilitating in the protagonist's everyday life, the model for which probably came from the past. The drama, therefore, is not reported as a 'transference cure' but as an example of co-creating meaning around a superficial transference process. Later, illustrations of transference processes reported in the next chapter concentrate more on the therapist's importance in a 'real' relationship with the group member.

The clockmaker's son

The protagonist of this drama was Pino, a slim, bearded, and engagingly raffish man aged 35 who seemed to enjoy good relationships with other group members. The group in question was a 'personal growth' group that had been running for about eight months. Dennis had been called in to conduct a weekend session. His contact with the group, therefore, was of recent origin, and his relationships with members were not deeply formed.

Pino's sharing in the group at the end of the sessions that had run thus far had concerned his relationship with his former wife and their children, who were now living with her in another part of the country. On the day prior to this psychodrama, Pino had been passed over by the group when he had put himself up to be a protagonist. Then, in the drama of the session preceding the present one, the elected protagonist had chosen Pino as her brother, of whom she was jealous because he got the most attention in the family. (See 'The lady of Spain' in Chapter 2.)

At the commencement of the session, when the group is settling into discussion after lunch, members begin to notice Pino. He makes angry asides to the people around him, but when asked what the matter is, he refuses to say. One of the group members urges him to come and play with her. The playground metaphor that she introduces is taken up by the group. Another member asks him to stop sitting in the 'playground' wriggling his feet in the gravel, and to join her on the merry-go-round. He refuses. Another invites him to do something. He refuses angrily. Another says she wants him to be a protagonist, but doesn't want to take responsi-

bility for him. Others in the group appear to be caught in a similar dilemma, focusing on Pino, who becomes coy.

Soon Pino stands up, and moves to the middle of the group. The director remains seated. Pino says that he doesn't know what he wants to do, but he wants to do something. He waves his arms around. He jumps up and down with rather unconvincing exuberance: 'I'm here, I'm here'. He ceases, and wanders round again, a little boy lost. One of the group, Meryl, asks if he would like to sit down beside her. He becomes angry, and tells her that he wouldn't, that he's not going to share the floor with anyone now that he's there. He wanders up and down some more, then addresses the director:

P: I want to punch you, but I'm frightened of your power.
D: I am not interested in being punched.
P: (Pacing round the group, addresses the director again) You're not here. I want to talk to the group without you listening.
D: (Plays along, and hides his head in a pillow)
P: (Pleased) What I normally do in circumstances like these is to see if anyone else is unhappy. I get a little group of discontented people around me, and subvert from the inside. (He approaches each group member) Do you feel he's too bossy? Do you think he's too loud? Don't you think he's a smartarse? (He simultaneously pleads with them to join him, and sends himself up in so doing)

The group reply in their divers ways. One says: 'It's your own stuff, Pino; don't involve me.' His acting as commentator and 'little psychologist' to himself appears to be an inadequate way to warm people up to him, to give him the support and attention he desires. The group members seem to be getting embarrassed. The behaviour of Dennis, the director, is also doubtless influential: he remains seated on the floor. As he explained later, he too was not warmed-up enough to 'join' Pino in the director role. One member, however, Simone, agrees to go with him in his little army: 'I'll go with you'. After a few minutes, however, she too sits down.

On the sidelines, Dennis begins constructing his hypothesis about Pino in his original social atom in terms of the major roles he has so far demonstrated: coy attention-getter; angry male who does not want rivals; irresolute brooder caught between action and inaction. From what sort of original social atom might these roles come? He decides to test a hypothesis that might tie the roles together. The central role seems to involve a rivalrous, irresolute child who battles an older person for attention.

D: In what way do you feel powerless?
P: I don't know.
D: (Suddenly) They're all mine; you can't have any of them.

P: What? What do you mean?
D: The women here. They belong to me. They're all mine; my wives.
P: (Looks amazed, but for the first time makes eye contact with the director, and seems steadier, less 'floating' in his manner.)
D: (Continues) Which one do you want to fight me for?
P: (Understands immediately) That one. (Points to Meryl)

When Meryl comes forward, Pino suddenly puts his head in his hands and groans. The director asks him what is happening. Pino replies that when a woman gets too close to him, he gets overwhelmed. The director asks whether he has a particular scene in mind where this feeling was strong. Pino sets up a scene involving himself and his former girlfriend Sue (Meryl) in a country cottage where they have been living for about eighteen months. Briefly, the scene involved Pino feeling 'stuck' in the relationship and frightened by Sue, who made too many demands for closeness. She also was a heavy smoker, and, when upset, would take to the whisky bottle.

Pino could not bear these habits, but was torn between wanting to control her and wanting her to be a free spirit (a not unusual male dilemma). Pino and Sue's interactions are typical of a 'complementary couple': she blames him for his lack of responsiveness, he is guilty but critical, and guilty about being critical. They argue for a while in somewhat desultory fashion, and it becomes clear that this scene repeats Pino's earlier irresolute actions in the group: it is not able to go anyplace.

Pino seems stuck in a repeated dynamic between his desire for closeness and his fear of closeness, and between desire to control Sue and his fear of controlling her. The dilemma might well stem from his early childhood. If this is so, the director has a choice of scenes from the recent or distant past. As it is usually more powerful to work with early rather than recent scenes, Dennis asks Pino to bring his mother and his father into the scene. This procedure involves two other people being anachronistically imposed on an existing scene (which had taken place about three years previously). Although Pino's mother and father were never physically present at the actual argument between Pino and Sue, it is dramatically legitimate to superimpose them on a current interaction, to act as a chorus or reflection on the events there, as it were. Two parts of the past are thus overlaid, so that news of difference may be brought to the protagonist by means of the double description. The anachronism allows similarities and differences to be noticed.

To take the role of his father, Pino chooses a woman in the group, Angie. For the mother, he chooses Simone, his original ambivalent ally when he was trying to raise a subversive army against the director. Dennis asks Father what is going on with his son. Father says that he does not know, *but that his 'wife knows more things', and that he is going down to the back shed to fix some clocks. The father appears to be inadequate to his parenting roles and all but absent as a person. The director puts the same question to the mother. She seems dithery and fluttery, and begins a conversation with Pino that is subtly dismissive of her husband.*

During this discussion, Pino starts walking with his mother to a corner of the room. He walks very close to her, and gives her very slight and apparently random nudges in the direction that he wants her to take. They are talking all the while, and both Pino and the mother appear oblivious to their own actions. He is almost herding her as a sheepdog, but the movements are subtle and unobtrusive at first. In role reversal, he as mother does not resist. Eventually, she is in the corner, looking rather fearfully over his shoulder back out towards the room. They can no longer be unaware of what they are doing.

Pino spreads himself over the corner and puts out his hands on either wall, thus 'caging' her in an attitude that has every appearance of sexual dominance. In role reversal, Pino as Mother complies with all these movements, but mutters rather weakly about Pino's actions being a little improper, and that she should be seeing to her husband.

After a few of these exchanges, the director is more firmly convinced that the conflict may be similar to an even earlier one involving rivalry with another man for a woman's undivided attention. The evidence is coming not only from Pino's initial warm-up in the group, but from the material of the drama itself. He makes a guess that at some stage Pino had his mother all to himself. He turns to Pino and says:

D: *It was better before he came along, wasn't it?*
P: *Yes.*
D: *After all, you're only little.*
P: *Yes.*
D: *About how old are you Pino?*
P: *I'm 4.*
D: *Has your daddy been away?*
P: *He's been in the war and then he's been sick.*
D: *What about you go to a scene where he is back at home.*

In this next scene, Pino and his mother are standing by the father, who is bent over a table mending his clocks. Pino begins to beat on his father's back, crying 'You shouldn't have come back, you shouldn't have come back'. He also starts beating his mother, who has (in role reversal) been rather ineffectually expostulating with him.

This description illustrates ways by which directors and protagonists collude as co-producers of a drama. They work on a mutual influence process. Dennis' change of language from 'your father' to 'daddy' acts as a cue for the protagonist to 'regress'; it is an embedded command to go back in time. He is not so much 'leading the witness' as in fact responding to Pino's verbal and physical cues, and constructing hypotheses about the appropriate place and time for those sorts of cues to be manifested. Director and protagonist follow–lead in the process of co-constructing a reality. Dennis is not yet highlighting the differences between Pino's code book and the therapeutic code book, because the therapeutic code book is not yet in operation. Dennis is acting mainly in the role of producer at this stage, though what he produces, of course, is largely dependent on his therapeutic hunches.

Despite the noisy shouting, the text-book psychological 'truth' of the events, and the apparent psychodramatic fullness of the interaction (crying, beating, etc.) the enactment still has an inauthentic air. Pino seems to be putting on a show, and yet he does not seem to have a choice about the sort of show he puts on. He is repeating the dynamic scene earlier between him and the rest of the group: of not knowing what he wants to do, but wanting to do something. His anger still concerns not wanting to share the floor with anybody. It could be said that this battle is metaphorically similar to one that as a child he did win, but did not really want to win, and could not afford to.

There is no necessity to see a so-called 'Oedipal' struggle in terms only of sex. Generational boundaries, role definitions, limitations of individual power (impotence/omnipotence) are all involved in the family's developmental life cycle. The child must master complex triangles of father, mother, siblings, and self from birth onwards. Sometimes the conflicts involved become more evident during the Oedipal period. When boundaries become uncertain, new rules are learnt very early, and so is the belief that these rules are immutable. Later, it is quite possible to substitute players, so that although the components of the system are new, for example the director or the girlfriend, steps are taken that these new people will not disturb or interfere with these previously learnt rules.

D: *No matter what you do, you can't sustain it for very long. You find yourself planning the next move. You feel your authenticity slipping away.*

P: *Yes.*

D: *That's particularly so with her, isn't it? You don't know whether you want to make love to her or beat her up. Neither feels right. But being with her is unbearable too. Doing nothing is terrible, there's no relief. But no action seems right.*

P: *That's exactly how it is.*

A family helps an infant develop healthy roles by maintaining clear interactions. Ideally, the parental coalition is strong, generational boundaries are distinct, and individuals are treated with respect and caring. Some of these ideal conditions appear to be missing in Pino's case. It appears that when he was very young he must have assumed some of the roles and functions of his father. Although these roles initially may have been very gratifying, they seem not to have been completely serviceable to either Pino or his mother. The absence of appropriate boundaries between him and his mother in his early life appears to have resulted in their constructing a cage for them both later on. In his adult life it seems impossible for Pino either freely to enter an intimate relationship or freely to break away, as was evidenced by his relationship with his girlfriend early in the drama. For Pino, personal space is confused with interactive space. The only possibility for co-existence becomes an intrusion into the space of others (as shown in his early behaviour with the group), the loss of his own boundaries, or the attempted demolition of others' boundaries.

No single person, whether lover, parent, or child, can meet all the needs of another person. But we do try for this in our infancy, and perhaps also in later life. The knowledge of limits can only be communicated to a child if the parents themselves possess it. When they do, the child is helped to give up impotence/omnipotence polarities, and learn to negotiate. As Beavers remarks, when another person such as one's mother sets limits, the child 'learns that mother needs others, and therefore that those others are not enemies but allies. He learns this as he experiences himself not as a dangerous intruder, but as a welcome addition to the parental relationship' (Beavers, 1977, p. 199). Pino's anxiety about 'sharing the floor' suggests that others are not, in his view, welcome additions to the 'parental' (director's and group's) relationship.

Had Pino been raised in a different household, and perhaps one where external circumstances such as war service and illness had not interfered with normal developmental patterns to the extent that it did, he might have had a better chance of learning the importance of renunciation in order to obtain gratification in close relationships. One person is not able to form a satisfactorily wide sociometry for another: more complementary roles are called for than can be provided by a single other person. This is true of parents, lovers, spouses, children, or friends. Therefore a child needs early on to deal with triangular demands by negotiation, and thus avoid the impotent/omnipotent polarity. Pino has been seen to swing between one role or another throughout the drama.

There are several options open to finish this drama, which was stimulated by Pino's rivalrous feelings (transference) to the director. It seemed important that the director take pains to define relationship limits, and to make clear what it is he cannot deliver. An elegant 'sonata form' conclusion might have been to develop the role of the father and to create an effective division between the father and mother as spouses and the child subsystem (Pino). This process was not adopted because the father was too shadowy a character to build up at this stage. To have done so, Dennis would have needed virtually to have taken over the course of the drama to a degree not suggested by cues from the protagonist.

Instead, Dennis decides to help Pino have a different experience of being mothered: to provide him with a psychodramatic new code book so that he can experience the differences. The 'firm mother' had been a significantly underdeveloped role throughout the drama, and was a role notable by its absence even in the original scene. Dennis asks Pino to pick a woman from the group who would make a 'good parent'. Pino picks Joyce, a very practical young woman who, as it happens, is in real life a single parent with a 4-year-old son.

The first action is a re-enactment of the original scene as it was. Pino is asked to stand out of the action and watch it with the director (the mirroring technique). The auxiliary becomes Pino and starts beating the mother in the way that Pino had. He demands that the mother attends to him rather than to father. Then the scene is replayed. This time Joyce insists that he stop, and when he does not, carts him out of the room and gives him a good slap. She is efficient and clear. In effect, Joyce is conducting role-training for Pino's mother, though, of course, only Pino himself is present in the psychodrama.

The psychological undercurrents are quite complex at this stage. First of all, in terms of transference, Pino's original dispute with the director is now forgotten. It is long in the past, relegated to irrelevance by the 'working alliance' that was generated when Pino commenced the psychodrama. At the same time, both the director and the new auxiliary playing the mother are involving Pino in a 'corrective emotional experience' (Alexander, 1946). The director talks to Pino as they watch the action, 'coaching' him on important experiences in living. The new mother is also offering an even more direct, corrective, emotional experience, and Pino acts towards her as to an actual authority figure. The so-called transference is now three-way: towards the director, towards the mother in the psychodrama, and towards the new psychodramatic mother. Finally, the director is working as a family therapist, in setting up new structures involving generational boundaries, and producing enactments in both the new with Joyce and the old with the psychodramatic mother code books. These two code books are juxtaposed to provide news of difference.

Pino now goes in the scene as himself, and gets the same treatment from Joyce, his transformed mother. He then role-reverses as the mother, and modelling himself on Joyce's behaviour, deals out that treatment to the

young Pino. He then goes back to the mirroring position beside the direc-
tor. He watches the whole thing through once more. He looks different, the
drama is over. When he is rearranging the room and putting the props back
in their rightful positions as chairs at the end of the drama, he says to the
director: 'I enjoyed that slap.'

In terms of systemic therapy, the aim of an intervention is to repunctuate
a sequence of behaviour between a set of members, so that experience can
take on different meanings. By encouraging family members to enact new
ways of talking and behaving with each other (that is, learning and practising new roles), a change in the overall context of meaning and expectation can be achieved. So Pino's mother gives him a good slap, instead of
colluding with him against her husband. The family sequences that have
been in operation since the child was born have led to certain characteristics of the individual self that are in turn fed back into the system. Certain
behaviours, whether verbal or nonverbal, such as the mother's ambivalent
acceptance of Pino as lover/husband, are read into the family as cues or
markers. These cues cause sets of expectations or perceptions to be brought
into play, which stimulate further predictable patterns of behaviour. Of
course, these expectations are generally determined without conscious
thought or intent, which means that powerful but tacit assumptions are at
work in the family most of the time.

Pino's drama suggests once again the possibilities for conceiving interactions in systemic and structural terms, even simple terms such as drawing
boundaries. Pino's relationship with the director was not a significant one,
and the psychodrama could in no way be construed as a 'transference
cure'. The relationship with the director was used as a trigger to launch the
drama. As it turned out, Pino's dynamic with Dennis and the group at the
very beginning of the drama was repeated over and over throughout. We
began with the puzzling topic of transference, however, and it is time now
for us to return to that issue.

Psychodramatic and interactional views on transference

Moreno held no particular affection for the notion of transference. Taking
Freud's definition: 'A transference of feelings upon the personality of the
physician ... it was ready and prepared in the patient and it was transferred
upon the physician at the occasion of the analytical treatment', Moreno
claims that if the definition had been made from the point of view of the
patient, then the description given by Freud could be reversed without
change, except by substituting the word 'physician' for the word 'patient' and
vice versa. The definition would then become:

A transference of feelings upon the personality of the *patient* ... it was ready and prepared in the *physician* and it was transferred on the *patient* at the occasion of the analytical treatment ... His feelings do not originate in the present situation and they are not really deserved by the personality of the patient, but they repeat what has happened to him once before in his life.

(Moreno, 1959, p. 6)

As Moreno would have it, transference is an interpersonal phenomenon, and countertransference is merely transference 'both ways'. Countertransference has long been regarded as the reaction of the analyst to the patient as though the patient were a significant person in the analyst's early history. The dangers of the therapist having a dislocated view of the patient and using the therapeutic encounter for his or her own ends are obvious. Moreno's redefinition of countertransference does not eliminate the notion that therapists approach clients with their own role structures, some of which may be helpful, and some of which may not. But he makes the whole process more realistic and egalitarian.

The intense contact between therapist and client does take on strange forms of yearning and need that are not totally explained by Moreno's redefinition. His formulation, while a little facile, perhaps, is nevertheless satisfactorily recursive. It is limited by its simplicity, however, in that it does not discuss the crucial hierarchical elements of relationship to a role, which makes the reversal not quite so parallel. The therapist and client *are* equal as human beings, but there are nevertheless structural elements in the roles of therapist and client that remove the meeting from being a simple encounter. There is much that is not equal when one goes to see a therapist.

Moreno does offer a timely corrective to traditional transference notions, however, by his pointing up the importance of contextual factors in definitions. As well, his switch-over brings with it a freshness to the discussion and is characteristic of his perpetual attempts to de-pathologize the patient. His redefinition provides a more thoroughly systemic idea of transference: he eliminates the persistent and unsystemic bias in traditional therapeutic literature that holds therapists as the ones who define the therapeutic situation, and who (countertransference literature aside) seem to assign to themselves a status of uninvolvement. The time that a therapist spends with a client, he suggests, should count for something because the time is real time and part of the lives of both people. The opposite of this type of relationship is an authoritarian relationship where the time spent with the other is not a 'real' part of the life of the therapist or person in authority.

The concept of tele is important in Moreno's writings and now requires further explanation to that given in Chapter 1. It is unclear whether Moreno wants the concept of tele to be a substitute for, or in addition to the notions of transference and countertransference. As we have seen, he did not esteem these psychiatric concepts very highly and probably dismissed them a little easily. Tele is Greek meaning 'at a distance'. Kellerman remarks that 'This peculiar choice is no exception from the obscure psychodramatic terminology, which has been largely influenced by classical Greek drama ... (it) is unorganized and sometimes inconsistent' (Kellerman, 1979, p. 41). According to Moreno, tele is 'insight into', 'appreciation of', and 'feeling for' the 'actual makeup' of the other. Whereas empathy is a 'one-way feeling into the private world of the other person', tele is two-way, although for tele, each of the partners needs empathy. It is an appreciative mutual exchange; a flow of feeling between one or more people. It is not a relationship from the past but a spontaneous process proper to the here and now.

In a therapeutic context, claims Moreno, the patient certainly may project and displace fantasies on to the therapist. But part of his or her ego is not consumed by this regression; rather, it 'feels into' the therapist. This part appreciates intuitively what type of person the therapist is, and the amount of kinship or lack of it with the therapist. With luck and skill, this admiration of the therapist for his or her real qualities will develop as therapy progresses, and the transference aspect will become gradually more irrelevant. When the status of the patient as the one who has the projections is removed 'we arrive at the simple, primary situation of two individuals with various backgrounds, expectations and roles, facing each other, one potential therapist facing another potential therapist' (Moreno, 1959, p. 5) — an utterly ecosystemic notion, if you like. If the therapist is wise, kind, strong, and knowledgeable, then the patient's appreciation is not transference but an insight gained through a different process, which concerns the actual make-up of the other's personality.

On the other hand, if the therapist has the feeling of superiority and a certain godlikeness, and if the patient experiences this from the gestures that are made and from the manner of speaking, then the patient is attracted not to a fictitious, but to a real psychological process going on in the room. That is, if the therapist is habitually obscure, ungiving, mysterious, and consistently interprets whatever the patient says about any topic as either the resistance or transference, or even resistance to the transference, then the patient is certainly reacting to something real in the relationship.

In most forms of psychotherapy, the therapist's personality is highly significant, and of course influences the type of treatment he or she uses. Ideally, each person should be assigned to a therapist who is suitable to him or her, though it does not often work out that way. Poor clients using government health services, for example, do not have the luxury of such choice. Moreno insisted that all therapists are not appropriate for all patients: treatment outcome will be dependent, to a large degree, on an advantageous tele process: both parties of the relationship must be drawn to each other because of their genuine characteristics. The ideal of Moreno's recommendation that each patient be carefully assigned a therapist through sociometric choice based on a desirable tele relation must remain a dream; the best that most patients can ordinarily achieve is to 'shop around' for someone who suits them, and even this process is beyond the reach of many people who are suffering severe difficulties in living and are shunted from GP to psychiatrist to clinic.

Conclusion

To play down the notion of transference is not to deny that people do construe others, including therapists, in ways that are uncomfortable and do not seem to make sense. An analogy might be to consider the therapist as the moon and the client as the earth. We all know that when we are able to see a 'full' moon, it is because the earth is not casting a shadow on it — that is, we ourselves are not standing between the light source and what we are looking at. When the moon is not full, in fact we are looking partly at the moon and partly at our own shadow. If our dysfunctional preconceptions are 'in the way', that is, if we have reasons to construe an authority figure in certain ways, we will only see part of the other person.

In any relationship, however, there is no 'pure' knowledge of the other — knowledge is always a relationship of two. The analogy with moon and earth must go both ways, of course — therapists also look partly at the moon, and partly at their own shadow. A third element, the therapeutic system itself, must also be taken into account. Reality is always constructed. Therapy sometimes helps us make constructions that are more helpful than the ones we habitually use. Possibly we can see more of the full moon, and less shadow (or total eclipses), but it is still 'our' moon.

In Morenian terms, a 'transference' relationship differs from a 'tele' relationship in the degree of relevance, accuracy, immediacy, and appropriateness of what is experienced in the relationship. Tele relationships are more modifiable by what actually happens than a relationship highly based on projection or transference. But what is real and what is transference always overlaps. All transference contains reality elements, and all telic relationships have transference elements. In therapy, the 'working alliance' (Bodin, 1979) that is necessary must be found in the reality side of the relationship (Greenson and Wexler, 1969) — otherwise the whole social structure between the two parties is in danger of collapsing. Many schools of therapy would be content with a 'working alliance', and consider clients' attitudes to the therapist as good data indicating how they want the other person to be. Systemic therapists would derive hypotheses from the data, and work forward in the normal fashion, by questions, interventions, and so on.

There are many ways to skin the cat of so-called 'transference'. It can be regarded as one of several, limiting personal constructs, and be relegated to a fairly low position on the treatment spectrum. 'Transference' thoughts and images produce unnecessary discomfort and suffering, and lead to self-defeating behaviour. The cognitive-theory process is to clarify the distortions, self-injunctions and self-reproaches that disable the client, and to get at the underlying 'rules' on which these crippling thoughts are based. Working through the transference becomes essentially a problem-solving exercise, the aim of which is to undermine the transference rather than establish it. Transference is regarded as a distortion, and people have enough distortions in their lives already without a therapist abetting the process. Unnecessarily limiting personal constructs towards other figures in the client's life are treated in similar fashion to unnecessarily limiting constructs towards the therapist. A 'working alliance' is all that is necessary to keep the client in treatment in such a way as to follow the therapist's interventions. In general, cognitive and personal-construct therapists seek to undermine the philosophical and ideological foundations of transference: they are thinking processes that bind the client in defeat, and force him or her to behave in a compulsive and undignified manner.

Therapists who work intensively with individuals or groups can indeed attract powerful unconscious attitudes from their clients. Sometimes they wittingly activate this process, working by means of the transference. Sometimes the activation is unwitting and occurs by the mixture of the therapist's personality, and the roles and tasks of leadership. Even in the first instance, however, clients 'pick up' some of the therapist's actual roles, personality, and inner life. The distortions in this case might be exaggerations, but are based on what is actually there. Therapists can act 'professionally' as 'opaque' figures, or can actually be ambivalent persons who like to have people guessing about them in order to help them with their guessing about themselves. They may act out these roles outside the therapy room as much as in it. They might even have become therapists so that they could safely act them out in their working hours. Perhaps ultimately we choose our therapeutic modality to fit our basic, personal and social orientation.

Therapists do not uncover objective 'facts' about clients, but inevitably elicit particular information in keeping with their own theoretical frameworks and the types of situations that are set up. The clients' productions are a mix of the therapeutic form of enquiry and the patient's/client's particular context of historical happenings and personal fantasies. The 'truth' of what is happening to the patient is filtered both by the therapist's personality and by the ideology of treatment. While the client may have factual biographical information to reveal, for example, of having been beaten up at home, the meanings of such past events are arrived at between the therapist and client at any particular moment of treatment. Just as there are no objective 'meanings' to an Oedipal conflict, nor are there even to

171

being beaten up. Therapeutic reality is always a concoction, negotiated interpersonally. In therapy, one gets a new map of reality, rather than a new reality. One hopes that this new map leads to more pleasing realities for the client in the future.

Chapter ten

Transference redirected

Say, do you have any brothers?

Client to therapist

Because transference processes are so complicated, so emotional, and so mysterious, they cannot quite be explained by any system of therapy, whether it be psychodrama or psychoanalysis. The intense client–therapist bond can only be expressed analogically, not digitally; that is, the attachment is an experience of relationship, not a message or an ideological statement. Hillman (1964, p. 19) suggests that transference can be better understood by comparing it with the model of secrecy, silence, and 'against all others' which is operative in other profound works of the soul — the creation of art, religious mysteries, passionate love. Participants in the unique relationship of long-term therapy share 'a common mystery as do lovers, explorers, initiants, who have together been touched by the same experience'. Throughout this book, I have referred to this experience of mystery as 'epiphany' or 'revelation'.

The intense therapeutic relationship is a disquieting one, containing a mixture of uncomfortable and pleasurable feelings. The sense of yearning and need, so carefully built up, is never quite met. These feelings of disjunction, and the yearning for conjunction are elemental emotions, essential fibres in life's fabric. Some therapists say they are fit matter for therapy, and indeed that therapy should be based around them in the person of the therapist. Other schools of therapy find such a view exploitative of the most precious tendencies in human life, and suggest that there is no need to direct these feelings towards the therapist — they should immediately go outward to the social atom, to the real bonds in the real world that form the matrix of the client's being.

The relationship that two people build up in individual, intense, long-term therapy often does have the characteristics that Hillman describes. Long-term, intense, individual therapy requires from the client an actual living through, or living out in time, the encounter of the new relationship. If a client's experience of childhood, say, is not one of being emotionally fed, held, or contained, and someone is prepared to do that, and to let the client experiment with the relationship without threatening to go away, the client naturally develops a deep bond with that helping person. A long-term relationship with a sensible and stable other person who is totally committed, at least during the hour of therapy, to one's wellbeing and personal expansion, can be a helpful as well as a deeply moving experience. It can also be a frightening experience, not only because of the scrutiny involved, but because of the structural ambiguity of the therapeutic situation and possibly the personal ambiguity of the therapist him or herself, which may be a subject forbidden of negotiation.

No systems view, and especially no psychodramatic view, need deny the phenomenon of repetition of the past — an attempt to recycle particular types of interactions that seem inappropriate to the present context. In a family-therapy session, for example, one only has to ask clients to draw a genogram to see the links of attitudes and characteristics carrying through the family line. Transference reactions, then, can be regarded as a form of attempted solution. People find themselves in dysfunctional relationships because the spontaneity required for creating a new type of interaction seems more painful than maintaining interactions as they are. People are restrained, by a network of presuppositions largely out of consciousness, from construing new situations in a fresh light. The personal-construct system of the client may have its origin in the client's early family life, or it may be of more recent origin — constructs on experiences that have made a person, say, overly suspicious or overly dependent on others for guidance and entertainment.

Whatever the origin of the restraints on the client viewing the world differently, so-called transference reactions, if and when they present themselves in therapy, need to be understood as a three-way process, the meaning of which is to be found in the context and in the interaction between therapist and client. They are not something pathological within the client that must be worked through and got rid of. They are roles called up in particular circumstances towards particular other people. For them to be a fit subject of strategic therapy, they must somehow represent a problem, rather than a general orientation. Strategic psychodrama does not take on the client's whole being and attempt to fix it according to some model of a realized or enlightened person.

To hold a strategic position on transference processes does not make it necessary to deny that people distort reality to fit interactions they have had in the past, or that they wished they had had in the past. A strategic therapist is not blind to the phenomena towards which transference-based therapists point. Rather, the issue in individual therapy becomes whether working on the transference itself is an ethical, efficient, and viable way of conducting therapy. The issue in group therapy is similar — are the concepts of transference as applied in groups useful and explanatory, and is a transference-based group treatment an effective way to conduct group therapy? Whatever the merits of transference-based individual therapy may be, it will be suggested in this chapter that although transference phenomena certainly present themselves in groups, direct attention to these phenomena and encouraging member–member interaction is preferable to an 'opaque' leadership style.

Group-transference therapists aim to create (or say they find) conditions in which the therapist represents the entire social atom for each group member. All interactions in the group, therefore, are really 'about' the leader. Later, we will offer an extended critique of this point of view. In the following drama, the reverse of this position can be seen to apply: interactions apparently towards the leader can actually concern the whole leader–group system. Member-to-member interactions are not necessarily sour-grapes activities to compensate for loss of the leader's singular attention. The drama of 'The woman who wasn't born' highlights the embedded nature of the leader's role as member of the group system, a point discussed at greater length in the companion volume to this book, *Forbidden agendas*.

The woman who wasn't born

Petra is normally a very calm and competent group member. She is in her late thirties, has five young children, is a post-graduate psychology student, and holds down a part-time job as well. She is one of the group's sociometric stars because of her devotion to the goals of the group, and her ability to 'be herself', no matter how foolish that may seem to others or indeed to herself at the time.

On the day of this drama she was very distressed, unlike her usual efficient and other-directed self. She told the group that she was afraid she was 'falling apart' in her personal life, and expressed extreme alarm at Duane's (the director's) imminent departure for a period of three months. The topical concern in the group had also seemed to narrow towards this issue since the start of the session. The members soon focused on Petra in her distress, and she emerged as a 'natural' protagonist, that is, one elected unanimously, rather than by formal sociometric procedures.

In the interview, Petra describes how she had been humiliated in front of a training group led by a different director several months previously, and how she had 'never recovered' since. She tells the group that she had lost all that she had gained in the previous year and had also lost her relationship with the current director. The director asks her to nominate what it was that she had lost. Petra says that she had lost her ability to look people in the eye.

The director asks her to select someone from the group who can be her ability to look people in the eye. She does so. 'What else?' the director asks. Hesitantly, Petra says that she has lost her love of herself. Someone is chosen for this role. More rapidly now, Petra says that she has lost her competence, her physical strength, and her sense of herself. 'There's another thing, but I can't think what it is', she says. She puzzles for a while. 'It wouldn't be your creativity, would it?' the director asks. 'That's it, that's it', she says with excitement and relief. Even the naming of 'creativity' has a profound effect on her. Once it has been named, it seems as if creativity becomes once more her ally. She selects people from the group to play thse qualities, and positions them at varying distances from her.

Petra has selected her own six pillars of wisdom, although at this stage they have been chosen as parts of herself that are alienated from her. The visual impact is striking, although not wittingly set up in any way: the auxiliaries are indeed standing like pillars of wisdom around her. The director waves them away before Petra has a chance to interact with them. This apparently arrogant interference with Petra's drama is, in fact, simply and literally following Petra's original cue that she had 'lost' these qualities, and that she was 'falling apart'.

In thus following the protagonist's metaphor, Duane is not acting unilaterally, but merely shortening the drama and tracking the protagonist's and audience's 'energy' levels. It did not seem appropriate to Duane to have an intrapsychic drama (that is, one overtly dealing with 'parts' of the protagonist) at this stage, since such dramas tend to be relatively flat and can get very mixed up: 'Which part am I now?' the actor in such a drama often asks. Generally speaking, it is better to populate a drama early on with historical figures, and to give it a scene. Without persons and a situation to respond to, the protagonist tends to flounder, and the drama becomes abstract and dry.

All dramas, of course, are intrapsychic in that the acted-out roles and characters such as mother or father, although based in history, are ultimately constructions of the protagonist's reality. As such, they become part of her thinking about herself and her dealings with others (Leutz, 1982). Some of these roles are regarded as 'like me' and some are rejected as 'not like me at all'. One of the aims of therapy is to reincorporate all projected roles, including kind, loving, tender, and creative roles as parts of the self. It is easy to fall into the trap of regarding the projected roles to be owned as from the 'shadow' only — the dark, cruel, sadistic, insensitive, or selfish parts. Duane's experience is that people are all too ready to admit to these and to say that that is what they are really like. The kind, loving, and tender parts of themselves give them much more trouble. In Petra's drama, therefore, Duane decides to keep the six 'pillars of wisdom' waiting in the wings, as aspects of herself needing reincorporation later. Had Petra reacted very strongly when the director waved them away, this in itself may well have become the important moment of the drama, and would have been pursued. Petra offered no resistance to their dismissal, however.

Petra is invited to establish the scene of her humiliation with the visiting director, but as soon as she is asked to choose the person who precipitated this three-month crisis, she changes course and says that she wants the present director himself (Duane) to be in a scene with her.

She is working very quickly now, apparently having already dealt with that earlier troublesome event by making a leap to a situation even more relevant than the one that precipitated her distress. Duane is now faced with a problem that is personally and technically difficult. If he asks Petra to choose an auxiliary to be himself, the drama will be somewhat weakened, but will be easier to direct. The disadvantage of this course is that the director has to stand by and see an auxiliary speaking and acting as him, using words put into his mouth by the protagonist. The advantage of this 'outside' position, on the other hand, is that the director is relatively uninvolved in the action and can see clearly what is going on. The director's hypothesizing and producer roles are thus able to be maintained. When some of the projections are enacted, the director can then meet the protagonist in an encounter, as in the instance of 'The avenging angel' (p. 187).

A second option is for Duane to enter the drama himself as an auxiliary, knowing that if it is truly a transference matter that is stimulating the protagonist, the scene will move elsewhere, probably to family-of-origin. If the director does agree to be cast in the drama, he must find his cues for the role as would any other auxiliary. Thus he must be himself, and yet be also the projection of himself, mouthing sentiments and attitudes with which he almost certainly will not agree as being true to him. Moreover, he has either to direct from within the role, or to appoint an assistant director to conduct that section of the drama where he is an actor.

A third option is for Duane to occupy the role, but to do it as himself. He thus goes into encounter with the protagonist without using the psychodramatic method at all. The difficulty here is that although he honestly attempts to encounter Petra, he is still in some sense directing, and still managing the group. These roles can never entirely be given up. The third option, however, has the advantage of giving the protagonist a chance to encounter another human being who is at that time a problem to her, and to hear the honest responses of that other person. It seems, therefore, that this third option is very valuable, and should either be used on its own, or be incorporated either before, during, or after the drama.

In Petra's drama, Duane chose the second option of being in the drama himself, and calls for an assistant director from the group to conduct the next part of the session. When this is done, Duane enters the drama as an auxiliary. Petra talks to Duane, saying how much she wants to be special to him. In role reversal:

Petra (as Duane):   *Don't be ridiculous. Who are you anyway? Look,*

	I've got plenty of groups to run, and lots of people in
	each group want to be unique, to be special. They all
	want me to love them more than the others.
Assistant Director:	*Reverse roles to yourself. (She does)*
	Tell him you're special.
Petra:	*I can't. I feel like the adopted one.*
Assistant Director:	*Say that again.*
Petra:	*(Screams) I feel like the adopted one.*

This section of the drama took only a few minutes to enact. Its form was that of a dialogue between a cruelly rejecting top dog and an abashed, insignificant underdog. Such dialogues can become repetitive, locking in both people as victims of a servant-and-master routine. It appeared that it would be so in this instance too, so the director decided to move on. He asks Petra if he can come out of role, and now take on the direction of her drama. Petra agrees, and sets up her family-of-origin in relation to father when she was a child. By this action, Duane is now moving to a scene containing fairly obvious transference ramifications, and away from one directly involving himself.

Petra says that to do as Duane asked would be very hard, and that she did not know her family's relationship to father. She does not seem, for the moment, to be directly concerned with Duane as such. Duane asks her whether she could set up the family's relationships with mother, if those with father present such difficulty. In this case, Duane is not asking for a typical social atom that has the protagonist as its nucleus, but more for a circular-relationship social atom with another family member, the mother, as nucleus. The shift in thinking is therefore away from an individual and into a systems orientation.

Petra chooses auxiliaries as her family members. She is from a large family with six siblings. She makes a family sculpture with them in their relation to mother. Petra herself is on the outer fringe. Duane asks Petra to role-reverse as various siblings and to comment on the position of other siblings (not on their own position). He is hoping to create a dynamic understanding of the family that will be helpful to Petra, but which will not necessarily have her at the centre. The format that Duane uses in this instance is a psychodramatic variation of circular questioning.

From one of these sibling comments, it is established that there is a play-group of three, a sort of 'top group' in which Petra desperately would like to have been included. A scene is established where these three — Angie the eldest sister, Mark, a brother, and Lucy, an asthmatic younger child, are playing family games in a corner of the chicken pen. Petra asks to join them in the game. Contemptuously they give her a minor role as the uncle and banish her to a different part of the backyard. She sits alone in an improvised shelter, quite miserable, but stoic and not despairing.

Meantime, the three others concoct a plan. Petra has the family nickname of 'Wait for Me' because she is always trying to catch up after having been excluded from some activity. The children decide that they will put it around that Petra has been adopted, because she is so different from them — she is plump and they are skinny, her hair is brown and theirs is fair. 'What does adopted mean?' asks one. 'It means you haven't been born', replies the eldest, who, of course, is Petra in role reversal. There follows a discussion of whether Petra really was or was not born, and the children conclude that she probably was not, or that at least their parents were not her parents. They go with this news to poor old 'Wait for Me', still in exile from the chicken house, which has become so desirable as the top group's lair.

Petra still does not despair at their latest cruelty, and although this moment of casual viciousness would seem an ideal staging ground for a psycho-dramatic battle-royal, Petra declines to fight for her existence in this way. Instead, she stubbornly holds on to it, disputing with the other children, arguing that she must have been born. Her sense of herself, of her existence, seems miraculously unshaken, but her pessimistic sense of her place in the social order is further confirmed.

The other children do not care about her logic. They go off, grinning. The director asks if there is anyone with her in her shelter. 'Only the cat', Petra replies. The director encourages Petra to 'console the cat'. He realizes that it would be impossible for her to receive love at this stage, or to be consoled. She has had to make herself too tough to survive the other children's cruelties. His injunction is similar to a so-called paradoxical injunction in family therapy, and has a similar effect. Petra quickly warms to her role of consoler, and then, at last, is herself held and consoled in role reversal as the cat. After all, it is not too threatening to be a cat being consoled and held by its mistress. This scene continues for some time, with continued role reversals to check its authenticity.

Petra is now warmed up to being loved and to loving. The director asks if there is anyone in the family she would like to have with her now. Instead of choosing father or mother, or even older sister, Petra chooses Lucy, the asthmatic 'special child'. In surplus reality they talk to each other and hold each other though they did not do so in the reality of their childhood. In time, this section of the drama is also finished, with Petra having reincorporated her own 'special child' role, a role that is, of course, as yet not fully developed.

Duane then asks for the reappearance of the auxiliaries playing the six characteristics of Petra that she had feared losing. The six pillars come back

179

on stage. One by one she interacts with them, first as herself, and then in role reversal. The intrapsychic drama has real power and meaning now, once the family one has been played. She spends time with 'physical strength', for example, and as that role advises herself to eat better, rest more, and so on. As herself, Petra says that she doesn't need to resolve to do these things, she will automatically do them 'when all the rest is right'. She also lingers with the auxiliary playing 'sense of shame', and says that for a long time she hasn't been able to look people in the eye, but that now she doesn't need her any more. But the longest interaction is with her 'sense of herself', who, as it so happens, is played by the person who was Lucy in the family drama. There is a real battle between Petra and this role. It is not easy to make friends with this one. Eventually the two have a cup of tea in a garden. They eat cakes. Petra at last hugs and cries and laughs in the face of her re-met 'sense of self'.

The sonata is nearly, but not quite complete. Just as Petra has returned to the six pillars of her wisdom, so she must go to the time of the original introduction of the theme — her meeting with the director. She interacts briefly with him with openness and love. At the same time it is clear that he is now largely irrelevant to her — she has done her work in the family, and he is in his proper place once more.

The following week in the processing session, Petra reported that she had spent a whole day during the week in bed, caring for herself. She had also been assertive with her supervisor at work, had confronted a teacher of one of her children, and dealt with her relationship with a girlfriend with whom she had had years of 'unfinished business'. She felt less stoical and more resentful of rejection and hurt, where her love was not appreciated, not reciprocated. She was gradually changing her ideas about love, which she had formed in her background as a devout Catholic. She now saw love less as hard work, an act of the will, a grind: 'If I say "I love you", I immediately have to say "Prove it"', she commented. Love had always been an obligation, an act of the will rather than of the heart, and was to be backed up by acts of service and mortification. In a way, love had always meant self-hatred. 'Now I have the glimmer of an idea of another love, which is easier, more fun.'

To enact a drama in the original social atom is merely a way of working metaphorically, putting a new construction on history. Reconstructing events and reframing interactions in the original social atom is only useful if it ultimately leads to adequate roles in the client's current social atom — as it seemed to do with Petra. The past is used as a way of warming up to the here-and-now. To consider that the present is really a warm-up to the past, a stance apparently held by psychodynamic workers, seems an inappropriate one to take towards mental health or towards adequate roles in the person's current social atom.

Arguments against transference interpretations of group process

An essential understanding in psychodynamic methods of working with groups is that the therapist is the centre of the group's desires. Freud (1921) argued that although the leader is always a potential source of fantasized, libidinal gratification, the group cannot have him or her because of the presence of the other members. So leaders must be 'shared'. The unconscious wishes of the members are frustrated; they turn away from the leader and towards each other for possible gratification. The turning away from the 'primary object' (the leader) towards a substitute one is similar, in Freudian mythology, to what occurs at the time of the passing of the Oedipal phase. Transference wishes are deflected on to other members, where they find at least partial gratification for their frustrated needs, and can bury their hatred or desire for the therapist in fellowship with each other. Members attempt to act out, and try to get others to act out their unconscious roles and conflicts.

According to the Bion/Tavistock opinion, group conflict is a result of the members' unconscious transference wishes for the leader. When groups do not want to work on the purpose for which they started therapy, they are said to form a hidden group, a 'basic assumption group' (Bion, 1961). Conflict over the leader is regarded as the chief issue in a basic-assumption group. This conflict can take several forms: the 'dependency group' looks for an omniscient-omnipotent leader who will magically cure them; the 'fight-flight group' want a Solomon, a dynamic figure who will be able to preserve the group's existence and save it from disintegration; and the 'pairing group' are in mystical gestation, coupling for the purposes of reproduction so that they can bring forth a messiah or saviour for the group.

In the same tradition, Ezriel (1952, 1973) argued that transference in the here-and-now reveals the nature of the unconscious object relationships, which are the source of infantile conflicts. The interpretation of the transference must take in the 'required relationship', the 'avoided relationship', and the 'calamitous relationship'. The avoided relationship relates to the therapist, because only in him/her can the member endow the fantasized qualities no human being could in reality possess. The calamity is embedded in the theme of the sessions beneath the topical concerns. The required relationship exists in the interactions between group members.

Even 'moderate' authors such as Kibel and Stein believe that most group interactions concern the leader:

Unconscious transference in the group may also be expressed as character traits. As such, they constitute resistance phenomena. In fact, much of the transference attitudes that members show in relation to each other can be viewed, theoretically, as resistance to the expression of the original forbidden transference wishes for the leader.

(Kibel and Stein, 1981, p. 420)

In other words, relationships within the group tend to regress from ordinary ways of choosing and rejecting to a series of regressive identifications with an idealized leader. Members become totally preoccupied with the leader (little wonder, if the leader continually makes interpretations to that effect). The group interactions are viewed as 'fractionated manifestations' of that regressive phenomenon. The people in the group become 'part objects', whilst the therapist remains the 'synthesized whole object'. Early on in the group, members will express the aim to merge with the leader, who is unconsciously represented as the earliest ego-ideal model, the model of the first half-year of life. Members may unite around wishes to merge with and devour the leader, to possess and control him (Saravay, 1985). The fact that the group members' wishes for him or her are frustrated, becomes agonizing, but leads inevitably to interaction in the group and interpretation by the leader that are eventually productive. The group bond or tie to the leader will always advance or regress in phase, synchronized to the same developmental stage, as components of the prevailing group transference.

According to several group analytic writers, such as Ezriel (1952), Whitaker and Lieberman (1964), Foulkes (1964), and Anthony (1967), a predominating unconscious wish or fantasy unites the members in a certain group phase and imposes a common influence on their behaviour. These phases were thought closely to resemble the stages of infantile development, so that the psychosexual zone symbols, defences, resistances, symptoms, object relations, ethics, and ideas are common at any one time and are determined by the shared unconscious fantasy or wish that unites members in relation to the leader. The members accept the leader as their collective ego-ideal and superego, and consequently regress from object ties to identification within their egos to unite together as a group. They are filled with anxiety over Oedipal striving towards the leader, their common ego-ideal, and as a result regress to form an ego-identification with each other.

In contrast to these notions, research evidence and clinical experience suggest that a broad range of therapeutic factors, rather than encouragement of a regressive transference neurosis are important in group work. Catharsis, learning to trust others, and learning how one relates to others are also extremely helpful. In longer-term therapies, a broad range of factors have been found to be salient, including universalization, altruism, guidance, and existential factors, as well as catharsis, insight, and inter-personal learning. Yalom (1975) fosters a sense of reality in his groups and has a concrete focus for the group's activity, such as learning how to react and behave more constructively. These un-esoteric goals and procedures are supported by other moderate elements within the psychoanalytic move-ment, who suggest that group leaders do not dwell on the immaturity of the transference relationship, but find ways to make the group members' even-tual relationships more adequate and pleasurable. As in individual psychotherapy, there is currently more stress on the importance of real interactions between therapist and group members.

In the psychodramatic conception of the group process, it is understood that a leader's task is to produce contexts that call forth creative and spon-taneous roles from the participants. A pyschodramatic group session, therefore, is woven not simply out of the individual's or group's neurotic systems. Now it is true that most schools of therapy have in common a focus on the 'resistances' to healthy, happy wellbeing, but their understand-ing of the nature of these resistances differs: many psychoanalytic models, as I have suggested, are based on the notion that the group members' unconscious stirrings focus on their wish for gratification of their depen-dency needs by the therapist. A psychodrama group leader makes no such assumption. To a psychodramatist, the lack of role flexibility of the 'opaque' leader would be unbearable.

Both systems recognize that group members take up various roles for each other; in the case of psychoanalytic groups, this phenomenon may be understood in terms of displacement, projection, identification, and split-ting of internal objects into parts. The psychodramatic understanding is sometimes similar, in that the 'internal objects' are concretized and acted by auxiliaries. The expression of this understanding, though, is typically psychodramatic, viewing the enactment not so much in terms of pathology as in encouraging the person's desire to expand their role repertoire. Nevertheless, it is fair to say that each therapy frequently works towards the eventual integration of formerly denied, rejected, or sought-after roles within the person.

Psychodrama directors do not so much work to evoke group trans-ference reactions, as to resolve them when they do arise. A 'cure' through the transference is not part of the psychodramatic philosophy, as we have seen in the preceding chapter. The analytic method favours a passive/ interpretative leadership style, in order that fantasy can have free rein, and that thereby the transference neuroses can be brought about. The pyscho-dramatist, on the other hand, tends to be active, giving plenty of 'personal-ity' and behaviour for members to interpret. Psychodramatists tend to adopt a high profile, and put out more cues as to what they are thinking and feeling; the process is more 'transparent'. They might join in the sharing phase of a psychodrama, for example, and reveal details of their own lives. They may use personal experience in the form of an anecdote to warm the group up.

Many of the insights on group transference from analytically based group therapists need to be studied according to the type of social structures that they establish, as we have repeatedly stressed. It seems natural enough that if most interactions in a group are interpreted by the leader in terms of transference, then the group will become preoccupied with transference, thereby yielding more actions to be interpreted. If leaders give few cues as to what they are thinking, it is natural that group members will become preoccupied with what they are thinking. So the cycle goes on, with no way for alternative data to emerge.

A group epistemology depends on several factors: the actions of the therapist, the culture of the group, the particular needs and talents of each member, the personal constructs (including displacements, projections, etc.) that operate towards each member from other members, and the real relationships that are operating towards and from all. Provided therapists do not set themselves up as gods and assume awesome power over people's lives, these other factors will usually be just as important as therapist-centred constructs. When transference material emerges, instead of it having uniform meanings in a predetermined mode of unconscious expression (e.g. Kleinian, Freudian), it has more chance of being appreciated in its own terms, and the spontaneous and creative importance of it can be brought out.

By now it will be obvious that a systemic approach is incompatible with the group-analytic view. Whatever tension the group is experiencing is experienced and 'caused' by the whole group, including the leader. The leader is not outside the system. The group does not exist without the leader, and the leader does not exist without the group. While it is quite possible or even likely that the leader may be part of the 'desired relationship' of the members, it cannot be argued that he or she alone is based in reality (the 'work group') while it is the members who must wander aimlessly in their 'basic-assumption' groups. The group mythology is to some extent a joint production and takes in both fantasized relationships and the reality of the context.

The analytic form of psychological apartheid does not always make for good theory or rewarding practice, and transference-based therapy has a better chance of success, and more theoretical validity, in an individual, rather than a group therapeutic context. Most clinical observations on transference come from those exhibiting a certain style of leadership. Given that one gathers evidence on social behaviour according to the social structures that one sets up, the psychoanalytic observations are not surprising. It is quite reasonable that group members will be dazed, bewildered, fighting, flighting, and joining if the leader is perceived as punitive, withholding, or even 'opaque'. In fact, simply being opaque is sufficient to be seen, with some justice, as punitive and withholding. Causality in human affairs is circular, not linear. If one is lost in the desert, *of course* one looks for someone to lead one out to the promised land. But the desert itself is partly the creation of the therapist. With experience, members might get streetwise, or desertwise, and give up their search for a messiah. This is often, perhaps not without reason, called a 'cure'.

People's 'improvement' in a psychodrama group tends to hinge on the group having a structure that is systems-sound, and within which people are able to develop newness in their interpersonal systems. In a group where people are given scope to develop real or 'telic' relations with each other and with the leader, the leader will of course occupy an important but not necessarily a preoccupying position. Not all members are equally obsessed about their relationship with the leader. Moreno, as a result of sociometric testing of the perceptions of group members about their own status and that of others, found a very great diversity of opinion: some members underestimate their own status and overestimate the status of the therapist and other members of the group. Some do the opposite, and consider themselves as most attractive and acceptable to the therapist or to other members of the group. Some think they are unattractive to the therapist, but attractive to the group members. The degree of accuracy or distortion varies from member to member, and no doubt would also vary over time and according to mood. It is evident from this type of research that not all members are equally obsessed about their relationship with the leader. If leaders set it up so that members become obsessed with them, by interpreting all behaviour in that light, then fairly soon such a dynamic will actually prevail.

The cardinal rule of any analytically oriented therapy is that resistances are dealt with before the transference (to a therapist) can be interpreted. To a psychodramatic group leader, it is theoretically and therapeutically unacceptable that the very character traits of the members (their more or less permanent role constellation) are considered as 'resistance phenomena'. Nor can their member-to-member interactions be regarded simply as disappointed transference reactions, to be worked through prior to interpretation of the transference towards the leader. While it is most important to recognize all social transactions from the group members as expressions of how they construe events, it does not seem helpful to assume that transference to the director is the sole dynamic force behind all group interactions, nor that group interaction is a result of the inhibition of the overt expression of desire for the leader.

The true subject of therapy in a group is the ways in which members construe all people in their lives, including, but not exclusively so, the leader. In one-to-one therapy, therapists working by 'process', rather than strategically, may indeed gradually become the focus of many of the clients' transferred longings and constructs: towards father, mother, siblings, significant others, and the 'powers'. But to suggest that this process in this type of therapy is validation of a theory of transference is to base the theory on very limited evidence. It is like studying the prevalence of homosexuality in the community by taking the male population of a prison as one's sample: although most inmates might practise homosexuality there, the context is all important. Analytic leaders finding abundant evidence for transference in their groups is as little a triumph of evidence as sociologists finding homosexuality in prison and extrapolating homosexuality to the whole society.

In a formally constituted therapy or training group, the leader does take many roles for the group members, which stem from their original social atom, and sometimes it is helpful to explore these. But by concentrating on only the pathological side of this process, the group is continually chastened, reprimanded, and the members gain the impression that they are mad or bad, or more usually, both. Such an assumption increases the dependency dynamic on the group and on the leader. The psychodramatic assumption, that each member is potentially a creative genius, albeit with certain 'resistances' to becoming that, seems a better place to start.

Mixed psychodramatic/here-and-now procedures

A theory of displacement needs to be based on a recognition that the therapist and client, or group, are part of the same system. In a one-to-one setting, the error is to assume that the client 'produces' the transference, rather than it being a joint production of client, therapist, and setting. The 'resolution' of the transference involves the two of them getting out of it; renegotiating their relationship. Similarly in a group: to assume that the designated leader is always the 'therapist' and the members are always the 'clients' is to ignore the fact that the leader and the group are bound together; not merely that the group is bound to the leader. For this reason, any evolution in the group through various stages requires a co-evolution of the leader. The leader's relations with group members change, as well as the group's relations with the leader. If the group is to develop, the leader must also develop. In fact, the group may develop before the leader develops. Once immersed in the progress of the group, the leader is fighting for individuation and belongingness as much as any member, although it is to be hoped that in a therapy group the intensity of the leader's battle will usually be considerably less than that experienced by the members.

Sometimes the leader can become the 'patient' of the group; in any case, the group is acting out from the leader's system, whether that be functional or pathological, or a mix of both, as with most of us. There does not seem to be any way around this. Any member of the group can become a therapist to any other member, as Yalom (1975) consistently argues. Moreno (1959, p. 9) suggests that we must differentiate between the overall 'conductor' of a session — the leader — and the 'therapeutic agents' who are the leader and the group members. He makes three postulates: (a) the group comes first and the therapist is subordinate to it; (b) therapists, before they emerge as therapeutic leader are just another member of the group; and (c) one person is therapeutic agent of the other and one group is therapeutic agent of the other. Statements like these suggest not so much an appealing egalitarianism on Moreno's part — a sort of quirky democracy — as a thoroughly systemic understanding of the therapeutic process.

The psychodramatic method offers several possibilities for dealing with authority-role issues in a group: for example, directors are not role-limited to the 'opaque-therapist' style, forced into giving only group or individual interpretations. They can be themselves more, allowing themselves to be seen by the group, and can be flexible in their methods of working: socio-dramatically, psychodramatically, by the strategic interview, by news of difference, or by encounter. Leader issues are generally less important anyway, as directors actively attempt to build relationships within the group so that transference towards them does not become the over-riding concern in the group. If it does become important, there are ways to deal with it.

One such way is to mix encounter with psychodramatic enactment. The psychodramatic enactment can give depth and range, allowing more imaginative freedom, while the encounter with the director promotes reality-testing. This format, which at first glance looks like attempting to have the best of both worlds, cannot be produced at will. The director, as always, must follow the cues from the protagonist: sometimes these will lead to a full-blown psychodrama that only involves the director at the beginning, as in 'The clockmaker's son' (p. 160); sometimes the relationships are essentially concerned with peers, as in 'The woman who wasn't born' (p. 175); sometimes only encounter will do — the protagonist gives no cues to going anywhere else, and the struggle must be with the director. In the drama of 'The avenging angel', a mixture of procedures was used, quite without premeditation, to work out the relationship between Pauline and the director. The encounter is now briefly described.

The avenging angel

The group concerned is a trainee group in its second year of study. Pauline, the protagonist in this instance, had progressed in her training from a silent, but apparently angry noncontributor to being a leader in a faction that demanded more action, more self-disclosure, more 'gutsy' psychodramas. She was bitter towards other group members for 'slowing things down', for their timidity and half-heartedness. At the same time, she said that she and the other 'good people' in the group could not do any serious work because

of 'the lack of trust in the group'. In the weeks preceding the present incident, Pauline had stepped up her attacks on her enemies, and at the same
time had also managed a major and courageous psychodrama for herself.
She was certainly 'on the move'. Next step, the director.

A few minutes into the general discussion at the beginning of the session,
Pauline said that she wanted to 'sort things out' with the director. The
director agreed to attempt this, already getting the feeling that the issue
might not be so much one of transference as a stage-appropriate part of
Pauline's emerging assertiveness towards the world in general. Pauline
began her drama with the accusation that in the past the director had 'put
her down'. The dialogue taken up here is a few minutes into their interaction.

P: Anyway, I'm equal to you.
D: (Taking a chance) No you're not.
P: (Taken aback) Yes I am. (Becomes thoughtful)
D: You're not my equal in any way.
P: Well, I'm equal as a person; I might not be equal in skills and in
      learning, but I'm equal as a person.

The director is now in a quandary. He realizes that Pauline has a chance of
learning new roles in this defiance-based mode of working out her dependency and anger towards the director and hopefully to other intimidating
people in her life. At the same time, it does seem a bit 'over the top' to tell
Pauline that she is not his equal as a person. Should he continue? Will the
dispute become simply a childish fight? He fantasizes punishment from the
group and judgement from all the gods of humanistic psychology and
modern literature. He decides to go on:

D: No, not even that is true.
P: (Momentarily confused and crushed) Well, I want to be.
D: (Heart in mouth) But you're not.
P: I am equal with you as a person. I feel like a child with you; I hate it.
D: Choose someone from the group to be that child. (Pauline does so)
      Now reverse roles, and become this childlike person.

Pauline begins a dialogue with an older, more mature person in whom it is
obviously safe to confide, and with whom the boundaries can be explored.

P: (As child) I feel little when I get too close. I feel frightened that I'll
      cross some boundaries that I'm not allowed to cross. I don't know
      what they are. (Angrily) I don't care what they are! (Reflectively) But
      I want to know what they are.

The older 'Pauline' has supported her to this point, and then suggests that both of them can ask the director what the boundaries are. They re-merge into one person, and now Pauline confronts the director once more about the boundaries between the two of them.

The question of equality is now irrelevant and well in the past; a 'real' encounter seems about to take place with Pauline operating in a new role, for which 'resolute clarifier' might be a good title. The encounter is valuable for its own sake (to clear the air), and also because it becomes the role test for the new role that Pauline has learnt: can she maintain her role of resolute clarifier with this frightening person? It is difficult and painful for Pauline to sort out the partly transference, partly real wishes that she has for the director. It is difficult and painful for the director to say that he does not reciprocate her desires. The interaction can be labelled an 'encounter' rather than a hierarchical therapeutic interaction in that the director attempted to respond as far as possible 'as a person'.

To have managed the interaction as a therapist might have entailed further psychodramatic interaction with Pauline's family-of-origin, or further teasing out of what Pauline's feelings were and of whom they reminded her, or circular questioning concerning reactions to her position in the group among the other member-siblings, or telling Pauline that a relationship could not be countenanced because of their respective positions as director and group member. All these methods are legitimate, and need to be used from time to time. But somehow a tripartite way of working seemed advisable in this instance: the emergence of the transference roles and provocation on the part of the director to expand them; the brief psychodramatic development allowing two polarized roles to develop fully and then to integrate; and the final role-test/encounter with the director dropping as many of his 'wise therapist' or 'unattainable god' roles as possible, and facing Pauline with his own strengths, frailties, and attitudes.

At the end of the encounter the group seemed relaxed and relieved, which is usually indicative that the enactment has been adequately cathartic and is not carrying an unnecessary load of 'unfinished business'. Such an atmosphere also suggests that they had been able to manage the role transitions that the director had made, as well as those by Pauline.

In the processing session the following week, Pauline was questioned on her thinking and activities during the week. She claimed that she felt 'free, adult, and not confused'. 'Being little', she said, 'is confusing. I never know what expectations there are.' Her feelings of being 'grown-up' had generalized during the week, and did not apply simply to the director. This result suggests that the transference to the director is more in the nature of a test case — a measuring stick for autonomy.

P: I feel strong today. It's a lot to do with my conflicts with men.
D: What sort of men?

P: *With all men.*
D: *What difference does it make to you when you feel like that?*
P: *I feel powerful. I'm in charge. It's my life.*
D: *With whom did those feelings manifest themselves in the past week? (Etc.) How were you able to make those changes? (Etc.) The director continues with strategic questioning.*

In the processing section, the director is going through the 'improvement routine', making sure that the differences become information for Pauline — that is, that the differences make a difference. The questions concern more interactions in her social atom than her 'introspective self', so that the framework is more systemic. The director questioned Pauline around the issues of who first noticed the differences in her social atom, and the changes other people had to make now that she was different. He asked questions along the lines of whether the 'old' Pauline or the 'new' Pauline suited her sort of person best, and so on, thus creating news of difference by means of double description. As we are concentrating here on the process of the drama itself, especially as it relates to transference processes, however, we need not concern ourselves so much with follow-up at this stage — the general structure has been covered in Chapter 4.

It is unlikely that any of the three segments of the session, taken on their own, would have been adequate to effect the change in Pauline. The provocative first section was nearly enough to bring Pauline out of her alternatively avoiding and approaching disposition towards the director. Although it provoked her to a defiant assertion of equality, that assertion was not a thorough one. It was shaky, and because still defiant, not adequately integrated.

The second phase of psychodramatic interaction with the self that was 'little' actually strengthened her ability to be nurtured and supported without threat. In turn, as the role-reversed 'big' person nurturing her smaller self, she could learn nurturing and supportive roles, and could eventually forgive herself for her dependency. The supportive and childlike roles then linked to form an adequate, spontaneous person well able to deal with conflict, to seek clarity, to assert herself without needing to be defiant, and to be open to the other person. These roles she brought to the encounter with the director. For his own part, Duane had to call up adequate roles as 'a person' to meet Pauline as fully as he could without giving in to the far easier repertoire of 'wise therapist' and 'powerful leader' roles. The third stage — encounter, was not simply a role test, therefore, but also served to maintain the integrity of the relationship.

Use of self by the director — transactional resolutions

Finally, difficulties in perception between the leader and the members of a group (transference and countertransference) can sometimes be managed without 'technique', as it were. Yalom (1975) suggests two major ways of transference resolution that do not rely on obscurantist psychodynamic interpretations. The first is consensual validation, where the members check out their interpretations of the therapist with each other and arrive after a time at a 'reality-based' view, where each person's viewpoint is modified by the views of others. Yalom's second procedure is that of increased therapist 'transparency'. It is to this latter procedure that we now turn, it being a particularly Morenian solution.

'Transparent' directors deal with their groups as real persons in the here-and-now. They share their feelings; they acknowledge or refute feelings attributed to them; they demonstrate respect for feedback, and look to their own shortcomings. Thus the process between therapist and member is not very different from the one that the therapist encourages the members to have with each other. 'After all', says Yalom, 'the therapist has no monopoly on authority, dominance, sagacity, or aloofness, and many of the members work out their conflicts in these areas not with the therapist (or *only* with the therapist), but with other members who have these attributes' (Yalom, 1975, p. 204).

So here is another role for the psychodrama director, and a frightening one at that: the role of 'person'. In a transparency/transference interaction the member is minimally a 'member', the leader is minimally a 'leader'. Although leaders should be terribly good at being just people, in fact often they are not, and have to fumble around and do things wrong, just like anyone else. The question 'Do you love me?' is one that can be painfully threatening to a therapist, or indeed to anyone whose love is sought but not especially returned. Even worse, says Yalom (1975, p. 213), is the group's question to the leader: 'How much do you love each of us?'

This question, and its cynical answer, was posed, it will be remembered, by Petra, the 'woman who wasn't born', when in role as Duane the director. In the long run, as we saw, the question was not as important as it had first seemed, and the drama ran back to other family matters that became of more importance than Petra's relationship with Duane. But did Duane pull the oldest therapeutic trick on Petra, and get himself out of an embarrassing scrape? It is hard to say, and the interaction at large points up the difficulties of working in a nonstrategic fashion. Therapy creates therapy, unless the problem is the focus. Duane was known for his flamboyant and overintimate style, which may have accentuated Petra's problems in the first place.

People who lack a sufficiently reliable parenting figure in their original social atom with whom to relate and identify tend to construe events in an extremely bi-polar fashion: they 'defend themselves psychologically by splitting' — to use terminology from another school. Such group members are the most vulnerable to alternating idealization and devaluing of the director; there are few therapists who have not been at the receiving end of these alternating currents of love and hatred, apparently inexplicable in their vagaries. People experiencing the extremes of these feelings do seem to need someone who stays calm in the midst of their fears, even though they have become a monster, even though they want to destroy the world. At this stage they need a mature and cohesive parent figure who is in tune with their changing needs: that is, they need a mirror or double.

Sometimes the group itself can act as a mirror or double: it can serve as a 'transitional object', by which the fantasy relations with some high-up person, such as the director, are mitigated by the experience of real relationships with real people. It is as if a member is somehow able to make other group members parts of him or herself, and use the other members as extensions of their own ego functions. Experimentation is allowed in this special setting. The person's connection with the leader is still strong, but there may be less need to submerge one's personality to please the therapist; after all, there are other fish to fry. Members may also experience less fear of being engulfed by the therapist than in a one-to-one encounter. Other people take on roles of early authority figures, so that the here-and-now interaction with the director becomes more intelligible. Consider the following fairly typical psychodramatic interaction with a client who has underdeveloped self-nurturing roles:

D: *When you were a little girl did you have any toys you really enjoyed?*
P: *No.*
D: *Any pictures you really liked?*
P: *A book of fairy tales.*
D: *Go and get it. Does your mummy read to you?*
P: *Yes.*
D: *Whereabouts? In bed?*
P: *Yes.*
D: *Is anyone else there?*
P: *My brother.*
D: *How about you choose someone to be your mother and someone to be your brother.*

This interaction is, of course, standard procedure. The 'internal objects' become living auxiliaries. The director slips back as the 'transference object' and group members fill up the roles occupied by historical figures from the protagonist's past. Protagonists have the chance to role-reverse as idealized or dreaded parents, and to experience those states from the receiving end of the adulation or hatred.

As well as this factor (the director consistently acting as the producer of the protagonist's fantasies, rather than as the object of them) operating to make the transference processes more diffuse, there is the consistency of non-psychodramatic interaction with other group members through group work itself: exercises in pairs and threes, etc. Interactions in the group become diffuse and multilayered. Support is seen as available from the peer level as much as from the authority level. Because relationships with the other group members have to be worked out outside the relationship with the authority figure, some sort of consensual validation on the 'reality' of the therapist can be reached with the other group members.

Let us not get too idealistic here. This fortunate situation where the intense preoccupation with the leader is defused by the various functions of the group does not always prevail. For some members, the director is and remains utterly central, and they look only to him or her. Not even this phenomenon validates the omnibus theory of group transference, since the leader is only important in this way to a few members, not all. Even then, it may not be *the* leader that is important, but *this* leader. With another, they may not care so much. We are back to the tele, the particularity of interaction.

In the instances where a leader is subject of particular intense feelings by a member, it may be better to tackle the intensity and apparent distortions head-on, person-to-person. Sometimes there is no ethical choice. A group member who is very angry with the director, for instance, may not agree to be diverted to the alleged 'origins' of the interaction, such as in a family-of-origin psychodrama. Such persons may, quite rightly, suspect a trick, or a power-play, or a subtle way of invalidating their perceptions and making out that they, rather than the interaction, are pathological and need to be examined. In such denials, madness lies for both parties, although only one (the group member) may appear to be mad. To another member, the suggestion that they 'work' on the interaction as a problem may fall on deaf ears. He or she might habitually and in general suspect trickery wherever he or she goes, and will be suspicious of being in such a 'powerless' position as that occupied by a protagonist. To be a protagonist in this instance is tantamount to an admission that their construct system is invalidated, and that they are alone in their view of reality; not a nice position for anyone to be in, and calling for great tact and gentleness on the part of the leader.

In some of these instances, nothing less than an encounter with the therapist will suffice. By encountering the therapist, both parties attempt to deal with the real or tele relationship at the same time as the transference relationship, and try to speak frankly about any displacements they may have from other relationships. The interaction can generate much heat, while the therapist and member attempt to contact and disclose their felt reactions to each other. This meeting can be difficult for them both, as indeed such meetings are even outside a group setting. To add to the embarrassment of it all, about a dozen people are listening to the leader's faltering attempts at humanity.

Mick, the member, might say to Dot, the director: 'I am attracted to you.' Dot might reply: 'I am/am not attracted to you.' This type of reply, of course, has a very different effect on Mick from 'What does it mean for you to have the courage to say you are attracted to me?' The latter reply might make Mick even more attracted, if it was Dot's air of psychological omni-science that attracted him in the first place. Or Mick might be very angry with Dot and give her a list of her crimes, to which she might say heatedly, 'That doesn't belong here, to me. Don't do that to me.' This reply once more is very different from an empathic response such as 'So you feel I am a liar and a cheat, and it makes you angry that I ...', which may make Mick more confused than ever. He *feels* so mad at her, yet she *seems* so kind and wise.

The director attempts to act in the dual roles of 'equal human being' and 'therapist'. The latter role is inescapable: even by her self-disclosure she is trying to effect a clean-up of relationships in the group. That is her job. She models responsiveness to her inner truth in the relationship; she is prepared to be silly and wrong; to make mistakes; to stumble over her words and even to eat them; to show her irrationality, vanity, or fear. She also demon-strates support and acceptance of the members by the giving of herself. This, too, is part of her job. Even when she is most 'human', she still acts strategically, however. She is there as leader of the group, and nothing can do away with that structure — it is, after all, the basis of her relationships with those people, and without it they would not even be acquainted.

Dot's way of working with a member is not indicated in every case, as we have seen. Several examples have been given ('The woman who wasn't born', 'The avenging angel') where the director becomes the focus of the person's construing from past interactions, but then quickly steps out of the way of direct encounter, and into a psychodrama. At other times, the constructs truly seem to be about the director as such, and the system they have set up with group members. At these times, the interactions are best dealt with by using themselves fully, and translating the transference relationship into a tele relationship, even if that relationship, because of the frailty of us all, is bleak and unglamorous. We are, as King Lear found to his great despair, but poor forked animals.

Chapter eleven

Psychodramatic applications in family therapy

Let me take you to a place of relative safety

Spock, *Star Trek*

Introduction

So far we have been describing clinical and revelatory functions of psychodrama where the protagonist enacts a family-of-origin psychodrama in the midst of a group of strangers. Even though this form of therapy may be more interpersonal, or even systemic, than many other forms of individual therapy, the real-life members of the protagonist's system are nevertheless not there to object, propose, modify, or cry 'unfair!' instead, protagonists are at centre stage, and command the action in accord with how they see it. Their own phenomenology becomes the 'truth' in the system that is portrayed. This is why, one assumes, the Morenos instructed trainees to use encounter methods when the actual participants of a protagonist's drama were present (Guldner, 1982, p. 47). They acted out perceptions of the single protagonist and took their cues, not by copying a consensual reality that others (e.g. the rest of the family) would attest to, 'but by concretizing the feelings and perceptions that are true for that protagonist. The aim is concretization and reduction of conflict in and handling of the phenomenal reality of the protagonist' (Seeman and Weiner, 1985, p. 146).

What changes must be made when the members of the social atom are actually present? In the first place, the production techniques and therapeutic requirements when a whole family attends therapy present a markedly different set of challenges and limitations to a director. In its traditional form, psychodrama makes the phenomenal reality of the protagonist vivid, concrete, and conscious. This reality of the protagonist is experienced as being in the present, whether or not the incidents being enacted took place in the past, present, or in the anticipated future. 'Enactment' in family therapy, on the other hand, reveals patterns that are going on in the present, though they may have their roots in the past. In family therapy, the 'we', the family construct system, is more evidently in charge of each individual, rather than the individual being at the centre of the 'we'. An individual's sense of being at the centre is modified by other individuals who have a similar belief. The phenomenological truth of any particular member does not take precedence when everyone is there.

For family therapists, truth is most importantly the meaning underlying the interactional patterns that they observe. The nature of the 'audience' has changed, too, from that audience of relative strangers who look on empathically while the protagonist 'works', to actual family members who have a vital interest in the process and outcome of the drama. The interests of closely related people can be in serious conflict, as we all know from our own families. In individual therapy, this factor can be ignored, to a degree. But in a system such as a family, the question for the therapist becomes 'how to be biased towards everybody?' The answer, of course, is by circularity. At least with the whole family present, true circuits of interaction may be evoked, rather than the pseudocircularity necessary when there is only one protagonist who indicates in the role reversal what the other members would say and do.

Even persons who apparently 'control' the family by their symptoms are themselves controlled by forces within the family so that they have those symptoms. Where does it all begin? Who can be satisfactorily blamed? In the context of the whole family's presence, an extended psychodrama with an individual protagonist, which involves the rest of the family as auxiliaries is clearly out of the question. Quite apart from the production difficulties involved, such a drama is theoretically and practically unsound, and can lead to chaos in family structure. When the whole system is present, each member of that system is the protagonist. Therefore individual psychodramatic interventions, when made, need to be brief and rapidly to relate back to the whole family.

An exception to this proviso may occur when multiple families are present (Laqueur, 1980). A single protagonist works on the group theme, choosing members of other families to represent members of his or her own family (Guldner, 1982). By not being involved directly in a family member's drama, other members of the family could see or have 'mirrored' their process, Guldner reports. The 'seeing from a distance' enables them better to recognize the structures of the system and to follow prescriptions given to the psychodramatic family that they have witnessed.

The aforementioned restrictions may seem very limiting indeed. As a consolation for the discouraged reader, it could be said that the power and intensity engendered by a full psychodrama is quite unnecessary when all the family members are present. There is intensity enough in their very presence all together. In such a setting, the slightest action method, if well conceived and well timed, can have dramatic and far-reaching effects. Strategic therapy is superficially quiet; but not so on the 'inside'. Almost any interaction takes on a significance that is commensurate with the importance of the members to each other. Family members are likely to have intense affective experiences in the waiting room, the therapy room, on the drive home, and in the ensuing period before the next appointment.

It would seem from the aforementioned, that action methods, rather than any kind of full psychodrama, are indicated. Even the use of action methods, however, is as an adjunctive technique when the whole family is present. Action methods have not developed a theory and practice of their own where they could claim to be a family therapy superior to the verbal forms that now dominate western therapeutic family practice. Often these verbal methods are quite satisfactory on their own. Action methods do have immense potential for illustration of difference and for analogical interventions, however, that make them powerful aids to verbal methods in working with whole family groups.

The increased freedom and spontaneity within action therapy enhances opportunities for the emergence of new symbols and relations within the family system. An enactment has the power to blur distinctions between actuality and possibility. Even if the enactment is defined by the family as not being real, it is nevertheless so absorbing that the moments of action are more intensive and significant than most moments of everyday life. Thus the distinction between actuality and possibility becomes less obvious, and the family is thereby freed from some of the restraints on change. Their networks of presupposition are changed, to a degree, by the method itself: 'this is happening, so it can happen'. What then, are some of the benefits of action methods with a whole family?

Advantages of action methods

(1) Enactment changes the mode in which the family commonly expresses itself. Subtle emotion, for example, can be expressed physically and openly, rather than through covert body language and speech. If a family is overly verbal and intellectual, members have the opportunity to change from a verbal mode, and therefore thinking-style, into pictures and action. Imagination and spontaneity take on concrete form, and recursively feed into the family's concept of itself.

(2) Action methods can be used as analogic representations of differences in the family. The method is capable of illustrating intangibles more clearly than most other techniques. The subtleties of emotional distance, for example, can be expressed on a line, and so can most comparisons, such as first-to-notice/last-to-notice the symptom, or most/least pleased with the identified patient's improvement.

(3) It dramatizes roles and role perceptions. Members observe what each other do, how it is perceived, and how their roles are reinforced (Sherman and Fredman, 1986). The transactional nature of family roles, for example, becomes clearer: someone cannot be

197

helpless unless someone else is prepared to be helpful. The family and the therapist, therefore, have the advantage of action diagnosis, which may be more useful than the diagnostic methods they have hitherto employed.

(4) It can re-create the past and bring it vividly into the here-and-now, thus allowing re-editing of family myths. Similarly, it can bring into the therapy room family who are dead or absent, and around whom are invisible loyalties that profoundly affect the working of the family in the here-and-now. An absent father or a deceased grandmother, for example, can be evoked and reacted to.

(5) It can be used to enact fantasies of the future, and can help 'contaminate' those fantasies when they are dysfunctional, such as suicidal fantasies. The unanticipated consequences of an action such as suicide can be made real, and can be developed in the family context.

(6) The transactional and systemic meanings of family behaviour can be uncovered and elucidated by role analysis. Understanding the interpersonal context of a role, such as the role of juvenile firesetter and the effects of that role on the rest of the family, can lead to fruitful hypotheses about family functioning.

(7) The family is enabled to act out rituals that may concern rites of passage, or may be ways of marking differences, thereby enabling the family to make distinctions.

Subsequent sections of this chapter will elaborate some uses of these seven modes, though by no means exhausting their possibilities.

Establishing enactment

Establishing enactment as one of the therapeutic procedures that will be used in therapy suggests to the family a multilayered symbolic representation of their current state. The content of the family's problem definition is only a small part of the total mapping of that system; action methods tend to focus on the unreported aspects of their lives, and conveys back to them the rich complexity that ordinary interactions acquire within the therapy frame. Thus the literality of family definitions is challenged by the symbolic diversity of alternative mappings (Kobak and Waters, 1984). The symbolic potential of the therapy frame is developed as the family comes to tolerate the divergent nature of the therapist's perception and understanding of the family. The family becomes aware that their initial view of the problem is subject to change and revision. They may even glimpse alternative ways of being together, but this glimpse is only useful if they are also allowed to see the ways in which they *are* already together.

In establishing an action-method sequence, the therapist uses the freedom made available by the symbolic setting to react on the basis of imaginative alternatives to what the clients are presenting. Their own view might be rather restrictive and fearful. By action, one can establish a setting that the family does not anticipate; the therapy itself becomes the first of many ways of being out of the rut. The therapist aims for divergence from the expected and understood rules that govern the family's view of reality. The family is led to the less certain and less predictable territory that will involve them in new definitions of themselves. As anything might happen, an atmosphere of risk, excitement, and uncertainty builds up. Just as therapy itself is betwixt and between normal day-to-day social states, the use of action methods increases this sense of 'liminality' (Turner, 1969), the sense of potency and potentiality, of experiment and play.

The process of enacting a family myth allows the myth creator to have a more explicit picture of how their fantasies would be if enacted, and also allows the passive members (those who are involved in the other person's myths but do not know it) to see the fantasies in which they are wittingly or unwittingly involved. Only seldom is the goal of enactment in family therapy to achieve a catharsis on the part of the protagonist. Enactment, however, can be most useful as a way of helping a single individual or an entire family to define their own system more clearly. In this case, it is usually a fantasy system that is being defined. The action needs to be kept relatively brief, otherwise its systemic meaning will become obscured, and the session will become individual therapy for one member. Extended therapy with one person could foster the systemically dangerous notion that one member is 'to blame', or that if when that member 'got better' the rest of the family would no longer have any problems. Therapists themselves can lose therapeutic neutrality through excessive concentration of time and energy focus on one member. The family itself is already doing that.

When therapists re-edit the family mythology by means of drama, they elicit the fine tracery of presuppositions, personal constructs, and expectations that make up the members' 'map of the world'. These maps establish the rules for information about occurrences or persons within the family. They operate largely unconsciously, and limit the amount of information that can be received, and therefore the courses of action that can be taken. All we know is based on perception. We *recognize* what we know, however, by making patterns. These patterns, in turn, restrain us from further perception unless they are given the OK, as it were, by an existing pattern.

Sometimes the mythology of the whole family — the family-construct system (Proctor, 1985) — can be dramatized. But as each member tends to have a different version of 'our family', dramatic chaos can result as individuals chime in with their notion of how things should be. The multiple perspective is obvious and inevitable: each person takes up different roles for every other person with whom they are in relationship. Thus every child sees the mother or father differently from the way other children in the family see them; and certainly the child's version is different from the way mother 'sees' herself and father, and father views himself and mother.

How a person is viewed depends partly on the outer constructs of the role (father, mother, son, daughter), which are partly socially and partly culturally determined (Duhl, 1983). The second set of elements is the personal and inner construing of the person: how they have decided to construe these socially and culturally designated roles. The third set of elements is the actual interactions that build their own network of present positions and stem from that network. In such instances, the director needs to be the conductor and central organizer of the images. When there is no agreed-upon central myth, it is allowable for one member to set up his or her version of reality, and allow the others time to comment afterwards.

The boy in the grave

Alan is a suicidal boy, aged 14, who had made three attempts prior to his referral by the school counsellor. The incident to be described was only one part, albeit a useful one, of Alan's successful treatment, which involves a brief psychodramatic enactment of the fantasy of one family member, in this case Alan himself. Alan and his family were seen by a therapeutic team of four persons, with one person conducting the direct therapy, and the others acting as consultants behind a one-way screen. Present at this third session (of six) were Alan's sister Leanne, his older brother Dan, his mother, and his stepfather, Lyall.

Aldridge and Rossiter (1983) have detailed some effective questions to ask suicidal people. For example, to describe what sort of flowers they would like at their funeral; what they would be wearing when they died; where they would be buried; who would attend the funeral; what clothes the mourners would be wearing; and so on.

Attempts were made to build up Alan's picture of what other people's lives would be like after his death, using the types of questions suggested by Aldridge and Rossiter. The questions fell flat, however, as Alan had little idea of the details of death. His difficulty in warming up to the role of dead person was perhaps indicative that his attempts at suicide and his suicidal ideation were more a process than an actively imagined outcome. It was as if he imagined the process of dying, but not the 'process' of being dead. He was not able to conjure any clear or detailed images of the funeral parlour or the cemetery. Nevertheless, he was a serious suicide risk, and had escalated the severity of his previous attempts.

Naturally, no attempt was made to act out the actual suicide, as such an enactment can be a form of rehearsal, rather gratifying and quite dangerous. It is important not to 'energize' the person too much or too quickly, as the energy can be used in the service of the angry and helpless roles, giving a manic burst that may enable people to end their lives. The same principle applies to homicidal ideation.

Nor does it make sense systemically or interpersonally to enact the actual event — the important systemic implications come in just before or just after. The actual moment of death is not systemically interesting, whereas even a second before or afterwards is. An appropriate time and scene must therefore be found after the action, even if it is straight afterwards, as their helpless body hits the floor, or an hour afterwards, when they are found. That is the stage when other people undeniably come into the act. Who finds the body? Who is most/least affected?

Obviously, role reversal with relevant persons from the family is called for. By means of role reversal, it is also possible to enact scenarios of how the plot would have ended if the person did not suicide. Role reversals can be made at points in the near, mid, and distant future. The suicidee thinks of the act not only as an escape but as a release. (It is also dyadic, a form of murder of someone else, as we shall later elaborate.) In the escape/release dialectic, it is a movement not only from, but towards, in some cases. This is especially true if severe physical suffering is causing the person to think of killing themselves.

With some clients (not Alan) it may be appropriate and safe to explore the release aspect of their suicide. Such an exploration invokes the client's creativity, and is therefore a generally helpful process anyway. They may explore ways within the social atom to achieve the release that they seek. If the social atom is such a desperate failure, there may be ways 'within' the person for attaining the release that they want — for example, inner peace.

When asked whether he would be cremated or buried, Alan was again stumped, but he replied, 'Buried, I suppose'. He did not know any cemeteries, so his family was asked in which cemetery the burial would most likely take place. The actual interment was not acted out, since once again, Alan had no idea of this process. So he was requested to lie in his grave and place his family around him, standing at the edge of the graveside. He was then asked to detail the amount of 'upsetness' of each member at this time, and to rank them in terms of upsetness and ruined life.

The therapeutic team subscribed to the theory of suicide-as-murder (Everstine and Everstine, 1983) in which the suicidal person actually attempts to kill another person by killing themselves. Their angry revenge is anticipated as sweet because while their own death is swift, the other person's goes on for the rest of their lifetime. Suicide, in the interactional view, is not the result of increased depression to the extent that the person can no longer bear to live, but actually a desire to hurt someone else with whom the suicidal person is extremely angry. The suicidal ideation needs to be dealt with respectfully as part of the client's warm-up, and their suicidal roles considered as part of their total role structure, at least at that time. Everstine and Everstine maintain that from the premiss that suicide occurs in an interactional context, three other premisses follow:

1. Suicide is an event which is intended to send a message from one person to another.
2. There is a specific person who is expected to receive the message of suicide; for that person, above all, the suicidal act is performed.
3. The primary content of the message being conveyed is anger.

(Everstine and Everstine, 1983)

Alan nominated his mother as the person 'most upset' on the day of his burial, and outlined with great precision how upset the other family members would be then. The time scale was then shifted to three months later. When asked how people would be feeling in three months' time, Alan reported the picture to be 'pretty much the same', with the family still in shock and the mother most upset of all.

The time scale was shifted again. At a year later, his older brother was 'over it' and his twin sister was affected, but recovering. His stepfather was now living as if nothing had ever happened. Mother was still massively affected, however. Even when the scene was shifted to ten years further on, mother's life was still more-or-less ruined, although the others were now living with hardly more than an occasional thought of him.

Alan's enactment also provided scope for a series of questions to the rest of the family about the impact his death would have on them. When the family had all sat down again, they were asked whether they agreed or disagreed with his assessment. Mostly their opinions about the effect of his death concurred with Alan's; mother confirmed that she would be 'deeply affected' throughout most if not all of her life if Alan killed himself. Therefore Alan's fantasy was not actually unrealistic about the effect on his probable main 'target' — mother — though it was highly unrealistic about the effect on the other important person — himself. It seemed clear that when he thought of killing himself he did not consider actually dying. He was vividly accurate about the effect on other people, but had almost no fantasy of being actually dead. He knew almost nothing about the trappings of death.

These themes were kept alive during the remaining sessions, and tripartite interventions were made from the team about Alan successfully killing himself, his making further unsuccessful attempts, or his ability to find other and more creative ways of showing his mother how angry he was with her. The enactment affected not only him but also his mother, of course, who became less bound up with his displeasure and her responsibility for it. She announced in the subsequent sessions that she was taking a firmer stand with Alan, and that while she would be tremendously grieved if he were to kill himself, she would not herself die. On a year's follow-up, Alan has made no more attempts.

Enactment of fantasies

Dysfunctional families generally have rigidly assigned roles and have lost their capacity for creative games. If the actual image is part of the dysfunctional system, such as suicide, the therapeutic enactment can help 'contaminate' the image. Whitaker (in Held and Bellows, 1983) remarks that 'contamination' involves an exploration of the fantasy pursued in detail in order to destroy it as a worthwhile solution. One might wish quite strongly to contaminate a suicidal fantasy, but not every fantasy is destructive and therefore to be contaminated. When a family's dilemma is presented to them in the form of drama, they have the chance to alter the script, should they so desire, or to keep it the same.

Andolfi and Angelo (1982) conceive of family therapy itself as such a drama: the therapist enters the family system in the role of a theatrical director who revises a play — the family drama itself. Andolfi and Angelo take a more severe and confrontational line than most writers on the family's motivation for seeking help. The therapist, they suggest, is invited to accept the family's paradoxical request to help them change without changing — they want even greater stability so that interactional patterns and individual functions become progressively more rigid. Although the request for help is conceived in dialectical terms by Andolfi and Angelo, the authors do seem to weight the no-change pole of it. By entering the family drama, therapists hope to reinterpret the meanings that are played out.

It may not be necessary to go quite this far. Therapists can prompt a re-write of the family script by their own experimental behaviour: double description, directing enactments, interrupting and reframing interactions, or exaggerating or ignoring particular items. By amplifying the various roles and functions of the family players, and by asking appropriate questions and devising appropriate interventions, the family's own version of its script becomes clear to it, thereby leaving room to change.

The interventions amplify, but do not come down on one side of the dilemma between staying the same and being different. It is clear to the family that the therapist will look at old problems through new lenses. In the drama itself, the individual family actors evoke roles that may have been grossly underdeveloped because of their strong emotional implications. But because of the safety brackets around the enactment (it is only drama, after all, and it takes place within a therapist's room), and because of the therapist's own attitude towards spontaneity, painful themes and embarrassing roles can be played out with less of an expectation of grinding through the ugliness yet again. The family becomes curious about how their actions will be seen; how they will see them, even. The poor identified patient, the bad or mad person, begins to hope that he or she may not be seen as wrong this time around.

In re-editing a family drama, therapists also risk exposure, since they are directly utilizing their own fantasies in relation with the family. Elements supplied by the family are reintroduced in the form of images, actions, or scenes that stimulate the family members to offer new information or to make further associations in a circular process. The therapeutic relationship becomes intensified as the critical elements of the family's script are brought together and reorganized by the therapist's suggestion (Sherman and Fredman, 1986). The therapist emphasizes some elements that have previously gone unnoticed, and relegates to the background others that have been overemphasized. Sometimes the enactment can be quite light-hearted.

The example of 'The boy in the grave' and the one that follows illustrate the usefulness of drama as a form of play. The essence of drama, as against actions that take place in real life, is that the activities occur in a novel setting, and do not result in the usual consequences — for example, Alan's actual death by suicide. The therapist and the family experience a widened sense of freedom to experiment with new possibilities. Roles can be revised, dominance hierarchies overturned, and rules of interaction broken. Behaviours that bring special excitement or meaning can be repeated, and hidden desires or fears can be concretized. Enactment within a session can lift the sense of immutability with which the family is burdened, as we shall see.

The zealous father

Mr Swingly was the divorced father of two girls aged 15 and 12. Freda, aged 15, was the identified patient, who had been referred for family therapy because she was constantly spending whole nights away from home without her parents' knowledge of her whereabouts, and because she would go to school in uniform with a change of clothes in her school case, visit the lavatories, and be out of school in street clothes before 9 a.m.

Mr Swingly was born and raised in Germany, and had fought as a volunteer on the Russian front. At the end of the war, aged 16, he made his way on his own from Russia to southern Germany, and had had a hard life there until he emigrated at the age of 25. He had very strict notions of bringing up children, and even though divorced for ten years, still wore his wedding ring. He said that if he found any boys fooling around with his daughter, 'they would not go home on a stretcher, they would go home in buckets'.

The team hypothesized that at least one of the effects of Freda's absconding was to bring mother and father together, as they telephoned police, drove through the suburbs at night looking for her, and so on. Mrs Swingly lives three doors down from her former husband in the same street. Mr Swingly visits Mrs Swingly every night, even though Mrs Swingly has a live-in lover.

The girls described living in Mr Swingly's household, if he had his way, as 'repressive and old-fashioned'. Mr Swingly was asked how he would like his daughters to be. He replied that he wished that they could have been brought up by his grandmother in the 1930s. He would like them to cook, sew, sing, and have all the domestic arts.

He sits in a chair; the girls pretend to bring him soup and special cake; they sit at his knee while he pats their heads and calls them his beautiful daughters. The girls, in their New-Wave haircuts and modern dress, enjoy the enactment — being fully what he wants them to be, for once. Mr Swingly also enjoys it, but becomes more aware of the fantasy element in his wishes for them. The scene acts as a simple example of concretization of an image so that the family members can see one of the central myths that has been running the family dynamic for some time. Its mere presentation was sufficient for this purpose.

It would not be accurate to say that in this case, the outcome of which was still positive at a two-year follow-up, the enactment clinched the therapeutic outcome. It was a useful way, however, of providing a definition of something that was actually happening, at least on the fantasy level. It led to a series of questions about how Mr Swingly could console himself for the disappointments of his daughters growing up, as well as reward himself for his pride; what he would need to say to himself if things did not turn out (as they most assuredly would not) as he had hoped, and so on. Once more, the dramatization is an adjunctive technique, rather than the mainstay of therapy.

The separation of the play or drama element from real life produces, as we have seen, the possibility of transformation and disruption of rigid structures and apparently immutable patterns of thought. This is because the ordinary consequences of a sequence are not realized. Although the separation from ordinary reality establishes the potential for action methods to be different from other interactions, however, the task is by no means finished. The actuality of differentness and spontaneity in working things out is still to come. This transition can be problematic, as there is a tendency to move from anti-structure towards an even more solid, known equilibrium. The possibility of spontaneity has to be maintained in the follow-up to the sculpture or enactment. The play-by-action inevitably ends, but the play-by-words, the dialectical reformulation, must go on until it is part of the family's own solution.

Role reversal and role analysis

By means of psychodramatic role reversal, protagonists see reality through the eyes of the other person, and experience the other's role emotionally and physically. In enacting the role, and speaking back to themselves, protagonists enter a complex psychological area: they suggest the way they view the other person, the way they view themselves, the way they view the other person's view of themselves, and they implicitly comment on the relationship as a whole. When an individual becomes part of a whole, the other parts of the whole are seen as affecting the behaviour and experience of all the parts. Being an action method, role reversal allows clients to think, feel, and act out interactions rather than merely talking about them.

In the context of a classical psychodrama, since their viewpoint is the only one being enacted, protagonists may or may not gain insight into the viewpoint of another. Where role reversal takes place in a real, social-atom context, such as a family, and two parties actually present are involved in the reversal, the chance of adopting genuinely different viewpoints is greater, since the other person is there, ready to say, 'That's not what I think' or 'That's not it at all'. The results of role reversal with the other person present should be a greater understanding of and empathy towards the other person, and how one's own behaviour affects that person. But in fact, this result often does not eventuate, and sometimes leads instead to more, rather than less, deeply entrenched positions. How can this be?

In the first place, role reversal that goes against structure or generational holons — parent/child, for example, probably defeats its purpose from the outset. Perhaps this is because in some way a child ought not to know what it is like to be her parent, and the parent somehow ought not to know what it is like to be the child of themselves. In the second place, live role reversal seems to imply that the way out of a dilemma or conflict is 'more communication'; but more communication, family-therapy-as-encounter, is not a method favoured by contemporary systemic theorists. This is not to argue that 'communication' in a family is bad — far from it. But as a form of therapy it has its limitations, and is not used as a method of choice by strategic, systemic, or even structural family therapists.

Third, role reversal can further polarize people's positions — they hold their own view even more strongly now, but they do so in a somewhat guilty fashion. One might role-reverse with an African famine victim, feel the torment, and then go back to one's own role simply thankful that one is oneself and not them. Even with very skilful warming up and interviewing-in-role, person A finds it very hard to get into the role of person B when they know that person B, in turn, is going to be them. They are watching out that B does not get their own position wrong. People reversing roles seem to need freedom so that they can play around with possibility; if they are too constrained watching how the other person is playing their own role while they are playing the other person's, this freedom seems to get lost. Perhaps this is why role reversal tends to work in psychodrama, where one has complete control over what B says back, but not when B is actually there.

Finally, role reversal in the presence of the other has 'change' or 'therapy' signs hanging from it that are visible from miles off. It has been the position in this book that the greatest moment for change comes when the system has been helped to define itself according to all its connections. If the message embodied in any particular exercise is: 'See the other person's point of view and then you will change', each party to the exercise is likely to react as an organism does when a foreign body invades it — unless it recognizes the body as 'mine', it tends to throw it out. One strongly holds a point of view precisely so that one does not have to change, and one is suspicious of any intruders who look like they will tamper with one's cherished personal constructs.

Where it is actually roles rather than persons that are the subject of role reversal, the fun and the no-change elements tend to be heightened, and the threat to one's personal-construct system is diminished. People do create reciprocal roles in relationships: care giver/care receiver, leader/follower, coper/hopeless one, persecutor/victim, and so on. In repetitive conflicts, such as those that bring people to the therapist's door, each person tries harder in the role that they already occupy; when it does not work, they try even harder, and become stuck in that pattern. Let us say that a disputatious married couple is the unit of treatment, and the therapist has decided that role reversal will be helpful. Instead of John being asked to act as Mary, and Mary as John, they are asked to exchange one of their roles — for example practical doer and feckless dreamer.

The therapist might relabel these roles as one 'in charge of work' and the other 'in charge of fun' (Sherman and Fredman, 1986). The couple is asked to reverse roles so that the practical doer is put in charge of organizing the family fun and the feckless dreamer is put in charge of organizing the family tasks. John and Mary thus find themselves disengaged from their usual patterns and have the opportunity to practise new behaviours if this will be to their advantage. They may be asked to enact a scene there and then with each of them in their new roles, or else assume the new roles at home.

Getting partners to exchange roles needs to be done with care and as a result of a specific hypothesis about how the roles as currently shared are unhelpful and contribute to the parties' dysfunctional lifestyle. It is not enough that the therapist's ideology has it that roles should be evenly shared. Roles may, in fact, be quite uneven, and yet perfectly suit the involved parties. 'Complementarity' (Minuchin, 1974; Minuchin and Fishman, 1981) is a term used for the balanced, reciprocal nature of inter-personal behaviour. As a technique, it demonstrates how the action of one person affects the action of the other. It is a form of 'double description' (White, 1986a, b) where the behaviour of one member is described, but responsibility for it is assigned to another. Bateson (1958) suggests that people who have long-term relationships become involved in two types of interactions — symmetrical and complementary interactions. In a symmetrical interaction, the behaviour of one party is followed by similar behaviour from the other: one person shouts, and the other shouts louder. A complementary interaction, on the other hand, is characterized by opposite responses that link up with and complement one another. One person shouts and the other becomes even meeker.

There is nothing wrong with either complementary or symmetrical styles as such — they have suited countless couples over countless generations. But sometimes it is helpful or even necessary for dyads to introduce more complexity into their interaction. Couples who demonstrate a pre-dominantly symmetrical pattern of interaction can learn to use a more complementary pattern with each other — say to replace mutual recrimination either with mutual requests, or for one party to request and the other to comply on three days of the week, and the reverse to take place on the other three, with the seventh day being a symmetrical day or a 'free day'. Where family members show predominantly complementary behaviour patterns, the complementarity can be reversed, or the couple can practise symmetrical behaviour. Harper, et al., (1977) describe alternating symmetrical with complementary behaviour as 'parallel' interaction.

This crossing over of functions is often used as an intervention in itself for entrenched patterns that are causing distress. The role reversal in these cases is usually one-sided — that is, the identified patient has taken up a certain role, and others in the social atom are asked to take it up too. A man with a history of compulsive embezzlement, for instance, is confounded when other members of the family are instructed to 'fiddle the books' once every month or so (Chubb and Evans, 1985). A woman with an entrenched habit of lying is taken aback, and stops lying, when the two friends who brought her to therapy are asked to lie to her once or twice a week. The effect of these two interventions appears to come about, not so much from being in someone else's shoes, but from having someone else be in one's own, and this is not merely in a therapy session, but in one's whole life. When someone else is in one's shoes, perhaps, it can seem less like the comfort of being understood and more like the discomfort of a crowd. There seems to be only one thing to do — vacate one's shoes!

An advantage of role reversal is the scope it gives to experiment freely, to try out behaviour, to stand in for another person and experience their personality from their point of view. These aims are best achieved if the other person is not present, or if the other person is present but the role reversal is done in some scene in the future — this latter process will be outlined shortly.

Role reversal with absent members

Role reversal to an absent person, let us say Simon Biggles who died in Bali (see Chapter 5, p. 85), is not simply a matter of telling that person to 'be' the deceased Simon — one will only get puzzled looks and exclamations of 'This is silly', or 'I'm sorry doctor, but I just can't do it' for one's pains. A full warming-up process needs to take place. Thus the most fruitful time to suggest a role reversal occurs when it is as if the absent person is somehow present in the room anyway, and can clearly be seen as influencing what is going on at the time. A statement can be made to this effect: 'It is almost as if he is here, isn't it?' a place is then chosen — usually an extra chair is put in the circle, but the family members can be asked:

If Simon were here, where would he be in this room? Would he be seated here with us, or over there by the fireplace, or on the floor playing with the children? Where would he be?

These questions, of course, are already beginning to assume the physical presence of the other person, and are establishing a place and perhaps a typical posture for that person. Other questions can be asked, such as: 'What would he be wearing?', or 'What would he think of the goings on, right now — what would he make of you all being here with me in this room talking about your family and the difficulties you're having?'

These questions deepen further the sense of presence of the other person, but are not actively the interview-in-role. That, of course, must be done with the person him/herself. But having asked the questions, it is easier for the therapist to give leads to the family member after role reversal:

Could you go and stand over there where you said Simon would stand, and I'm going to talk to you as if you are him. I'd like you to talk to me as him. Good. Hello, Simon. (S: Hello.) Your wife said that this is where you would be in the room — is this actually where you want to be? (S: Yes, this is the spot.) I guess your wife knew you pretty well to pick that. (S: Yes.) She said that you would be wearing your.... Is that what you've got on?

209

*Look down and tell me, etc. Thus the interview-in-role begins, with more
realism and less likelihood of failure because care has been taken with the
warming-up process.*

With the absent person now present in the form of positive hallucination,
the actual significant point of the role reversal can commence. The lead-up
to this would usually be by means of a cue-in, as had been the warming-up
interview. The director might say something like:

*Mr Biggles, in this room we've been discussing Ralph getting expelled
from school, and the fact that he's pretty withdrawn most of the time. Your
wife is pretty worried about all this, and I get the impression he misses you
a lot too. What do you think is going on with him and with Theresa at the
moment?*

S: *(To therapist) I suppose he's missing me.*
Th: *Could you say that directly to him?*
S: *(To where Ralph has been standing) I suppose you're missing me.*
Th: *Reverse roles. Ralph, your father says that he thinks you're missing
      him. Is that right?*
R: *It sure is.*
Th: *Say that to him directly — there he is, standing right over there by
      the fireplace.*
R: *(Crying) I miss you heaps.*
Th: *Maybe you can tell him a few ways in which you miss him ... the
      times you remember, or things you remember him by.*

There is usually little need for role reversal in this phase, if Ralph or Jane
are adequately warmed up. Occasionally, the therapist may stand beside
Simon and act as a double, emphasizing or repeating something he has
said. If it is appropriate, Simon may also be encouraged to say good-bye
(Kaminski, 1981). This phase of letting go of the other person by actually
saying the words good-bye can be very painful and very difficult for
people. They usually need great tenderness and empathic joining from the
therapist at this stage.

The farewell has real point, apart from the obvious one of helping Jane
and her family with their grief: it can develop new perspectives, so that
'missing Simon' can now become part of the dialogue between therapist,
Jane, Ralph, and Theresa. Simon and his current influence on the family
can be referred to directly, and the therapist may even incline his head
toward the fireplace whenever he speaks of him. Just as he has been
included, the fact that he is no longer there can also now be emphasized in
the therapeutic questioning, and the reality and peculiar problems of the
family as a single-parent family can begin to be dealt with.

Grief is not the only reason for evoking an absent member of the psychodramatic method. Family-of-origin influence, and in particular, the influence of one member, can also be concretized and made part of the therapeutic process, as is illustrated in the case of 'the loyal son'.

The loyal son

The Bardwells are a young couple and have come to therapy because of emotional and sexual difficulties. The husband is disabled from polio, and requires a wheelchair. Mrs Bardwell is able-bodied. As the sessions progress, it becomes very clear that the influence of the husband's mother is most relevant. She had been Larry's major caregiver since birth, and had had much to do with building special facilities for him, taking him to and from school, and so on. It is not appropriate to invite Larry's mother physically to therapy, since the presenting and actual issue concerns an adult couple, and the boundaries between son and mother are already too diffuse.

Larry seems caught between loyalty to his mother and loyalty to his new partner. Jill is angry at Larry's mother and at Larry because she is continually made to feel inadequate and 'not good enough'. She has lost her job and spends most of her time in front of the television, smoking. When Larry goes to bed, she stays up until the early hours of the morning. When he wants to get up in the morning and needs her help to go to the bathroom and to get breakfast, she is comatose. He lies in considerable discomfort until she wakes up. Their sex life is at an end, although it was rich and exciting before they were married.

Larry's mother, and to a lesser extent his father, currently influence this couple. If the mother's physical presence is to be evoked, care needs to be taken lest the session degenerate into a blaming one, with very poor systemic basis and little chance of being useful. Apart from temporary relief, it will serve Larry and his wife ill to have mother in the stocks, as it were, and to throw fruit at her. The more she is made the villain of the piece, the more the question arises of why the couple are so loyal to her.

In the author's experience, the warm-up to the mother needs to be tightly controlled. Where role reversal is used, the mother needs to be questioned mostly on her beliefs — beliefs about sex, care-giving, mother–son and mother–daughter-in-law relationships, fears for Larry, and so on. Then a chair can be left for mother in the circle and the issues of loyalties can be raised — the dilemma of being loyal to two women for Larry, and the dilemma of being perfect, thereby causing Larry to lose his mum, or being a self-sacrificing slattern, so that he might keep her. The 'cool' warm-up to mother is sufficient to last over several sessions, if the chair is always placed in the same position. The placement can itself be a therapeutic milestone, of course: 'Do we still need mother here this session,' the therapist asks, 'or should she take a back seat?'

Rituals

Rituals are prescribed symbolic acts that must be performed in a certain manner and a specified order, and may or may not be accompanied by verbal formulae. Apart from their formal elements, they also contain an element of emotional experience (Van der Hart, 1983). Rituals can be repeated or once-off. A repeated ritual can be something so minor as the therapist's appointment card at the end of a family session, putting a child to bed, saying grace before meals, or a couple having a bath together. The aim of a once-off ritual is more elaborate: it is to enable people to make a transition or to correct previously unsuccessful transitions. Once-off rituals can be compared to traditional rites of passage in certain cultures; indeed Kobak and Waters (1984) have suggested that family therapy itself is a rite of passage.

Rites of passage are sub-divided into (1) rites of separation; (2) transition rites; and (3) rites of incorporation (Van Gennep, 1909). These rites both mark and aid transitions from one state of being to another, especially the life-cycle rites associated with the movement of the individual through the life course — birth, puberty, marriage, and death. Most transition rituals have the structure of separation, transition, and reconciliation, but one of these will be more emphasized according to the particular life phase. At a burial, separation is dominant; at initiation, transition is the most important; and in a marriage, the notion of reconciliation is highlighted.

A walk down memory lane

The 'memory lane' procedure is a useful one where the therapist hypothesizes that the family's difficulty is, at base, an overreaction to an ordinary developmental phase. In effect, it is a visual and acted analogue for the passing of time and the changes that time necessitates. The aim is to allow the family to define themselves more clearly as existing over time.

The Riccardi family came to therapy on the advice of their GP. Mrs Riccardi was presenting as depressed and was having apparently psychosomatic headaches, that were becoming more frequent and severe. Mr Riccardi worked in a government department as a clerical assistant. Their eldest daughter, Thea, aged 11, and their son, Aled, were doing quite well at school, but the youngest child, Monique, aged 6 gave the appearance of high anxiety and was reported as refusing to play or interact with other children.

In the first two sessions, Mrs Riccardi's despair became a major theme. She was disappointed with her marriage and with her life, and was very worried about Monique's fear and nervousness. After some questioning about the early years of their marriage, Dale, the therapist, decided that a kind of moving history that could mark the differences between those days and these might be useful.

He told the Riccardis that he wanted to try an experiment with them to see whether they could make a sort of a film together depicting their lives. They agreed that this would be an interesting thing to do. When asked at which end of the room their lives together would have begun, they pointed to the screen end. Dale then sets up three chairs in a line down the room, but does not explain what he is doing. The Riccardis look on, intrigued. Their children are playing on the floor, sometimes watching, sometimes not.

The therapist has begun the warm-up. By indicating which end of the room they would start their life together, the Riccardis have already assented to the idea that a particular part of the room, in the here-and-now, can represent the beginning of a relationship in the there-and-then. Although he does not do it for exactly this purpose, the therapist, by placing the three chairs down the room, adds to their sense of involvement in a mysterious experience, bracketed from their normal understanding of reality.

The director now commences the interview-in-role. He asks Mr and Mrs Riccardi where they first met. It was at a speedway, apparently, on an outing organized by a youth group of their church. 'Do you have a car yourself? What colour is it? What kind is it? Is it your first car?' he asks Mr Riccardi. 'What do you like about speedway racing. How come you're here, then? Oh, I see. What are you wearing today?' (the day of their meeting) he asks Mrs Riccardi. He enquires about who was attracted to whom first, what was their first outing together, what were their early impressions of one another, and so on.

He leads up to the time they were engaged, and asks them to take one step forward, down the room, to represent that passage of time. After a few questions about that period, he asks them to take another step, to their wedding day. Again he interviews, asking whether they are nervous, what they are wearing, what regrets they have, and what is their dream for the marriage. He carefully rebuilds the reality of these early scenes from their courtship and honeymoon period, so that they have an emotional 'anchor' that might provide a rationale for their present life. After all, at least the original dream was love and happiness.

The couple are now thoroughly warmed up to each other and to their relationship. If the director had sensed that the crux of the problem was relationship or sexual difficulties that were none of the business of the children, he would have conducted the 'memory lane' session at a separate appointment when the children were not present. In the instance of the Riccardi family, however, his assessment was that this was a committed couple who were experiencing difficulties related to the developmental phase of their married and family life. The procedure is presented here with the full family, but any part of it may be singled out and emphasized, and it can be done with any part of the family configuration. The interview-in-role at the time of meeting, first date, engagement, and marriage, and the taking of a physical step emphasizes the journey the couple already has been on, and covertly emphasizes that things change.

If Dale so wished, he could at any stage have set up 'the dream' of the relationship by developing more fully the hopes and yearning of each partner. 'The dream' can take place on either side of the 'memory lane', and chairs, persons, or other props can be used. Each partner may set up the dream using the other person and themselves, or else using inanimate objects. An interview is needed, both with the protagonist and 'the dream as a whole'. Each partner can have an 'empty chair' dialogue with the dream, and role-reverse as the dream talking back to them. If this elaborate and probably private intervention is to be used, it is preferable that the children are not present. Contrast can be made between the dream and reality, and how the couple will best cope with the divergence.

Dale now takes the Riccardis one step further, representing the first year of their marriage. He asks questions that emphasize the freedom of that period, both financial, with both parties working, and in terms of time. He then asks how long it was after they were married that Thea was born. They tell him that it was three years, and he asks them to take three steps until they come to the first chair. (Again, the dream for the pregnancy and birth could be set up, though possibly not in the presence of the children, especially if they had been abused or unwanted.) The director asks Thea to come and sit in the chair. He interviews the couple about what it is like now to be a family, what the differences in their life, finances, time, and freedom are. Taking Thea in hand, they move two years (two steps) down to Aled's chair, and repeat the interview process as much as necessary. Then taking Aled in tow as well, they move to Monique's chair, and again interview.

Through the interviewing, and the physically moving down through time, as it were, the family are able to gain a sense that although things are not the same as they were, nor should they be. They have a context for their issues as being developmental, rather than just bad luck. They can draw distinctions between what is dream and what is reality. Their idea of causality for their woes, instead of being merely blaming, may become more complex. Furthermore, since time has been interfered with to this extent already, there is no reason why they cannot walk back up memory lane, shedding children as they go. They can return to the dream, and come out of it again. They can go back to easier and less exhausting days when they had only one child. They can go off on side tracks and explore possibilities — what if they had no children, what would their relationship be like?

The example has been from the Riccardis, a relatively problem-free nuclear family. But 'memory lane' is obviously a psychodramatic device, the structure of which can be widely applied. It is quite suitable, for instance, for blended families, with chairs off to the side representing former marriages, and elaborate interactions taking place about them. It can also be used as a before/after measure with a traumatic event, such as a death, illness, or divorce. It can be extended from the present into the future, and the family can be invited to walk a little further to see what happens. It can even have three branches in the future representing the family if the problem stays the same, the family if the problem gets worse, and the family if the problem gets better. Obviously, interview-in-role needs to take place at each of those points if the exercise is not to be a superficial one. The depth of warm-up is half-contributor to the efficacy of the exercise, and the systemic base of the questions asked when participants are warmed up is the other half.

Enactment as analogue

The Batesonian view that human beings respond primarily to difference or change has been an underlying theory of strategic psychodrama. The question for the therapist is how to present difference or change to clients so that the difference becomes information, or news of difference. A difference is always a relationship between two things or people; for example, 'Bill is fatter than Bob' implies a circular relationship 'Bob is thinner than Bill'; the circularity and difference in relationships can often be exemplified by action in space and time, rather than by words only, which are digital referents whose meaning does not quite capture the subtle essences of human interaction.

We have also observed that our sensory systems find it difficult to detect gradual change, because organisms become habituated to what is, leading us to be unaware of slow alterations. We may be slow to recognize a deterioration in our social affairs, for example, such as imperceptibly growing strains in a marriage. To reach our threshold of perception, the change must be of a sufficient magnitude for the difference to make an impact; it would suffice, though, if the difference were speeded up — then smaller differences can be noted. The ability of action methods to manipulate time — to extend it or collapse it — allows differences in time to become sharper.

Second, there are an almost infinite number of differences between one thing and another — between a golf club and a tennis racquet, for example. For differences to become 'information', they must be differences that are relevant — differences that make a difference, especially in terms of our response or behaviour. The important differences between a golf club and a tennis racquet become clear if we attempt to play tennis with the golf club or golf with the tennis racquet. Information is constituted, not just by any differences, but by critical differences. In therapy, therefore, the therapist triggers the release of information by enquiring about relevant differences: the questions are designed to confirm or disconfirm specific hypotheses that relate to the issues with which the family is involved.

The Milan Associates (Selvini Palazzoli *et al.*) have developed a form of questioning (circular questioning) that focuses on differences: 'By circularity we mean the capacity of the therapist to conduct his investigation on the basis of feedback from the family in response to the information he solicits about relationship and, therefore, about difference and change' (1980, p. 8). The cybernetic view of circularity does not consider any part of the system to have unilateral control. The behaviour of each part is determined by the behaviour of other parts as well as by its own previous behaviour. A circuit is a 'unit of mind' characterized by:

(1) a sequence of events,

(2) feedback structure, and

(3) is triggered by information.

Because of these characteristics, whenever the loop is drawn, there is potential for everything inside the loop to change or restructure itself when information is produced.

Penn (1982) notes that an important and particular effect that circular questions have on the family is that the questions compel the family to experience the circularity of the family system, and abandon more linear stances. Naturally, all family members feel themselves to be individuals with individual perceptions of the family dilemma; the circular questions act as a balance to this linear individualism. The questions are framed in such a way that members must give a relational answer to questions such as 'Who in the family first noticed that Anna was getting thin?' and 'Who most worries when mother begins one of her bouts of worrying?'

Sanders (1985) has developed a method of visual analogue that explores differences in ways that are suitable for families with small children. She maintains that there are families who are unable to answer many difference questions or to acknowledge that those that have been answered have any validity. Her methods are essentially sociometric, and draw on the work of Tomm (1984), who distinguished between questions based on spatial as opposed to temporal differences. He divides spatial differences into four categories:

(1) Differences between individuals, for example, 'Who is most pleased when Bill and Peter get on well together?'
(2) Differences between relationships, for example, 'Is Anna closer to Gavin or to Brett?'
(3) Differences among ideas, values, perceptions, and beliefs, for example, 'When people in this family become angry, does this mean that they care about each other more or less?'
(4) Differences in a time frame other than the present. This may refer to the past: 'When Dick was around, was Cain closer to mother?' — or the future: 'In two years time, which of the boys will feel least like fighting?'

Temporal differences are highly important in circular questioning. The questions aim to fix a point in the history of the system when important coalitions underwent a shift. The questions concern the consequent adaptations to that shift that were problematic for the family.

Essentially, the questions seek the differences in relationship the family has experienced before and after the problem began. To this extent, differences in relationship-over-time enactments make a new focus of sociometry, which is traditionally concerned with intimacy and choice. Generally speaking, temporal differences concern spatial changes that have occurred or might occur in the interval between two points in time. They may refer to:

(1) Two points in the past: 'Did Cain and Abel fight more before Dick walked out on their Mum, or did they fight more afterwards?'

(2) The past and the present: 'Is Anna (an anorexic girl of 16) more eager to please her dad now, or was she more eager two years ago when she was eating normally?'

(3) The past and future: 'If Harry had not left the family eighteen months ago to join the army, would Brenda be closer or more distant from mother when she leaves school next year?'

(4) The present and future: 'If instead of Harry leaving home mother had left home, what would happen?'

(5) Two future occasions: 'If mother stopped worrying about the fights, would Cain and Abel feel more or less compulsion to continue them?'

How does one devise which questions to ask? After all, there are an infinite number of questions that a family could be asked, but most of them will not be relevant. Penn (1982) suggests that the therapist note the 'cue' words in the family. In the problem-definition stage, the family offers cue words embedded in their statement of the problems. Father might say, 'His fire-setting makes my wife feel *sick*.' Mother might say, 'No one in this family *cares about each other*.' Son might say, 'It's totally uptight — there's no *freedom*.' And daughter might say, 'His firesetting is just his way of being *rebellious*.' The therapist attempts to make the problem-definition concern relationships; these cue words, therefore, are transposed into questions about relationships and differences in relationships: 'Who worries most when mother feels *sick*? Who in the family *cares least* about the others? Who is the person most accused of suppressing *freedom*? Who is most like your son in being *rebellious*?'

After the family has defined its problem by cue words, and the therapist has noted these words, the therapist attempts to discern the coalition align-ments around the problem in the present — hence the questions of the type: 'Who worries most when mother feels sick? Who in the family cares least about the others?' If the problem definition is firesetting, then certain standard questions might follow: 'Who is *most upset* about the firesetting? Who feels *more helpless* when Johnny sets fires? Who *notices first* when he sets the fires?' The answer to any of these questions defines a relationship.

The easiest family sociometric criterion is devised by ordering differ-ences to generate classification along a particular dimension — that is, the family can be asked, literally, where they stand on a particular issue — usually the problem as defined. A spectrogram of his form (see *Forbidden agenda*) is usually fairly intelligible to a family:

Let this end be 0 and this end be 100. Now, stand on the line somewhere according to your belief as to who is most worried about Johnny's fire-setting. Stand at 100 if you think you are the most worried person, and at 0 if you think you are not worried at all.

The criterion becomes circular if one family member is asked to arrange the others on the line according to how worried they are perceived to be.

Once one maintains that the process is basically a sociometric one, it is easy to see how Tomm's (1984) schema can be adapted. Spatial differences can be exemplified by a line. In one of the previous examples, the question 'Who is "most pleased" when Bill and Peter get on well together?' (p. 217) can be answered verbally, or can be answered physically and spatially. Furthermore, the question can be asked in circular form: that is, one family member organizes the others at various points on the line (see diagram) when mother stands outside and places members where she thinks they stand on the issue of being 'most pleased'. When she has completed this task, she herself may be asked to select a point on the line.

Nancy	Dick	Peter	Bill
x	x	x	x

least pleased   most pleased

The rest of the family can then take turns to direct the others to positions. Alternatively, the line can be established and a noncircular description can be required by the therapist: 'All of you, go and stand somewhere on that line to represent how pleased you are when Bill and Peter get on well together.'

The second form — differences between relationships, as exemplified in the question 'Is Anna closer to Gavin or to Brett?' (p. 217) can also be illustrated on a line, either in circular fashion by asking a third person (including Gavin and Brett) to place Anna, Gavin, and Brett on the line, or it can be done directly, by asking Anna to position herself somewhere between Gavin and Brett.

A sociometric division can be managed around Tomm's third spatial category: differences among ideas, perceptions, values, and beliefs. The question 'When people in this family become angry, does this mean they care about each other more or less?' can be asked as conversation, or the therapist might say, 'Go to this end of the room those who think it means they care about each other more, and stand at this end if you think that anger means they care about each other less.' Another question highlighting differences in beliefs might refer to a person rather than a process, for example, 'Who in the family most believes that Annabel will put on weight by the end of the year?' Members can then stand on a line from 'most believe' to 'doesn't believe at all'. Classifications and comparisons are constructed to follow changes in the family's coalition alignments. Once a classification has been established, notes Penn (1982), the therapist may then ask, 'Was that always true, was it ever different, or is it different now?' That is, differences in space are related to differences in time.

A difference in time frame can also be illustrated physically: using an empty chair for Dick, for example, and placing mother at a particular point in the room, the therapist can then ask 'When Dick was around (stands behind Dick's chair) was Cain closer to mother (moves Cain's chair closer to mother's) or further away (moves it back)? Closer? (moves) ... or further back? (moves) ... ' more or less like an optometrist trying several pairs of lenses for a patient. When the distinction is established, the therapist can then explore what else was happening at crucial points, and why family members perceive relationships differently now than they did then.

Action techniques are particularly suited for differences in time frame, because the event or person in the past can physically be represented by an object, such as a chair, and the past can then be evoked as present. The question can even require a little scene, which is easy to set up. For example, when comparing two points in the past, the question 'Did Cain and Abel fight more before Dick walked out on their mum, or did they fight more afterwards? (see p. 217), can be illustrated by five chairs for scene I to represent Dick, mother, Cain, Abel, and Kate and four chairs for scene II in another part of the room, to represent the family without Dick. Members need not occupy the chairs — the therapist can simply take them, almost as a little tourist party, between one scene and another. 'More fighting, then, or more fighting then?' the family might be asked.

Once information about differences has been established, the therapist can, at any stage, ask the family for an explanation or theory about why things have changed. These questions help the family make connections, and can lead to further distinctions illustrated by further actions, if need be. 'How does the family explain why Cain and Abel fight more after Dick walked out on their mum?' or 'Why is it that only Kate suggested that there had been less fighting?' The answers to the questions, and the differences in the explanations about the questions begin to weave a pattern, which is the pattern of the system. Shared and alternative epistemologies about the problem become evident, whilst, at the same time, perceived membership in the problem gradually increases.

It is now time to return to our major themes of passion and technique, revelation and therapy, and the place of psychodrama in bringing news of difference to people in difficulty. We have to ask: does technique rule out passion, and passion technique? And further: should psychodrama become a means of recovery of a lost world?

Chapter twelve

Heading for the exit

There is no such thing as a baby

Winnicott

Megalomania normalis

Moreno was probably right: the child in us never gives up its expectations to become the centre and ruler of the universe. As the years pass, though, we are all forced to become at least outwardly more humble: to bow before the 'stubborn structure of the universe', which we are no longer able to penetrate with the magic methods once at our disposal. As infants, we could make people appear with a cry, or disappear simply by shutting our eyes. Not so, now. But we never quite give up striving towards the fulfilment of our 'profound intentions to be forever connected with existence, to be all-powerful, immortal' (Moreno, 1959, p. 137).

According to Moreno's theory of child development, the infant inhabits a universe that is indistinct from the self. The child is fused with this 'first universe' and is the megalomanic centre of it. Very early in life, alas, a shock comes to this first world, and the infant discovers that what he or she perceives as the universe (fantasy) is different from what others perceive (reality). The first universe is broken, and young human beings find themselves in an unfamiliar 'second universe' in which they are alone. This is the lot of all of us.

To get over the shock, we thereafter try to make a bridge between fantasy and reality by realizing fantasies (Kraus, 1984). We had had no part in creating this second universe: it was there when we were rudely awakened to it. We must now create it for ourselves, making it contain at least some of our fantasy; the alternative is withdrawal and stagnation. To get back to the first universe, however, becomes our guiding (but covered-up) dream as adults. The adult longs for union, longs to return to the paradise of infant megalomania. Return to paradise occurs, if at all, only for a few moments, however; people must keep creating their new world, rather than attempting a return to that old one, no matter how exquisite it was.

The art of traditional psychodrama is to enable protagonists adequately to re-enact the lived-out and unlived-out dimensions of their private world. Their feelings and perceptions of reality are concretized, so that their inner conflict around their lost 'first universe' is reduced and their phenomenal reality is improved. It was an article of faith that this process would be curative, and Moreno held to his position with almost heroic passion. Even in the case of 'psychotic' patients, where the analytic and artistic imagination of the director could no longer follow the subject's flights of fancy, he invented devices where the subjects themselves could be made the chief producing agents. Few were greater champions of utter subjectivity than Moreno, and yet few held as dear the hope of a 'science' of social relations, where the modifications of that subjectivity by social interaction could be 'objectively' measured.

Moreno saw the essential 'I' in each individual as the creator. Psychodrama thus aims to raise people's consciousness of their immanent creativity, to help them become 'I–Gods', part of the supreme power ruling the world by spontaneity and creativity. In case this seems too utopian, it is as much an article of faith for family therapy, that notoriously hard-headed branch of therapy, as for psychodrama, that only by creating new realities can people emerge from their difficulties. Family therapists may not use the language of spontaneity/creativity, far less I–Gods, but the concept of spontaneity is nevertheless central to the philosophy of both therapies.

Psychodrama urges protagonists to become the individuals they dream of being, to transcend their mortality by contacting it more deeply. They fight the chains that hold them down, whether of family, education, employment, religion, or even the chains of logic itself. To be victorious in the struggle, they must not so much conquer the deadened system, as conquer that system's (the cultural conserve) internalized repression within them. Directors help protagonists to overcome this internal repression, and to allow expression of their act-hunger: by engaging fully in the fight to transcend earthly reality they must actually embrace it. The divine becomes immanent. Earth and paradise are not so different. In becoming the I–God, each person is uniquely responsible for whatever is created. Each is connected not only with the common principle of creativity and spontaneity that rules the universe, but with all the other 'I-s' who are also part of spontaneity/creativity.

Even the most singular and subjective experience of the self can be construed in some way as an interpersonal experience. The 'other', of course, need not be physically present. The interpersonal nature of a role suggests that therapeutic encounters with the person must simultaneously become a therapeutic encounter with the system. Thus Winnicott's remark, 'There is no such thing as a baby' is not as odd as it first seems: even a newborn baby is not only a baby but part of a natural dyad, or parental triad, or other system produced by hospitals, midwives, families, and indeed by cultural beliefs about babies. A strategic psychodramatist, more deliberately than a traditional psychodramatist, perhaps, accesses the patterns that connect the various members of the client's social atom and attempts to increase their flexibility.

Most people feel that they are the hub, the nucleus of their social atom. Though they might regard themselves as the helpless victims in that atom, or as controlling events within it, they are still the centre. Such is the nature of the experiencing 'I'. Therapists, however, whose job it is to look at other people's lives, know that clients are not the hub. In fact, there is no hub, only endlessly expanding galaxies of roles, of experiences into which private, social, and cultural forces have merged. They must work the difference between people's subjective 'megalomania normalis' and the therapeutic vision of them as but part of a complex system. Clients experience their lives immediately, completely, and in the foreground, while therapists, sensitive to their clients' subjective distress, nevertheless regard that distress as system-produced and somehow system-maintaining. Therapists have the twin commitment of encouraging people's 'full subjective one-sidedness', and of working with the system within which clients developed their various roles.

Revelation versus therapy: a return match

Seeman and Weiner (1985) have offered an extended critique of the practice of mixing psychodrama with family therapy. In particular, they are critical of the two meanings of the word 'enactment' when used in psychodrama and in family therapy. But according to some authors, such as Guldner (1983) and C. Hollander (1983), there appears to be little difference worth worrying about between the methods. Others (Dodson, 1983; S. Hollander, 1981; Remer, 1986) have written on the use of Morenian methods with family members, and Guldner (1982) and Laqueur (1980) have used psychodrama with several families present. It is doubtful, however, whether strategic or systemic family therapists would view the work described by these authors as being truly systems-based, or theoretically sound, for that matter. 'Family communications' or 'family encounter' might be all they would allow — they would reserve a different sort of definition for 'family therapy'.

Psychodrama in its present state of evolution as a systems theory may have to await further development before it is respected as more than an adjunctive method of working with families, as I have suggested in the preceding chapter. Despite Moreno having been a pioneer in the family-therapy field, the method is not currently regarded as having significantly evolved since those early days, and has suffered the lack of theoretical development and the sophistication that only a large number of people practising, researching, writing, talking, arguing, training, and refining can bring.

Leaving out working with whole families, for the moment, we may ask what contribution strategic psychodrama, itself only embryonic, may make to psychodrama itself. The directors whose dramas have been portrayed in these pages have attempted to explore the extent to which a director's strategic actions can fruitfully be grafted on to the client's 'full subjective onesidedness'. Protagonists one-sidedly interpret their distress as being produced by the system; a systems approach, however, more fully examines restraints on change and the ways in which the distress maintains the system. We have noted that the context and consequences of a person's roles, while implicit in the Morenian definition, are overlooked dimensions of role theory. A reading of such contexts and consequences, however, automatically propels one into a systemic analysis of roles. The five-part understanding of roles gives the information needed for 'the patterns that connect', and carries the potential for a full-blown contextual understanding. While the basis for a strategic psychodramatic form has been outlined, the process needs to be developed by many more writers, practitioners, and researchers.

By now you will have noticed a continual dialectic in this book: between passion and technique, aesthetics and pragmatics, analogic and digital communication, fantasy and reality, omnipotence and mortality, revelation and therapy. From our observations of directors helping protagonists negotiate their inside and outside worlds we have asked: is it legitimate to risk obscuring the revelatory and religious qualities of a psychodrama with a strategy? Can a therapy be passionate, and have a technique?

Perhaps it can, even in the most orthodox Morenian theory: for all the grand scale of his dreams, Moreno did try to reconcile for clients the fantasy of God with the reality of being human. He recognized people's desire to act out their psychodramatic roles, but he himself never encouraged this at the expense of social disintegration for the person. Moreno does not argue for persons to live under some megalomanic illusion that they are God, or for a private world that is ever seeking to engulf the person's social identity. The psychodramatic roles continually press to be expressed: such a pressure can lead either to creativity or, on occasion, to escapist counteridentitites, such as when a man dreams he is Fangio or a woman that she is the Queen of Sheba. These roles can be useful and enjoyable, so long as 'Fangio' does not wreck his Toyota or the 'Queen' does not catch cold waiting around for her fantasy attendants to pour her bath!

The point of both traditional and strategic psychodrama is to co-create with the protagonist a positive social reality. The client's destructive definition is abandoned, and replaced temporarily by alternative images that can break the circuit of redundancy in which the individual flounders. Strategic psychodrama offers a wider range of techniques to do this, and tends to look more rigorously at the context and consequences of the person's roles. It also tends to a cybernetic approach, attempting to ensure that therapy itself does not become part of the client's dysfunctional solutions.

In psychodrama as revelation, the 'full subjective onesidedness' of the protagonist is totally supported and explored. The drama is a personal epiphany, a revelation of personal history and potential, an education, a support for the passion to know the meaning of one's experience, and the drive to find, show forth, and enhance the inner spirit. These are all excellent pursuits. Psychodrama as therapy is neither 'higher' nor 'lower' than psychodrama as revelation: it merely has a different purpose — the solving of problems. The difficulty emerges if the two are confused, and revelation, or therapy for that matter, becomes part of the client's problem-causing solutions.

Given that skilfully conducted traditional psychodramas have usually something to add to the truth about people's existence, there is little reason why a client should not stay in a group that uses the psychodramatic method as revelation or theology as long as he or she likes. There are good reasons, however, as we saw in Chapter 8, why therapy should not be construed as part of one's life, and should be as brief as the problem allows it to be. One's education process is lifelong, and it is indeed most helpful to regard life and learning as one. It is not so helpful, perhaps, to regard life and therapy as one.

Creativity and spontaneity certainly do give life and spirit to the social atom. But let us try that meaning the other way round: appropriate functioning in the social atom actually enables adequate psychodramatic roles to develop. The successful management of the subjective/social dialectic characterizes good therapy. As well as supporting the individual's act-hunger to experience ever more psychodramatic roles, directors can also support adequate social structures that would enhance more complete expression of psychodramatic roles within the system. What comes first? When the protagonist's phenomenal reality is made present, concrete, and conscious, its repair can be social and structural, as well as subjective and personal. Nothing comes first, particularly.

Yet, to impose technique on the passion of protagonists acting-out their psychodramatic roles seems to offend against the tighest-held canon of action methods: the right of a person to live out their 'megalomania normalis' (Moreno, 1959, p. 139). Moreno remarks that the centrality of people's outlook, their self-reference, that is, reference to their matrix of identity, never ceases to operate: 'He remains a child as long as he lives'. An imposed structural shift within the system, or the presentation of a new code book introduced by the therapist, or a tightly constructed interview in the group certainly seems to imply a check being made to that 'megalomania normalis', and may pose a dilemma of warm-up. Moreno was in a somewhat similar dilemma when he developed sociometry, which he hoped would be the new 'science' of systems. But his grafting of sociometry to psychodrama was never complete, and certainly this present endeavour of grafting subjectivity and systemic thinking is only a first step — some useful implements for the kitchen, as I suggested in Chapter 5.

The network of relationships, the world of choice

In his concept of the social atom, Moreno, like Marx and like family-systems theorists, considered the person as primarily a social being bound in a network of relationships. He called himself a 'dialogical existentialist', viewing individuals as essentially connected in relationship. Indeed, social isolation was regarded as the primary condition for lack of spontaneity and creativity. His was far from a fascistic antiindivualism, however. The individual is not, or should not be, lost in this interconnection: both psychodrama and strategic therapy validate a rich fantasy life in every individual, and fully support individual enhancement.

Further to this recognition of the individual-in-relationship, Moreno added a cosmic focus — psychodrama as theology — where each person participates in a cosmological dialogue with the Godhead, the universal principle of spontaneity and creativity. He had a vision of millions of I–Gods co-creating the universe. Cut out the sense of a single Godhead, and one comes close to the ideas of Gregory Bateson, the hero of contemporary systems theory, who regarded the 'self' as only a 'small part of a much larger trial-and-error system which does the thinking, acting and deciding'; it is '. . . a false reification of an improperly delineated part of this much larger field of interlocking processes' (Bateson, 1972, p. 331).

Like traditional psychodrama, strategic psychodrama similarly works on developing the creator–individual in terms of the problem presented. To call this an individual 'Godhead', or to postulate a collective one, however, begins to impose something other than therapy on the client. One's philosophy about what it means for oneself to be a human being, or even one's hopes for humankind, are not necessarily the same as one's beliefs about change in therapy, and about the scope of therapy. Strategic therapies in general do not attempt to get a client close to the therapist's own ideals for human beings, and do not take on the other person's whole life more than is necessary. They are not there to tutor another person in how to be a human being, or to have the other show forth that humanity — that is the purpose of revelation, and generally belongs in settings other than therapeutic settings. The strategic psychodramatist is present to the protagonist or group member not only in his or her simple humanity, but as a therapist, there to deal with a problem or set of problems.

Let me not pretend that the distinction is clear cut, however. All successful therapy entails a transformation of consciousness, a redefinition of the problem, and usually an alteration of the client's view of the relationships between self and other. Even the resolution of one small problem may involve this. Furthermore, spontaneity is as much the basis of strategic psychodrama as it is of classical psychodrama, and so is working to connect and enlighten the client to some sort of larger context — in some cases that of life itself. And like any psychodramatist, strategic psychodramatists acknowledge their presence to clients in full-face encounter with them. They are open to the spontaneity of life itself. They are only therapists in so far as they themselves are capable of, or capable of generating in the other, greater spontaneity around the problem than the client already has.

Moreno created the first psychodrama stage as a laboratory for living — a forum for experiential theology. Strategic psychodrama does not quite do this: it creates a stage for experimentation in itself, a context for the unknown, the unpredictable, where the restraints on change may be at last dropped. The 'poetic universe' (Allman, 1982) or the 'enchanting universe of spontaneity' (Kraus, 1984) is restricted in its scope, but not its nature, to the resolution of problems. Both strategic and traditional psychodrama aim to create a world of play in which illusion and reality are one, and in which people come to recognize their connectedness with others, their 'dialogical existentialism'. Both types of psychodramas are 'ecological' methods, assisting people to shift their consciousness from a linear view of self to a more inclusive species consciousness.

When he went to the United States in 1925, Moreno translated his theology of the 'Godhead' into the 'science' of sociometry. He argued that faith in human fellowship and in the universal principle of spontaneity/creativity was a matter of survival of the human race as such. Who could say, these days, that he was wrong? Although strategic psychodrama restricts itself to problems, the distinction between it and traditional psychodrama is not one of pragmatics versus aesthetics. As may be clear to the reader who has persevered this far, strategic psychodrama is far from simple, far from blunt, far from crudely pragmatic. Both types of psychodrama recognize, or should recognize, persons in their contexts as part of the total fabric of nature. Both abhor, or should abhor, a linear mechanistic view of self and consciousness. If anything, strategic psychodrama is more systems-conscious than traditional psychodrama, and adopts a very open view about self and consciousness.

Strategic psychodrama and group work takes the challenge of clients stuck in their problem–solution cycle, and attempts to evolve a technique that helps the client grow, ferment, form, and re-form around the problem until the original network of presuppositions loosens and gives room for spontaneity. At least around the problem, the given world becomes more the created world, the intentional world, the world of choice. This world always exists within a network of relationships with others, but is less restricted by dysfunctional or unnecessary restraints from those human loyalties. The invisible loyalties are made visible, and the person is free to be loyal in a new way. Although strategic therapy may inevitably expand clients' awareness of the unity of life, and the 'playful connectedness' (Bateson, 1979) of all things, it does not set out explicitly to do that. Strategic psychodrama takes off its hat to psychodrama as revelation and psychodrama as theology, but it knows its own territory — the territory of the problem. The territory of the problem and the territory of the solution are not the same things. It knows that there is no worthwhile technique without passion, and that passion is impotent without technique.

A strategic therapist takes responsibility for directly influencing people towards specific goals. Strategic therapy is often distinguished (e.g. Rabkin, 1977) from those approaches that seek 'wisdom and enlightenment'. This distinction is important, since psychodrama as theology and revelation does seek wisdom and enlightenment. In 'A quiz for young therapists' Jay Hayley (1981) asks whether therapists should think of themselves as skilful technicians or as philosopher/humanists. He takes the example of a child who is wetting the bed. The philosopher/clinician does not review in his mind eleven ways to cure that problem. Instead, he thinks that the child is wetting the bed as a way of expressing his or her conception of the world. 'Is this child pissing on the universe?' he asks himself. A good question, but the therapist must also know the routine ways of curing a child of wetting the bed. If not, what are therapists for? Hayley arrives at his answer: it is all right to be a philosopher and a humanist if that does not interfere with being a skilful therapist. Strategic psychodramatists aim for a change in the joyless reflective sequences of interaction, and the creation of more alternatives for action. For a person in trouble, this will do as a definition of wisdom and enlightenment.

References

Aldridge, D. and Rossiter, J. (1983) 'A strategic approach to suicidal behavior', *Journal of Strategic and Systemic Therapies, 2,* 49–62.

Alexander, F. (1946) *The scope of psychoanalysis,* New York: Basic Books.

Allman, L. (1982) 'The aesthetic preference: overcoming the pragmatic error', *Family Process, 21,* 43–56.

Andolfi, M. and Angelo, C. (1982) 'The therapist as director of the family drama', in F.W. Kaslow (ed.) *The international book of family therapy,* New York: Brunner/Mazel.

Anthony, E. (1967) 'The generic elements in dyadic and in group psychotherapy', *International Journal of Group Psychotherapy, 17,* 57–70.

Bateson, G. (1958) *Naven* (2nd edn), Stanford: Stanford University Press.

Bateson, G. (1972) *Steps to an ecology of mind,* New York: Ballantine Books.

Bateson, G. (1979) *Mind and nature: a necessary unity,* New York: Bantam Books.

Bateson, G. (1982) 'Beyond homeostasis: toward a concept of coherence', *Family Process, 21,* 21–41.

Beavers, W. (1977) *Psychotherapy and growth: a family systems perspective,* New York: Brunner/Mazel.

Bentley, E. (1972) 'Theatre and therapy', in *Theatre of war,* London: Methuen.

Billow, P. (1977) 'Metaphor: a review of the psychological literature', *Psychological Bulletin, 84,* 81–92.

Bion, W.R. (1961) *Experiences in groups,* London: Tavistock Publications.

Bischof, L. (1970) *Interpreting personality theories,* New York: Harper & Row.

Blatner, H. (1973) *Acting-in: practical applications of psychodramatic methods,* New York: Springer.

Blatner, A. (1985) 'The dynamics of catharsis', *Journal of Group Psychotherapy, Psychodrama and Sociometry, 37,* 157–66.

Bodin, A. (1981) 'The interactional view: family therapy approaches of the Mental Research Institute', in A. Gurman and D. Kniskern (eds) *Handbook of family therapy,* New York: Brunner/Mazel.

Bodin, E.S. (1979) 'The generalizability of the psychoanalytic concept of the working alliance', *Psychotherapy: Theory, Research and Practice, 16,* 252–60.

Boszormenyi-Nagy, I. and Spark, G. (1973) *Invisible loyalties: reciprocity in intergenerational family therapy,* New York: Harper & Row.

Boszormenyi-Nagy, I. and Krasner, B. (1981) 'The contextual approach to psychotherapy: premises and implications', in G. Berenson and H. White (eds) *Annual review of family therapy (vol. 1),* New York: Human Science Press.

Bowen, M. (1966) 'The use of family therapy in clinical practice', *Comprehensive Psychiatry*, 7, 345–74.

Bowen, M. (1972) 'Towards the differentiation of a self in one's own family', in J. Framo (ed.) *Family interaction*, New York: Springer.

Braaten, L.J. (1974) 'Development phases of encounter groups and related intensive groups', *Interpersonal Development*, 5, 112–29.

Braverman, S., Hoffman, L., and Szkrumelak, N. (1984) 'Concomitant use of strategic and individual therapy in treating a family', *American Journal of Family Therapy*, 12, 29–38.

Brennan, J. and Williams, A. (1988) 'Clint and the black sheep', *Journal of Strategic and Systemic Therapies*, (in press).

Buchanan, D. (1980) 'The central concern model: a framework for structuring psychodramatic production', *Journal of Group Psychotherapy, Psychodrama and Sociometry*, 33, 47–62.

Campernolle, T. (1981) 'J.L. Moreno: an unrecognized pioneer of family therapy', *Family Process*, 20, 331–5.

Carter, B. and McGoldrick, M. (eds) (1980) *The family life cycle*, New York: Gardner.

Chubb, H. and Evans, E. (1985) 'Therapy is not going to help: brief family treatment of a character disorder', *Journal of Strategic and Systemic Therapies*, 4, 37–44.

Conrad, J. (1914, 1972) *The nigger of the narcissus*, Dent: London.

Coyne, J. (1986) 'The significance of the interview in strategic marital therapy', *Journal of Strategic and Systemic Therapies*, 5, 63–70.

de Shazer, S. (1982) *Patterns of brief family therapy*, New York: Guilford.

Dodson, L.S. (1983) 'Intertwining Jungian depth psychology and family therapy through use of action techniques', *Journal of Group Psychotherapy, Psychodrama and Sociometry*, 35, 155–64.

Duhl, B.S. (1983) *From the inside out: creative and integrative approaches to training in systems thinking*, New York: Brunner/Mazel.

Everstine, D.S. and Everstine, L. (1983) *People in crisis*, New York: Brunner/Mazel.

Ezriel, H. (1952) 'Notes on psychoanalytical therapy, II: interpretation and research', *Psychiatry*, 15, 119–26.

Ezriel, H. (1973) 'Psychoanalytic group therapy', in L.R. Wolberg and E.K. Schwartz (eds) *Group therapy*, New York: International Medical Books, pp. 183–210.

Farson, R. (1978) 'The technology of humanism', *Journal of Humanistic Psychology*, 18, 5–35.

Fine, L. (1978) 'Psychodrama', in R. Corsini (ed.) *Current psychotherapies*, Itasca, Ill.: F.E. Peacock.

Fisch, R., Weakland, J., and Segal, L. (1982) *The tactics of change: doing therapy briefly*, San Francisco: Jossey Bass.

Foulkes, H. (1964) *Group analytic psychotherapy*, New York: IUP.

Fox, J. (1987) *The essential Moreno*, New York: Springer.

Fraser, J. (1986) 'The crisis interview: strategic rapid intervention', *Journal of Strategic and Systemic Therapies*, 5, 71–87.

Freud, S. (1912) 'The dynamics of transference', *Standard Edition*, 12, London: Hogarth.

Freud, S. (1914) 'Recollecting, repeating and working through', *Standard Edition*, 12, London: Hogarth.

Freud, S. (1921) 'Group psychology and the analysis of the ego', *Standard Edition*, 18, London: Hogarth.

Freud, S. (1940) 'An outline of psychoanalysis', *Standard Edition, 23,* London: Hogarth.

Ginn, R. (1974) 'Psychodrama, a theatre for our time', *Group Psychotherapy and Psychodrama, 32,* 123–46.

Goldenberg, I. and Goldenberg, H. (1985) *Family therapy: an overview,* Monterey, Calif.: Brooks/Cole.

Goldman, E. and Morrison, D. (1984) *Psychodrama: experience and process,* Dubuque, Iowa: Kendall/Hunt.

Gordon, D. (1978) *Therapeutic metaphors,* Cupertino Calif.: Meta Publications.

Greenson, R. and Wexler, M. (1969) 'The non-transference relationship in the psychoanalytic situation', *International Journal of Psychoanalysis, 50,* 27–39.

Guldner, C. (1982) 'Multiple family psychodramatic therapy', *Journal of Group Psychotherapy, Psychodrama and Sociometry, 34,* 47–56.

Guldner, C. (1983) 'Structuring and staging: a comparison of Minuchin's structural family therapy and Moreno's psychodramatic therapy', *Journal of Group Psychotherapy, Psychodrama and Sociometry, 35,* 141–54.

Hare, A.P. (1986) 'Moreno's contribution to social psychology', *Journal of Group Psychotherapy, Psychodrama and Sociometry, 39,* 85–94.

Harper, J.M., Scorceby, A.E. and Boyce, W.D. (1977) 'The logical levels of complementary, symmetrical and parallel interaction classes in family dyads', *Family Process, 16,* 199–210.

Hayley, J. (1973) *Uncommon therapy: the psychiatric techniques of Milton H. Erikson,* New York: Norton.

Hayley, J. (1976) *Problem-solving therapy: new strategies for effective family therapy,* San Francisco: Jossey Bass.

Hayley, J. (1981) 'A quiz for young therapists' in *Reflections on therapy,* Washington, DC: The Family Therapy Institute.

Held, B.S. and Bellows, D.C. (1983) 'A family systems approach to crisis reactions in college students', *Journal of Marital and Family Therapy, 9,* 365–73.

Hillman, J. (1964) *Suicide and the soul,* Dallas, Tx: Spring Publications.

Hoffman, L. (1981) *Foundations of family therapy: a conceptual framework,* New York: Basic Books.

Hoffman, L. (1985) 'Beyond power and control: towards a "second-order" family systems therapy', *Family Systems Medicine, 3,* 381–96.

Hollander, C. (1983) 'Comparative family systems of Moreno and Bowen', *Journal of Group Psychotherapy, Psychodrama and Sociometry, 36,* 1–12.

Hollander, S. (1981) 'Spontaneity, sociometry and the warming-up process in family therapy', *Journal of Group Psychotherapy, Psychodrama and Sociometry, 34,* 44–53.

Howe, R. and von Foerster, H. (1974) 'Cybernetics at Illinois', *Forum, 6,* 15–17.

Jackson, D. and Hayley, J. (1963) 'Transference revisited', *Journal of Nervous and Mental Disease, 137,* 363–71.

Kahn, S. (1964) *Psychodrama explained,* New York: Philosophical Library.

Kaminski, R.C. (1981) 'Saying good-bye, an example of using a "good-bye technique" and concomitant psychodrama in the resolving of family grief', *Journal of Group Psychotherapy, Psychodrama and Sociometry, 34,* 100–11.

Keeney, B.P. (1979) 'Ecosystemic epistemology: an alternative paradigm for diagnosis', *Family Process, 18,* 117–29.

Keeney, B.P. (1983) *Aesthetics of change,* New York: Guildford.

Kellerman, P.F. (1979) 'Transference, countertransference and tele', *Journal of Group Psychotherapy, Psychodrama and Sociometry, 32,* 38–55.

Kellerman, P.F. (1984) 'The place of catharsis in psychodrama', *Journal of Group Psychotherapy, Psychodrama and Sociometry, 37,* 1–11.

Kellerman, P.F. (1987) 'A proposed definition of psychodrama', *Journal of Group Psychotherapy, Psychodrama and Sociometry, 40,* 76–80.

Kelly, G.R. (1955) *The psychology of personal constructs, vol. 1,* New York: W.W. Norton.

Kibel, H. and Stein, A. (1981) 'The group-as-a-whole approach: an appraisal', *International Journal of Group Psychotherapy, 31,* 409–27.

Kobak, R.R. and Waters, D.B. (1984) 'Family therapy as a rite of passage: play's the thing', *Family Process, 23,* 89–100.

Kopp, S. (1971) *Guru: metaphors from a psychotherapist,* Palo Alto: Science and Behavior Books.

Kraus, C. (1984) 'Psychodrama for fallen gods: a review of Morenian theology', *Journal of Group Psychotherapy, Psychodrama and Sociometry, 37,* 47–66.

Kubie, L. (1968) 'Unresolved problems in the resolution of the transference', *Psychoanalytic Quarterly, 37,* 331.

Laqueur, H.P. (1980) 'The theory and practice of multiple family therapy', in L.R. Walberg and M.L. Aronson (eds) *Group and family therapy,* New York: Brunner/Mazel.

Leutz, G. (1982) 'Correspondences between the psychodramatic theory of child development and the process and therapeutic goals of psychodrama', in M. Pines and L. Rafaelsen (eds) *The Individual and the group, vol. 1,* New York: Plenum Press.

Leutz, G. (1973) 'Recent developments of psychodrama in western Europe', *Group Psychotherapy, Psychodrama and Sociometry, 31,* 168–73.

Leveton, E. (1977) *Psychodrama for the timid clinician,* New York: Springer.

Lipchik, E. and de Shazer, S. (1986) 'The purposeful interview', *Journal of Strategic and Systemic Therapies, 15,* 88–99.

MacKinnon, L.K. and James, K. (1987) 'The Milan systemic approach: theory and practice', *Australian and New Zealand Journal of Family Therapy, 8,* 89–98.

Madanes, C. (1981) *Strategic family therapy,* San Francisco: Jossey Bass.

Masserman, J.H. and Moreno, J.L. (eds) (1957) *Progress in psychotherapy, vol. II,* New York: Grune & Stratton.

Maturana, H. and Varela, F. (1980) *Autopoiesis and cognition: the realization of the living,* Dordrecht, Holland: D. Reidl.

Minuchin, S. (1974) *Families and family therapy,* London: Tavistock.

Minuchin, S. and Fishman, H.C. (1981) *Family therapy techniques,* Cambridge, Ma: Harvard University Press.

Moreno, J.L. (1946, 1964, 1972) *Psychodrama, vol. I,* New York: Beacon House.

Moreno, J.L. (1947) *The theatre of spontaneity,* New York: Beacon House.

Moreno, J.L. (1953) *Who shall survive?* New York: Beacon House.

Moreno, J.L. (ed.) (1956) *Sociometry and the science of man,* New York: Beacon House.

Moreno, J.L. (1959) *Psychodrama, vol. II,* New York: Beacon House.

Moreno, J.L. (1964) 'The third psychiatric revolution and the scope of psychodrama', *Group Psychotherapy, 17,* 149–71.

Moreno, J.L. (1968) 'Universal peace in our time', *Group Psychotherapy, 21,* 175–6.

Moreno, J.L. (1969) *Psychodrama, vol. III,* New York: Beacon House.

Moreno, J.L., Moreno, Z., and Moreno, J. (1963) 'The first psychodramatic family', *Group Psychotherapy, 16,* 203–49.

Moreno, J.L., Moreno, Z., and Moreno, J. (1964) 'New Moreno legends', *Group Psychotherapy, 17,* 1–35.

Moreno, Z.T. (1967) 'The seminal mind of J.L. Moreno and his influence on the present generation', *Group Psychotherapy, 20,* 218–29.

Moreno, Z.T. (1968) 'Eye witness account of the Doctor Honoris Causa awarded to J.L. Moreno, Oct 14, 1968, at Barcelona University', *Group Psychotherapy, 21*, 180–3.

Moreno, Z.T. (1969) 'Psychodramatic rules, techniques and adjunctive methods', *Group Psychotherapy, 22*, 213–19.

Munro, C. (1987) 'White and the cybernetic therapies: news of difference', *Australian and New Zealand Journal of Family Therapy, 8*, 183–92.

Nichols, M. (1984) *Family therapy: concepts and methods*, New York: Gardner.

Papp, P. (1983) *The process of change*, New York: Guilford.

Penn, P. (1982) 'Circular questioning', *Family Process, 21*, 265–80.

Procter, H. (1985) 'A construct approach to family therapy and systems intervention', in E. Button (ed.) *Personal construct theory and mental health*, London: Croom Helm.

Rabkin, R. (1977) *Strategic psychotherapy*, New York: Basic Books.

Remer, R. (1986) 'Use of psychodramatic interventions with families: change on multiple levels', *Journal of Group Psychotherapy, Psychodrama and Sociometry, 39*, 13–29.

Rohrbaugh, M. and Eron, J. (1982) 'The strategic systems therapies', in L.E. Abt and I.R. Stuart (eds) *The newer therapies: a sourcebook*, New York: Van Nostrand Reinhold.

Sanders, C. (1985) '"Now I see the difference" — the use of visual news of difference in clinical practice', *Australian and New Zealand Journal of Family Therapy, 6*, 23–9.

Saravay, S. (1985) 'Parallel development of the group and its relationship to the leader', *International Journal of Group Psychotherapy, 35*, 197–207.

Seeman, H and Weiner, D. (1985) 'Comparing and using psychodrama with family therapy: some cautions', *Journal of Group Psychotherapy, Psychodrama and Sociometry, 37*, 143–56.

Selvini Palazzoli, M., Boscolo, L., Cecchin, G.F., and Prata, G. (1980) 'Hypothesizing-circularity-neutrality: three guidelines for the conductor of the session', *Family Process, 19*, 3–12.

Sherman, R. and Fredman, N. (1986) *Handbook of structured techniques in marriage and family therapy*, New York: Brunner/Mazel.

Stanton, M. (1981) 'An integrated structural-strategic approach to family therapy', *Journal of Marital and Family Therapy, 7*, 427–39.

Starr, A. (1977) *Psychodrama rehearsal for living*, Chicago: Nelson Hall.

Tomm, K. (1984) 'One perspective on the Milan systemic approach: part II, description of session format, interviewing style and interventions', *Journal of Marital and Family Therapy, 10*, 253–76.

Tomm, K. (1987) 'Interventive interviewing: part II, reflexive questioning as a means to enable self-healing', *Family Process, 26*, 167–84.

Tuckman, B.W. (1965) 'Developmental sequence in small groups', *Psychological Bulletin, 63*, 324–99.

Turner, V. (1969) *The ritual process*, Ithaca, New York: Cornell University Press.

Van den Berg (1975) *The changing nature of man: introduction to historical psychology*, New York: Dell Publishing.

Van der Hart, O. (1983) *Rituals in psychotherapy*, New York: Irvington Publishers.

Van Gennep, A. (1909) *Les rites de passage*, Paris: Libraire Critique. English edition: *The rites of passage*, London: Routledge and Kegan Paul, 1960.

Watzlawick, P., Weakland, J., and Fisch, R. (1974) *Change: the principles of problem formation and problem resolution*, New York: W.W. Norton.

Weakland, J.H. (1983) '"Family therapy" with individuals', *Journal of Strategic and Systemic Therapies, 2*, 1–9.

Weakland, J.H., Fisch, R., Watzlawick, P., and Bodin, A. (1974) 'Brief therapy focussed problem resolution', *Family Process, 13*, 141–68.

Whitaker, D. and Lieberman, M. (1964) *Psychotherapy through the group process*, New York: Atherton.

White, M. (1983) 'Anorexia nervosa: a transgenerational system perspective', *Family Process, 22*, 255–73.

White, M. (1984) 'Marital therapy — practical approaches to longstanding problems', *Australian Journal of Family Therapy, 5*, 27–43.

White, M. (1986a) 'Negative explanation, restraint and double description: a template for family therapy', *Family Process, 25*, 169–84.

White, M. (1986b) 'Anorexia nervosa. A cybernetic perspective', *Dulwich Centre Review*, 56–65.

Yalom, I. (1975) *The theory and practice of group psychotherapy*, New York: Basic Books.

Author Index

Subject Index